WAR ON SACRED GROUNDS

WAR ON SACRED GROUNDS

RON E. HASSNER

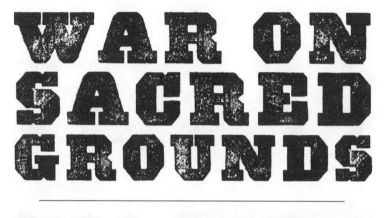

Cornell University Press
Ithaca & London

First published 2009 by Cornell University Press
Printed in the United States of America

Library of Congress Cataloging-in-Publication Data

Hassner, Ron E. (Ron Eduard)
   War on sacred grounds / Ron E. Hassner.
      p. cm.
   Includes bibliographical references and index.
   ISBN 978-0-8014-4806-5 (cloth : alk. paper)
   1. Sacred space—Management.   2. Conflict management—Religious aspects.
3. Religion and politics.   I. Title.

   BL580.H375 2009
   203'.50956—dc22

2009016720

Cornell University Press strives to use environmentally responsible suppliers and materials to the fullest extent possible in the publishing of its books. Such materials include vegetable-based, low-VOC inks and acid-free papers that are recycled, totally chlorine-free, or partly composed of nonwood fibers. For further information, visit our website at www.cornellpress.cornell.edu.

Cloth printing   10 9 8 7 6 5 4 3 2 1

The photograph on the title page is the Shahid Mosque in Baghdad, following the first phases of Operation Iraqi Freedom, on March 22, 2003. Photo by Mirrorpix/ Getty Images.

Für Meine Omi

Contents

Illustrations

1. The Dome of the Rock in the center of the Temple Mount/Noble Sanctuary bounded by the Old City of Jerusalem. The Western Wall plaza is on the bottom right of the image. Photo copyright David Silverman/Getty Images News/Getty Images.

Prologue

"A Terrifying and Fascinating Mystery"

Jerusalem

Walk with me through the dark alleys of old Jerusalem to the sacred site in the heart of the city. Leaving modern Jerusalem behind, we pass under an ornate Ottoman gate and enter the city within the walls. A small plaza, just by the gate, bustles with residents, tourists, merchants, and cab drivers. There are cafes here, a small museum, a youth hostel. Modern city life can penetrate this far beyond the gates but no farther. At the other end of the plaza, a small passageway, barely wide enough to accommodate two walking side by side, begins its descent into the Old City.

It is midday and midsummer but the path ahead is obscured in darkness. The jutting rooftops of the crowded houses block out the light. Shallow steps built into the pathway from local stone, slick with runoff water, make for hesitant progress. Narrower stairways and passageways branch off to our right and left, leading into gloom. As we descend cautiously, a loud group of tourists overtakes us and melds into a somber pilgrim party coming the other way. An elderly orthodox Jew grimaces disapprovingly. Three of the pilgrims are straining to heave a massive wooden cross up the stairs, pushing us forcefully against the walls of the alley. Two Palestinians, hot glasses of coffee in hand, seem oblivious to the street scene, focusing intently on their discussion, but raise their heads to look, blankly, at Israeli soldiers coming up the alley on foot patrol.

Merchants, loudly advertising crudely carved toy camels, religious trinkets, hookahs, and backgammon sets, add to the din. They seem to be lunging at us from all sides, touching us, striving, by means verbal and physical, to pull us into their stores. The next cross-alley brings an additional attack on the senses, as smells from the spice market and slaughterhouses waft into the dark passage. We avert our gaze from the goat carcasses hanging from metal hooks and the display of sheep skulls, eyes and all.

Our descent continues, past a group of yeshiva students, Palestinian schoolgirls, and a pair of Arab women, veiled and laden with shopping bags. The alley now passes under stone arches, reducing the light even more, our shoes sticking in trash and trickles of sewage. There is red, angry graffiti on the corrugated shutters of a closed store. The cold breeze from the far end of the cavernous passage is thick with mold, cumin, and incense. As the sounds behind us, an unintelligible mix of languages and tempers, mix with the sounds ahead, we catch a glimpse of saffron, beautifully laid out in a storefront; a merchant pouring steaming mint tea for his customers from a giant metal jug slung over his shoulder; two Franciscan monks arguing with a fishmonger; three children in Walt Disney t-shirts kicking a ball up the alley as an exhausted young man tries to maneuver a cart piled with warm bread down the same cobbled steps; a Japanese tourist group following a loud young lady holding up a red umbrella; a beggar, pleading at passersby; an Ethiopian cleric, fighting his way through the crowds; a settler armed with an M-16, leaning against a wall, smoking.

Just as the sounds, sights, and smells of the Old City threaten to overwhelm us, a stone gate appears at the far end of the alley, smaller but more ornate than the gate through which we initially entered. The sunlight passing through the gate is now the only source of illumination in the alley. Drawn to it, we step up and into the light. We cross a threshold.

Beyond this gate lies a world transformed. We have stepped up to the edge of a very large platform, open space as far as the eye can see, blinded by a sea of white polished flagstone. The eyes are drawn, first, up to the now open sky. Then, to the horizon, the hills rising east of Jerusalem, dotted with tombs, minarets, and church spires. Then, closer, to the perimeter of the platform, some hundred yards away, where cypress trees mark the boundary between this plateau and the bustling city. We hear distant children laughing, muted birdsong, hushed voices. Only then can our eyes focus on the monumental structure directly ahead of us, in the center of the platform. The Dome of the Rock, decorated with an endless mosaic of sparkling blue and gold stone, topped with a gleaming gilded dome, rises to the sky.

As we approach it, we are enveloped in silence. All movement threatens to grind to a halt. The few worshipers who have joined us on the platform silently mill around us, dazed. We reach the vicinity of the structure and the immensity of the plateau becomes apparent, stretching in all directions. The small shrines and clusters of worshipers that dot the sanctuary merely underscore how large and empty this space is. This expanse, in turn, emphasizes the vast presence of the dome at the center of the platform. This is the Temple Mount or Noble Sanctuary, formerly the site of the Jewish Temple, now a site holy to Muslims worldwide. It is breathtaking.

All around us seem to share in our exhilaration. Indeed, our emotions transcend time itself. Consider these impressions, recorded by the pilgrim Raymond D'Aguilers, upon arriving at this very spot nearly a millennium ago, after considerable travails. He describes the ecstasy among his fellow pilgrims, "the clapping of hands, the rejoicing and singing of a new song to the Lord":

> Their souls offered to the victorious and triumphant God prayers of praise which they could not explain in words. A new day, new gladness, new and everlasting happiness, and a fulfillment of our toil and love brought forth new words and songs for us all. This day, which I affirm will be celebrated in the centuries to come, changed our grief and sadness into gladness and rejoicing.... "This is the day which the Lord has made; we shall rejoice and be glad in it," and deservedly because on this day God shone upon us and blessed us.[1]

A serenity blankets us all, apparent in the expressions of those present, their deliberate motions, the reassuring nods as familiar faces are acknowledged and strangers are invited to join the small groups moving toward the shrine. Seated on a patch of grass, under an olive tree, a family enjoys a sunny afternoon. On the far side of the platform, by a mosque, a tourist guide attempts, for the benefit of his awestruck audience, to envelope the grand structures in a single, sweeping motion of his arm. We pass a scholar, engrossed in a religious text, glancing up occasionally to ensure that the shrine is still there, as real and majestic as it was a minute before. With our eyes raised to the clouds, without worrying where our next step will fall, we approach the dome, remove our shoes, and draw in our breaths in preparation for entering the shrine.

But there is something else. A different set of sensations, obscured from immediate perception. Perhaps we require a while to become attuned to this competing emotion. Some will notice it once their senses have grown accustomed to these new surroundings, others will notice it immediately upon entering the sanctuary. It is a competing sensation. Danger. A very real, very palpable anxiety that seems to emanate from the faces around us, from the structure towering above us, but most of all from below, from underground. There is a fear of violence in this place and it is coming from beneath our feet.

If sacred places constitute the meeting place of the heavens and the earth, then a description of their heavenly attributes tells only half the story. There is another story to be told here, a very earthly story. This story requires a reevaluation of our impressions upon arriving at the platform, indeed, a retelling of our journey. We did not pass through an ornate gate at the end of the dark alley. Instead, because we are not Muslims, we were turned away by the surly men guarding the entrance and sent several streets away to the tourist entrance. Nor did we pass smoothly from the alleys of the market into the sanctuary. Our entry onto the plateau, at the tourist gate, involved standing in line for nearly an hour in order to be searched by the Israeli police. We passed through a metal detector rather than a carved Mameluke archway. Our bags were emptied and our bodies were patted down, in a search not only for weapons but also for Jewish artifacts, lest we plot to desecrate the Muslim shrine with rival rituals. Jewish worshipers whose intentions are thus unmasked are prevented from entering the site by their own countrymen, their voices rising in anger.

The faces that had greeted us on the platform were not all welcoming smiles. There is a rage in the eyes of the Muslim overseers, who wish to banish all tourists. Frustrated at the foreign intrusion, they assert their authority by denying some visitors entrance into the shrines, charging others a fee, following tourists around the sanctuary, and bellowing admonitions and warnings. The visitors, unwelcome and irritated by the hostile reception, cower sullenly as the overseers approach. One tourist voices protest over his treatment by a guard and is immediately outnumbered by additional guards who have hurried to the site. Israeli police, previously relegated to the fringes of the platform, rush to intercede. At the sight of the armed men, representatives of Israeli sovereignty over this Muslim shrine, Palestinian fists clench and jaws set. Behind them is a gruesome memorial of previous clashes with Israeli forces on this site: Palestinian protesters have imprinted their hands, covered in the blood of the killed and wounded, on the whitewashed wall.

At the other end of the platform, a group of secular Jews who have made it into the sanctuary stare red-faced at the sight of a Palestinian bulldozer, digging wantonly into the plateau. The Muslim authorities are excavating an underground mosque and are discarding the archaeological remains unearthed in the process over the side of the platform. The priceless debris is gathering in large piles in the valley below. Before cameras can be pulled out, several locals scare away the nosy visitors. Elderly worshipers and parents with children, sensing impending trouble, hustle out of the sanctuary or into the safety of the dome. Their path leads past a small memorial to Abdullah I, the Jordanian king assassinated on this site in 1951 for negotiating with the government of Israel.

The danger is inescapable. It comes not only from the soldiers, the worshipers, the guards, and the visitors but from the place itself, from its very foundations. Beneath the platform, the ruins of prior sacred sites that once proudly crowned the Mount struggle for supremacy. It seems as though these sacred strata threaten to burrow their way up through layer after layer of earth and burst through the stone-paved platform at any moment, unleashing chaos upon anything and anyone on the surface. One imagines sensing, even hearing, the ominous grumbling from below. One can certainly see and feel the manifestations of that legacy in the faces of those above. A sacred site such as this is not merely a place where the mundane encounters the divine. It is also a place where the divine encounters the mundane.

Indeed, even the ecstatic description of this site by Raymond D'Aguilers requires a careful rereading. D'Aguilers was no mere pilgrim. He was a crusader and his visit to the sanctuary involved more than just "clapping of hands." It was July 15, 1099, the day on which he and his fellow knights conquered Jerusalem and butchered its inhabitants, littering the city streets with "piles of heads, hands and feet." Here is his impression of the sanctuary, the Temple of Solomon, placed in its appropriate context:

> Shall we relate what took place there? If we told you, you would not believe us. So it is sufficient to relate that in the Temple of Solomon and the portico crusaders rode in blood to their knees and bridles of their horses. In my opinion it was poetic justice that the Temple of Solomon should receive the blood of pagans who blasphemed God there for many years. Jerusalem was now littered with bodies and stained with blood, and the few survivors fled to the tower of David and surrendered it to Raymond upon a pledge of security. With the fall of the city it was rewarding to see the worship of the pilgrims at the Holy Sepulcher, the clapping of hands, the rejoicing and singing of a new song to the Lord...[2]

The scenes described by D'Aguilers on the Temple Mount are not without precedent. Consider this Byzantine testimony of the Persian conquest of the very same site, four hundred years before the crusades: "The enemy entered in mighty wrath, gnashing their teeth in violent fury; like evil beasts they roared, bellowed like lions, hissed like ferocious serpents, and slew all whom they found. Like mad dogs they tore with their teeth the flesh of the faithful, and respected none at all, neither male nor female, neither young nor old, neither child nor baby, neither priest nor monk, neither virgin nor widow."[3] Or this description of the final battle on the Temple Mount between the Romans and the Jews, six centuries before the Persian massacre: "Around the altar lay the dead bodies heaped one upon another; down the steps of the sanctuary flowed a stream of blood, and the bodies of those killed above went sliding to the bottom."[4]

Sinai

The twin attributes of attraction and repulsion, the tension between beauty and danger, are at the foundation of Western understandings of sacred space. The scene was set in Exodus, chapter 3, in the Sinai wilderness. Although this is not the first mention of a sacred site in the Hebrew Bible, this passage describing Moses' encounter with a fantastic vision while tending his father-in-law's flock captures the paradox of sacred places eloquently: "And the Lord's messenger appeared to him in a flame of fire from the midst of the bush, and he saw, and look, the bush was burning with fire and the bush was not consumed."[5] We need not speculate as to Moses' response for the text leaves little to the imagination: "And Moses thought, 'Let me, pray, turn aside that I may see this great sight, why the bush does not burn up.'" His curiosity springing into action, Moses is drawn to the site. He wants to take a closer look, investigate, perhaps even touch. But whereas the first verses focus on discovery and attraction, the next verses deal with repulsion and danger, as the voice from the bush issues a warning: "And the Lord saw that he had turned aside to see, and God called to him from the midst of the bush and said, 'Moses, Moses!' And he said, 'Here I am.' And He said, 'Come no closer here. Take off your sandals from your feet, for the place you are standing on is holy ground.'"[6]

Because sacred places offer access to the divine, they are attractive. At sacred places humans can aspire to communicate with the gods, receive healing and blessing, perhaps even witness a miracle or, at the most extreme, envision the divine. But because sacred places offer access to the divine, they are also dangerous.[7] Worshipers may come too close to the gods, or they may transgress the rules governing access to the divine. In so doing, they may incur divine wrath or the anger of other worshipers. Entrance into sacred space and behavior within it must therefore be closely monitored and any deviation punished. The decision to approach a sacred site thus involves very clear risks. Sacred stems from the Latin *sacer,* meaning "untouchable."

The German theologian Rudolf Otto used the Latin phrase *mysterium tremendum et fascinans,* "a terrifying and fascinating mystery," to capture this essential tension, inherent in all things sacred. The sacred is a mystery, according to Otto, given its numinous or "wholly other" character. This mystery is terrifying because it suggests a force without limits. It is fascinating because it entails comfort, miracle, and grace.[8] This duality, perhaps best captured in the English *awe* (for both *awesome* and *awful*), is reflected in the Greek term *deinon,* the German *ungeheuer,* or the Arabic *haram,* meaning both sacred and prohibited.[9] The same tension is apparent in the Hebrew *norah.* Here is how the Hebrew patriarch Jacob uses it, in Genesis 28. He has just dreamed of a ladder reaching to the heavens and has heard the voice of God: "And Jacob awoke from his sleep and he said, 'Indeed, the Lord is in this place, and I did not know.' And he was afraid and he said, 'How fearsome [*norah*] is this place! This can be but the house of God, and this is the gate of the heavens.'"[10]

Sacred places are both awesome and dreadful. That is the theme of this book.

WAR ON SACRED GROUNDS

2. Palestinians hurl shoes at Israeli police at the entrance to the al-Aqsa Mosque, July 29, 2001. Photo copyright Getty Images News/Getty Images.

Chapter One

On Sacred Grounds

Sacred places are sites of infinite beauty. Be they the medieval cathedrals of Europe, the great mosques of the Middle East, or the splendid temples of Asia, the structures that crown sacred places count among the greatest achievements of the civilizations that produced them, extraordinary in their artistry, architecture, and sheer investment of human effort. They are sites of supreme serenity and majesty, overwhelming the visitor in their scale, detail, and wealth.

At the same time, many sacred places have a history of extreme violence and bloodshed. Conflicts over sacred space have triggered ethnic and international conflict and have appeared as symptoms or as byproducts of existing conflicts. A dispute in 1852 between Christian denominations over rights in the churches of the Holy Land led to French and Russian intervention on behalf of the Catholic and Orthodox communities in Jerusalem, eventually triggering the Crimean War. In 1964, Hindu-Muslim riots in response to the theft of a relic from the Hazratbal Mosque in Srinagar, Kashmir, led within six days to 160 deaths, 600 injuries, and the mass exodus of 700,000 refugees into India and contributed to the outbreak of the second Indo-Pakistani war. In 1998, a suicide attack by Tamil separatists that destroyed Sri Lanka's holiest shrine, the Temple of Buddha's Tooth, terminated negotiations to end fifteen years of civil year and led to violent military backlashes against the movement and the Hindu population of Sri Lanka. In the decade following the Iranian revolution, pilgrim deaths in Mecca from violent protests, terrorist attacks, and one hostage crisis in the Grand Mosque exceeded one thousand. Over six hundred mosques were destroyed by Serbs during the ethnic war in Bosnia.

Around the globe, disputes have erupted over the ownership of sacred sites, the desecration or destruction of tombs, temples, churches, mosques, and shrines, and demands for free exercise of controversial rituals on pilgrim routes or burial grounds. These disputes afflict sacred places across states, regions, and religious traditions: it is difficult to conceive of a sacred site of significance that has not, at some point in its history, been subject to conflict and contention, nor is there a corner of the globe free of such disputes at present time.[1] Appealing to religious absolutes, conflicts at sacred places mobilize tribal, nationalist, and ethnic sentiments and lead to violence that spreads rapidly beyond the boundaries of the sacred place. As in Jerusalem, conflicts over sacred space are often at the core of longstanding disputes, thwarting attempts at peaceful resolution by offering opportunities for the escalation of violence.

In spite of the prevalence of disputes over sacred space and their grave consequences, the causes and characteristics of conflict over sacred space remain understudied. Indeed, conflicts over sacred places have yet to be recognized as an independent category of disputes worthy of special attention. Although the importance of specific conflicts has been noted by historians, geographers, students of comparative politics, and even lawyers and novelists,[2] no attempt has been made by political scientists to generate systematic and general findings beyond recognizing the mobilization potential of conflict over sacred space. The claim that sacred sites offer convenient resources for political mobilization, while sound, begs the question of how and why sacred places are conducive to mobilization.[3]

This volume is an investigation into the causes, properties, and potential means for the management of conflicts over sacred sites. My research is guided by two basic questions: Why are so many sacred sites plagued by intractable conflict? How can these conflicts be mitigated?

The Causes and Consequences of Conflicts over Sacred Places

Sacred sites are prone to conflict because they provide valuable resources for both religious and political actors. To believers, sacred sites offer the possibility of communicating with the divine, receiving divine favors, and achieving insight into the deeper meanings of their faith. These characteristics can lead to competition between religious groups who wish to control a sacred space in order both to exclude rivals from practicing potentially conflicting (and thus sacrilegious) rituals and to assert their own legitimacy.

Because believers value these sites, they become attractive targets for political actors as well. By controlling sacred sites, political actors hope to control believers, the religious movements they form, the leadership hierarchies of these movements, and their assets. The characteristics of sacred sites thus create the potential for conflict not only between competing religious groups but also between religious groups and political actors.

Conflicts over sacred places are particularly difficult to resolve because sacred sites pose an indivisibility problem: they cannot be shared. Political scientists have tended to dismiss indivisibility as an unlikely cause for conflict, arguing that most contested goods are entirely divisible.[4] Sacred places are one exception to that rule. They are indivisible because the religious prerequisites for safeguarding these sites from desecration require believers to have complete and exclusive control over them. Thus, competing groups may resort to violence in order to gain control of such a site.

If sacred places are highly contested but cannot be shared, how can these conflicts be controlled or even suspended? The mitigation of conflicts over sacred places requires recognizing that the religious elements of these conflicts are inextricably intertwined with their political elements. Sacred places translate religious ideas into political action. The management of conflicts over sacred sites thus requires cooperation between political leaders who are interested in promoting conflict resolution and religious leaders who are capable of shaping and reshaping the meaning, value, and parameters of sacred places to believers. At the very least, the mitigation of conflicts over sacred places requires consultation between political leaders and religious experts who can shed light on how the religious meaning, value, and parameters of a sacred site impact the political needs of a religious community.

Such a synthesis may seem counterintuitive to those readers immersed in a Western Enlightenment tradition that considers the separation of religion and politics to be a precondition for concord. Political leaders with similar preconceptions have sought to manage conflicts over sacred sites by means of purely political maneuvers, such as attempting to force competing groups to share a sacred space, dividing the space between competing groups or excluding one or more groups from a contested space. These strategies have consistently failed because they did not satisfy the underlying religious needs of parties to these disputes.

Political leaders who succeed in eliciting the cooperation of religious leaders are often able to manage conflicts over sacred places. They may even succeed in suspending conflict over sacred sites if they can mobilize influential

religious leaders who are able to redefine the meaning, value, or parameters of a sacred site in a manner conducive to conflict resolution. Because
a reconfiguration of sacred space along these lines requires the confluence
of political will, significant religious authority, and an appropriate win-
dow of opportunity, it is a relatively rare event. Where such cooperation has
occurred, however, the interaction between a society, its political leaders,
and its religious leaders offers insight into the dynamics of religious and
political decision making and into the intersection between religion, politics,
and conflict.

Methodological Challenges

Scores have lost their lives as a result of Catholic-Protestant violence over
marching routes in Northern Ireland. Hundreds have died in Jewish-Muslim
disputes over sacred sites in the West Bank and Jerusalem. Thousands of
Hindus and Muslims have been killed in conflicts over temples and mosques
in India. In regions such as South Asia, the Balkans, and the Middle East,
where political and religious boundaries often coincide, disputes over sacred
sites have sparked interethnic riots and armed confrontations that have exac-
erbated preexisting conflicts.

My primary reason for studying conflicts over sacred places is the potential
that these cases harbor for understanding how religion, politics, and conflict
intersect. An analysis of conflict over sacred space allows me to focus in on one
clearly defined instance in which a religious phenomenon, namely, the sacred,
is translated into a political outcome, namely, conflict. In so doing, I wish to
draw in equal measure on the disciplines of religious studies and political
science, building a bridge between two disciplines that have not enjoyed a
sustained interaction in the post-Enlightenment West.

The events of September 2001 brought increased public attention to the link
between religion and violence. Ill prepared for a nuanced study of religion,
many international relations scholars fell back on familiar tropes and resorted
to framing religious phenomena in traditional political terms. In these works,
religion is treated as yet another ideology, a form of identity, a manifestation
of soft power, or a transnational actor. Few of these analyses delve into the
content of religious beliefs, doctrines, practices, or rituals. Fewer yet attempt
to provide a causal chain that links the political phenomena that need to be
explained to their religious foundations.[5]

The primary obstacle political scientists face in writing about religion and
politics is methodological. In the absence of a continuous exchange between the

two disciplines, political science and religious studies have followed diverging trajectories and developed distinct and often incongruous ontological and epistemological practices. This is unfortunate because, as I intend to show below, religion and politics are inextricably intertwined. Not only can political ideas have significant implications for religion (a topic of investigation beyond the scope of this volume) but religious ideas can have undeniably political implications. This is particularly true in the case of sacred space where religious requirements are tantamount to political demands.

The mainstream of American political science scholarship remains committed to positivist, materialist, and pragmatic social science aimed at testing falsifiable hypotheses and conducting reproducible research. Political scientists strive for analyses that yield generalizable results and lend themselves, potentially, to prediction and policy making. On the other hand, students of religion in general and sociologists of religion in particular are as interested in material conditions as they are in the ideational factors that form the backdrop for these material conditions. They often abandon the pretense of objectively studying facts in favor of a subjective point of view that accepts beliefs at face value. Instead of trying to simplify or abstract from their subject matter, they tend to approach their area of research with an attention to detail, context, and complexity. This kind of analysis is not necessarily positivist, rarely interested in causal inference, and entirely unsuitable for prediction or policy guidance.

A study of sacred places that draws in equal measure on insights from the study of religion and the study of politics thus entails sacrifices as well as opportunities. Sociologists and anthropologists of religion would pause to consider the challenges in defining the key terms of their analyses, concepts like "the sacred," "desecration," and even "religion." They would also balk at addressing Confucian, Jewish, and Hopi sacred space in one and the same chapter. I have sought to define the key elements of this analysis as tersely, comprehensively, and pragmatically as possible and, in tension with my instincts as a student of religion, have attempted to draw conclusions about sacred space across religious groups as well as across space and time, often setting aside contextual differences in order to arrive at generalizable hypotheses, causal arguments, and modest policy implications. I have dodged altogether the responsibility of grappling with the definition of "religion."

At the same time, treating religion seriously poses challenges to political science methodology. Grappling with beliefs in miracles or in one's ability to communicate with the gods requires the introduction of flexibility into the standards of evidence and proof to which political scientist are accustomed. The nature of the available evidence permits cautious conclusions about likely causes, common trends, and probable outcomes, but the number of cases is too small and the range too varied to permit very rigorous comparative tests, particularly when dealing with the constricted universe of successfully managed disputes over sacred sites. Much of my effort, particularly in the second half of this volume, is therefore dedicated to producing and illustrating hypotheses rather than testing or falsifying arguments.

The result is a deductive argument with elements that may strike political science scholars as unusual but, I hope, not entirely alien. Sociologists of religion may find my efforts at generalizing and abstracting discomfiting but, I hope, not entirely illegitimate. Ultimately, I shall have achieved a modicum of success if students of politics and students of religion view my efforts with an equal amount of suspicion.

International Relations, Sociology of Religion, and Social Constructivism

The gulf separating the disciplines of international relations and religious studies need not be exaggerated. The emerging social constructivist movement, in particular, has opened avenues for dialogue between these two areas of study. Social constructivism's ability to partially bridge the gap between the sociology of religion and political science stems from its roots in both sociology and politics.[6] Constructivism emerged concomitantly with the resurgence of interest in religion and international affairs, as political scientists began experimenting with interdisciplinary theories that would enable research into questions involving ideas, identities, beliefs, norms, or culture. Rather than trace the causal impact of ideas, constructivism emphasizes the role of ideas in constituting identities and interests.[7]

Social constructivists problematize social facts and explore how agents employ ideas to shape these facts. Religion is one such fact and sacred space is one such idea. Agents constrain and shape social structures, which in turn constrain and shape agents, a process termed "structuration."[8] This process accounts for the institutionalization of identities and interests over time, as agent-driven and structure-driven effects reinforce one another. At the same time, structuration can also explain changes in identities and interests that emerge as agent and structure respond to one another.

Social constructivists share with students of religion an interest in how beliefs develop, spread through societies, and shape the identities of these societies.[9] Constructivists share with political scientists an interest in how ideas interact with material interests and power to constrain or enable action.[10] Later in this volume, I will employ this approach to elaborate how religious actors produce the social fact that is sacred space and how their ability to do so is constrained by the beliefs of their followers.

Social constructivism has successfully occupied some of the middle ground between sociology and political science.[11] But it has neither made an attempt nor succeeded at bringing the majority of scholars from both disciplines into its fold. Whereas some scholars in the field of religious studies take the construction and deconstruction of sacred space very far, other have no desire to take a critical view of religious structures or beliefs. Such scholars choose instead to adopt an interpretivist stance and study these structures as given. Applied to the case of sacred space, such an approach would lend insight into how believers view sacred sites, detail the functions this space fulfills for believers, explore how believers use the space, and examine conflicts from the vantage point of participants.

The political science community has received social constructivism with similar skepticism and has persisted in privileging material factors over ideational factors and emphasized causal arguments over constitutive logic.[12] Regarded through this lens, conflicts over sacred places result from bargaining failures. Force is introduced into these conflicts when parties cannot reach agreement on how to divide or substitute for these spaces.

These three approaches—the interpretivist, the materialist, and the constructivist—offer contrasting accounts of the causes of conflicts over sacred sites and diverging explanations for the role that religious actors might play in ameliorating these disputes. Used in isolation, each approach provides a distorting lens through which to view this problem. In the interpretivist account, sacred sites are coveted because they offer access to the divine, and religious actors are capable of shaping these sites because of divine power vested in them. This understanding ignores the political dimensions of these conflicts and places religion out of the reach of politics.[13] In the materialist account, conflicts over sacred places are mere real estate disputes, and religious actors become political actors in disguise. This position subsumes religion within politics and overlooks the ideational aspects of these conflicts. Finally, by focusing all attention on the construction of sacred space by religious leaders, social constructivists risk exaggerating the ease with which such space can be created, reconfigured, and abolished. Constructivists must be able to explain how ideas about the sacred differ from other types of ideas, what distinguishes religious leadership from political leadership, and how power constrains and enables the reconfiguration of these ideas.

These three accounts are contrasting but not contradictory. Indeed, the one does not make sense without the other. By combining insights from all three, I hope to arrive at an understanding that is as sensitive to the weight of religious ideas as to the processes through which such ideas are constructed and rede-fined, as well as their material underpinnings and their political ramifications.

Because I see these three approaches as complementary, I employ them in succession in the chapters that follow. In chapter 2, for example, I use an interpretivist approach to understand the functions that sacred space fulfills for believers, followed by a constructivist framework designed to explain how sacred sites become institutionalized. In chapter 3, I borrow the concept of indivisibility from political science in order to gain a handle on the challenge of sharing sacred space. Yet the three components of my indivisibility defini-tion rest on the interpretivist analysis from chapter 2. My efforts at weav-ing these theoretical strands together culminate in chapter 6, in which I use all three approaches to delimit the conditions under which religious leaders can reshape sacred space in a manner conducive to conflict resolution.

Power and the Sacred

The study of conflicts over sacred space that follows seeks to be as sensitive to the religious aspects of these conflicts as it is to their political dimension. By anchoring the analysis in a social constructivist approach, I can expose both the manner in which social beliefs and practices surrounding sacred space produce political outcomes and the way in which political capabilities and interests shape social understandings of sacred space.

At the same time, I wish to differentiate my analysis from prior research on the politics of sacred space in three important ways. First and foremost, I am more interested in the political ramifications of religion than in the reli-gious ramifications of politics. Second, I recognize the power of religious leaders to influence disputes over sacred space without requiring these actors to engage in interfaith peacemaking. Third, while I am interested in the con-ditions under which the parameters of sacred space can be manipulated, I do not regard this space as being infinitely malleable or without inherent sig-nificance prior to manipulation. It is worth dwelling briefly on these differ-ences in order to clarify what it is that I am *not* arguing in this volume. Three research programs in religion and politics that bear some similarity to my argument deserve scrutiny.

The first of these research programs, initiated by Roger Friedland and Richard Hecht, investigates the manner in which political power shapes sacred space.[14] Friedland and Hecht's work focuses on the manner in which political movements utilize sacred sites as nationalist resources in order to mobilize followers, forge a national identity, and legitimize their political programs.

This exploitation of sacred space is most effective, the authors argue, for those movements that seek to replace the secular underpinnings of a state with religious foundations.

The study of sacred space and its political ramifications in this volume seeks to complement Friedland and Hecht's analysis of political interest and its impact on sacred space. The difference between the two accounts is one of emphasis. I have placed religious actors and interests at the starting point of my analysis in order to investigate how religious principles regarding sacred space produce a political effect, namely, conflict. In emphasizing that political actors and interests configure sacred space in turn, Friedland and Hecht complete the structuration cycle: political agents shape and are shaped by religious structures, just as religious agents shape and are shaped by political structures. Given the significant strides already made in exploring how political power shapes sacred space, I have chosen to launch my analysis from the understudied aspect of this recursive cycle: the religious microfoundations of political violence. Consequently, the argument in the following pages places religious actors and religious ideas front and center.

A second research program in religion and politics, the study of faith-based peacemaking, bears some similarity to the argument proposed in this book. Douglas Johnston, R. Scott Appleby, Marc Gopin, Muhammad Abu-Nimer, and others have emphasized the potential role that religious leaders and religious organizations can play in mediating international and sectarian disputes.[15] These authors have suggested that religious actors are uniquely suited for promoting interfaith dialogue because they can draw on religiously embedded notions of justice, reconciliation, and nonviolence, while also credibly signaling their neutrality to warring parties.

The argument I propose below bears some similarity to this literature. Yet my focus in the coming pages is not on bilateral approaches to conflict resolution, in which religious actors act as intermediaries to bridge the differences between disparate religious communities, but on unilateral conflict management, in which religious leaders persuade their own followers to reconceptualize the meaning of sacred space in a manner that can reduce conflict over a sacred site. These same actors are intimately involved in conflicts over sacred places and can thus provide both opportunities for and constraints on the moderation of these disputes. If snubbed, they are as likely to aggravate a conflict as they are to mitigate it.

The third research program that I wish to differentiate my argument from is the poststructuralist study of sacred space. Poststructuralists have focused on the manner in which sacred places are read, legitimated, reinterpreted, and appropriated, as well as the political implications of these acts. The very definition of a space as sacred, according to some scholars in this tradition, is a political act tantamount to conquest and appropriation.[16] Sacredness is entirely contingent on power, and thus conflict and sanctity are synonymous: it is the struggle over the legitimate use and ownership of a space that makes it sacred.

In the absence of such a struggle, sacred space has no real substance. "Nothing is inherently sacred. Not full of meaning, the sacred, from this perspective, is an empty signifier," write David Chidester and Edward T. Linenthal: "Since a sacred space could signify almost anything, its meaningful contours can become almost infinitely extended through the work of interpretation."[17] Along similar lines, Jonathan Z. Smith writes: "There is nothing inherently or essentially clean or unclean, sacred or profane. There are situational or relational categories, mobile boundaries which shift according to the map being employed."[18] These authors seek to "subvert" the kind of interpretivist approach to sacred space that I use as the foundation for my argument in the next chapter by accusing it of "analytic naivete."[19]

I find this poststructuralist analysis of sacred space to be both counterintuitive and unhelpful in the context of seeking pragmatic solutions to conflicts over sacred sites. The suggestion that all actors are equally capable of shaping space at will is unpersuasive, particularly in the absence of a distinction between the respective abilities of actors to do so or a discussion of the manner in which precedent, tradition, habit, and path dependence constrain the abilities of even the most influential actors to shape space. In other words, poststructuralist approaches seem to overlook the fact that actors seeking to implement change face existing social facts that are resistant to change. The historical and social weight that rests on sacred sites, as a function of decades, even centuries, of continuous practice, grants these locations a very real permanence that can be difficult and costly to challenge. Symbols are not merely superstructure: power has a cultural as well as a material base.[20]

Poststructuralist approaches also tend to be hopelessly vague in their definition of sacred space: a leading study insists that an inventory of sacred space "would *have to* include the following sites: cities, homes, schools, cemeteries, hospitals, asylums and prisons, tourist attractions, museums, and even shopping malls."[21] Seemingly uninterested in providing an accurate diagnosis of the causes of conflict over sacred space, let alone offer policy recommendations for addressing such disputes, authors in this intellectual tradition are prone to adopting opaque language that can be difficult to decipher. What are we to make of the claim that sacred places "formed a recursive series of metaphoric equivalences"?[22]

Though the approach presented in this volume is distinct from the three research programs examined above, I have borrowed components from all three in constructing my argument. Where appropriate, I have incorporated lessons regarding the political foundations of conflicts over sacred sites in order to complement my focus on the religious foundations of these conflicts. Estimating the importance of a sacred site, for example, a task tackled in the next chapter, requires taking into account both religious principles and the manner in which political events, exogenous to these principles, have an impact on how a society values a site. I adopt the faith-based peacemaking literature's insight that religious leaders cannot be overlooked as one strives to resolve sectarian disputes. I will argue, however, that the power of religious actors in mitigating disputes stems not from their stance as neutral parties but rather from their implication in the construction and maintenance of sacred places. I also embrace the poststructuralist appreciation of the role that society plays in shaping and transforming the parameters of sacred space. Yet I qualify the ability of actors to do so based on their location in the religious hierarchy, the importance of the relevant sacred site, and the quality of change attempted. Unlike many in the poststructuralist tradition, I am less interested in changes in the manner in which sacred places are read or interpreted and more interested in changes in the rules governing access to and behavior within sacred places that are conducive to conflict resolution.

The first challenge facing a comprehensive analysis of conflicts over sacred sites is the variety of sacred places across religious movements. I introduce a semblance of order into the subject matter in the next chapter in two steps. First, I define the boundaries of the category of sacred places by introducing attributes common to all these places and by examining the functions that they fulfill for believers. Second, I classify sacred sites based on the extent to which they have become institutionalized. I then show that institutionalization determines the *centrality* and *vulnerability* of sacred places. Unlike alternative ways of categorizing sacred places, this typology permits an estimate of the importance of a sacred site to believers and, in turn, an evaluation of the likelihood of confrontations over these sites.

In chapter 3, my analysis turns toward political science for insight into why sacred places become contested in the first place. Unlike disputes over secular territory, conflicts over sacred sites must contend with an indivisibility problem. This indivisibility problem stems from the manner in which believers view their sacred sites and is anchored, in turn, in the characteristics of sacred space that I elucidated in chapter 2. Sacred sites are indivisible because believers perceive the sanctity of these sites to be dependent on their integrity, because believers perceive the boundaries of these sites to be unambiguously defined, and because believers will not relinquish a site in exchange for substitutes. Since these conflicts cannot be resolved by means of partition, sharing, or side payments, as would standard territorial disputes, conflict erupts whenever more than one group makes claim to a sacred site.

Chapter 4 analyzes how the potential difficulty posed by indivisibility is translated into a concrete problem whenever a sacred place becomes the subject of contest between groups. That such disputes are common derives from the value that sacred sites offer to competing religions, ruthless rulers, real estate developers, or conquerors. Five widespread historical trends create rivalry over sacred spaces, either among religious groups or between religious and secular forces. Disputes stem from the splitting of religions into rival factions, the fusion of opposed beliefs through syncretism, competition over sacred space as real estate, the use of sacred space as a force multiplier, and the vulnerability of sacred space as a social symbol.

Are conflicts over contested sacred sites inevitable? Because of the indivisibility challenge, cases of peaceful coexistence at sacred places are few and far between. Two exceptions to this pattern bear scrutiny: believers from competing religious groups can worship peacefully in one and the same space if that space is of exceedingly low centrality and vulnerability or if a third party is willing to invest significant resources to regulate access and monitor behavior. This last scenario, while common, offers a partial solution at best to the conflict between the parties. Rather than resolve the dispute, the presence of an enforcer merely constrains the groups' ability to express their claims by means of violent action. Resolution by fiat creates tensions that seethe under the surface, threatening to erupt as soon as one party perceives a change in the balance of power.

Chapter 5 is the first of three chapters in this book to offer case studies of policy responses to conflicts over sacred space. In contrast to the policy recommendations that follow in the second half of the volume, this chapter focuses on causes of conflict *mis*-management. The two cases examined in this section are the Indian government's failure to prevent disaster at the Babri Masjid/Ramjanmabhumi in Ayodhya in 1992 and the mishandling of the Israeli-Palestinian Temple Mount/Noble Sanctuary dispute in 2000. The Hindu-Muslim conflict in Ayodhya culminated in the destruction of the disputed mosque and led to sectarian violence across India, Pakistan, and Bangladesh. The Jerusalem conflict proved pivotal to the collapse of the Camp David negotiations and the ensuing intifada. Both cases demonstrate the futility of applying traditional conflict resolution approaches to sacred space, such as attempts at forcing groups to share disputed space or barring groups from that space altogether.

The second half of this book offers an alternative vision for addressing disputes over sacred spaces, anchored in an argument about the power of religious leaders to shape opinions about the meaning and significance of these sites. I present the theoretical basis for this argument in chapter 6, as I investigate the capabilities of religious actors and the limits thereon. Viewed from a social constructivist vantage point, sacred space, like other social institutions, is the product of social interaction. The initiation rites enshrining the laws, symbols, and social practices that define a sacred institution must, however, be constructed by experts, since they involve complex rituals that must take place in the presence of the divine. This should lead us to suspect that religious actors may be able to redefine sacred space in a manner supportive of dispute resolution. The ability of religious actors to reconfigure sacred space depends on a tripartite balance of power among the political leadership, religious leadership, and the community to which the site is sacred.

Chapters 7 and 8 offer two detailed case studies of the reconfiguration of sacred space by religious actors leading to successful conflict suspension. In the first case, conflict between Muslim and Jewish worshipers on the Noble Sanctuary/Temple Mount in Jerusalem was averted for two decades as the result of an unprecedented ruling by rabbinical authorities in the aftermath of the Six Day War. This ruling, issued in October 1967, prohibited Jewish access to this sacred site and thus drastically, if temporarily, reduced the likelihood of interfaith conflict at the site. The Israeli government encouraged this ruling and created the conditions for its proclamation.

In the second case, the intervention of Muslim religious authorities successfully resolved a dramatic hostage crisis in Islam's holiest shrine, the Grand Mosque in Mecca, in November 1979. The unique relationship between the House of Saud and the Saudi *ulema,* drawing on the historical bond between ibn Saud and the descendants of Abd al-Wahhab, enabled the ulema and the Saudi regime to collude in permitting the use of force in the Grand Mosque.

I conclude, in chapter 9, with the implications of my argument for the management of conflicts over sacred places and for the analysis of territorial disputes and religiously motivated violence more generally. Aside from obtaining information about the parameters of sacred sites from experts, I urge decision makers to consult religious leaders in order to obtain insight into the meaning and significance of sacred sites to believers. These leaders may even be able to assist in the management of conflict over sacred places by modifying the definition and significance of these sites to believers.

Beyond the immediate realm of sacred space, my analysis also has implications for the study of territorial disputes. The indivisibility of sacred places can shed light on the manner in which territorial disputes become increasingly resistant to resolution. Religious actors can imbue contested secular territory with religious characteristics so as to mobilize believers in defense of a territory. Disputed territory can even take on quasi-sacred qualities over time if participants begin conceiving of the space as civil-religious sacred space. Influential leaders can undo this process and resolve the most entrenched territorial disputes by persuading their domestic audiences to rethink their perceptions of the disputed territory.

I end this volume by discussing the future of research on religion and international relations. Concerned with current trends in the analysis of religion and international politics, I propose an approach that traces the pathways by which religion affects international affairs to their origins in the content and meaning of religion while at the same time offering generalizable implications at the international level of analysis. This *thick religion* methodology requires a sensitivity to theology, religious organization, iconography, ceremony, and belief but also a willingness to generalize from particular religious movements, regions, or instances to arrive at broader conclusions for the study of international relations.

PART I

Understanding Conflicts over Sacred Spaces

3. The interior of the Harimandir Sahib, the spiritual center of the Sikh faith, in Amritsar, India. The marble Akhal Takht, behind the Golden Temple, was reduced to rubble during Operation Blue Star in 1984. Photo copyright Martin Gray/National Geographic/Getty Images.

Chapter Two

What Is Sacred Space?

Small roadside chapels are sacred, yet so are cathedrals. Synagogues are sacred, yet so is the city of Jerusalem. Shintoists worship the spirits residing in rocks and trees but also worship Mount Fuji. How can we make sense of this variety in sacred places? In this chapter, I seek to introduce a semblance of order into the subject matter by circumscribing and classifying sacred space.[1]

The Phenomenon of Sacred Space

Emile Durkheim, among the first sociologists to study religion, argued that the distinction between the sacred and the profane is the basis of all religious movements.[2] All religious beliefs, rites, and places express either the nature of sacred things or the relationship between sacred and profane things. Religious phenomena, according to Durkheim, thus divide the universe into two classes, sacred and profane, that embrace all that exists but exclude one another. Other students of religion have noted the prevalence of sacred places across religions and have concluded that sacred space is an essential, perhaps the most essential, component in all religious traditions.[3]

Yet defining sacred space is difficult given the diversity of such spaces as displayed across the great religious traditions. Some sacred sites, such as temples or shrines, are constructed. Others are natural sites, like mountains or caves, that are made sacred by means of interpretation, not construction. The sanctity of a place may be communicated by the gods through a special sign, as with Mount Sinai, or the location may become holy because a religiously significant event took place there, as with the Via Dolorosa in Jerusalem.[4] It may have been imbued with sanctity because of the presence of relics, like the catacombs in Rome or the Shi'a shrines in Najaf and Karbala, or because it seems to reach toward, or reflect, the realm of the gods, like sacred rivers, mountains, forests, and lakes. Given that different religious traditions employ radically differing conceptions of time and space, it is not entirely surprising that they also exhibit sacred spaces that vary in shape, location, importance, and purpose.

Consider the following three sites, separated by continents, oceans, and centuries: the Bighorn Medicine Wheel in Wyoming, the Temple of Apollo in Delphi in Greece, and the Harimandir in Amritsar in India.[5] Though the three differ widely in their specific characteristics, all provide the same essential religious functions that, in all cases, give rise to similar tensions.

The Bighorn Medicine Wheel is located on Medicine Mountain in Wyoming at an altitude of nearly ten thousand feet. Of all the medicine wheels in the Americas, it is the best preserved and arguably the most significant.[6] It is a stone circle, 80 feet in diameter and 245 feet in circumference, composed of a cairn (a stone pile that functions as the center point) and twenty-eight radiating spokes. Six small stone piles, set along the rim, are aligned with the rising and setting of the sun and other bright stars at significant times of the year. The wheel is sacred to Plains Indian tribes such as the Arapaho, Cheyenne, Cree, Crow, Dakota, and Blackfoot. It is over seven hundred years old.

Some six thousand miles east, above the Gulf of Corinth, in the shade of Mount Parnassus, lie the ruins of Apollo's Temple at Delphi. For about a thousand years, before the site was abandoned in the fourth century CE, pilgrims would make the journey to Delphi to consult the Pythia, the prophetess of Apollo, the most famous oracle of the ancient world. Seated atop a volcanic fissure, said to contain the remnants of the slain dragon-snake Python, the oracle would utter incoherent riddles, interpreted by the priests of Apollo. All who wished to consult the Pythia underwent ritual purification in the Castalian Springs and then ascended the slopes of Parnassus, along the Sacred Way, through the *temenos,* the sacred area. The path was lined with statues, shrines, offerings, temples, and treasuries donated by victorious Greek leaders and communities in thanks for prophecies fulfilled. It led, in a zigzag manner, glittering with marble and bronze, to the temple. Visitors were taken to the main part of the temple, the *cella,* and thence into the inner sanctum, the *adyton,* where they would encounter the Pythia and, through her, communicate with the god Apollo himself.

Compared with the sacred area in Delphi or the Bighorn Medicine Wheel, the Golden Temple in Amritsar, India, is a relatively young shrine, a mere four hundred years old. It was founded by Guru Arjun, the fifth leader of the Sikh movement. The temple complex, known as the Court of the Lord, is made up of several ornate structures, arranged around a large, rectangular reflecting pool, called "the Pool of Nectar." They include the Akhal Takht (Throne of the Ever-Living God), several guesthouses, fruit gardens, pavilions, and a 130-foot domed tower. The centerpiece of the complex is the Golden Temple itself, the Harimandir, the most sacred shrine in the Sikh religion. This two-story building sits in the center of the pool, connected to the surrounding complex by means of a marble causeway. Its lower story is made of marble, inlaid with mother-of-pearl, onyx, lapis lazuli, and other gemstones, arranged in floral patterns. The upper floor is of copper, covered in gold and inscribed with quotes from the Sikh holy scriptures. During the day, pilgrims may worship the Guru Granth Sahib (Sikh holy book) in the Harimandir, where it is displayed on a divan below a gilded and jeweled canopy. At night it is ceremoniously carried to the Akhal Takht across the causeway in a gold and silver palanquin, showered with rose petals by the ecstatic crowd.

These three sites could not be more different in location, composition, age, and function. Yet all three share a salient characteristic mentioned in chapter 1. They are sites of "awe," paradoxically combining elements of wonder and attraction with an underlying sense of threat and violence. Set high in the Medicine Hills, inaccessible during much of the year because of snow, the Bighorn Medicine Wheel is a truly dazzling sight to behold, a place tinged with magic. Yet during my visit there, in August 2003, the serenity of the mountaintop was disturbed by a forest ranger who rushed to the site carrying a large trash bag. He had been alerted to an impending visit by a group of Native Americans who wished to worship at the wheel, and he was now hurrying to perform the routine clearing of the site of foreign ritual items. In the past, he has had to remove bones, goat carcasses, and other sacrilegious objects left in the wheel by nature worshipers, satanic cult members, or New Age religion practitioners who compete with the Native Americans over the use of the wheel. Clashes with local cowboys, who deny any Native American rights to the site and wish to see them barred from these lands, as well as conflicts with tourists who intrude on rituals performed in the wheel, have occasionally compelled forest rangers to carry arms while guarding the site. On the day I visited, minutes before the Native Americans arrived at the site, the ranger removed a Bible that had been placed in the center of the wheel by a visitor, weighed down with a rock for added emphasis.

Even in their desolate state, the Doric ruins of Delphi offer an imposing sight, with sweeping views of the Phaedriatic cliffs above, the Pleistos Gorge below and beyond, and the Gulf of Corinth. The notables of Hellas, Rome, and the neighboring Asiatic kingdoms, from Xenophon and Aristotle to Alexander the Great and Cicero, came here to seek advice from the Delphic Oracle before embarking on legislative, military, or economic ventures. Yet because of the power of the oracle located at this site and its ability to directly influence political and military affairs, Greek rulers fought time and again to control Delphi in a series of "sacred wars." The first of these lasted nine years and erupted in response to attempts by the Phocyan city of Crisa to levy tributes from pilgrims to Delphi. In the second sacred war, in 488 BCE, Athens assisted Phocis in reconquering Delphi from the Amphictyonic League. King Philip II of Macedon gained control of Delphi in the course of a third sacred war in 346 BCE. Persians, Gauls, the Pergamon dynasty, the Aetolian League, and the Romans made attempts at or succeeded in controlling the site at various points in history. Several of these conquerors fought to keep Delphi open to worshipers. Others wished to influence the oracle, control access to the information it provided, or, as in the case of the emperor Nero, loot it of its treasures. The worship of Apollo in Delphi finally succumbed to Christianity in 393 CE, when the emperor Theodosius declared the site closed and it was abandoned.

The dazzling complex that surrounds the Golden Temple in Amritsar became the setting for the first of many bloody clashes in 1757, when Amritsar was raided by the Afghan king Ahmad Shah. During continuous raids in the ensuing decade, the Afghans destroyed the temple and desecrated the sacred pool by filling it with slaughtered cattle. Amritsar was also the site of the 1919 Jallianwala Bagh massacre, executed by British and Gurkha soldiers under General Dyer against pilgrims visiting the shrine to celebrate Baisakhi Day. Over a thousand civilians, gathered in peaceful protest, are estimated to have succumbed to British machine gun fire that day. The massacre prompted Gandhi's Noncooperation Movement and paved the way for the Indian independence movement. In the 1980s, the Golden Temple became the focus of Hindu-Sikh clashes, prompted by the occupation of the shrine by armed Sikh separatists. A disastrous operation, executed by the Indian army with the intention of subduing the insurgents, ended with the destruction of the temple complex and the death of thousands of pilgrims. These acts, compounded by Indian acts of desecration, unleashed months of deadly sectarian riots across India and resulted, ultimately, in the assassination of Indian prime minister Indira Gandhi by her Sikh bodyguards.

4. The medicine wheel in Bighorn National Forest, Wyoming. Native American worshipers have attached prayer ties to the ropes surrounding the wheel. A Christian visitor has provocatively placed a Bible inside the stone circle. Photo copyright Ron E. Hassner.

Sacred places, then, are characterized by an extreme duality. Because they are attractive, they are coveted. Because they offer access to the divine, they pose the risk of desecration. Because they form social centers, they offer temptations to those who wish to control social groups. And because they offer terrestrial evidence of divine presence, they become arenas for competition between religious groups, each wishing to assert its ownership, rights, and rituals at one and the same site. Sacred space and violence go hand in hand. This violence is very real and can be measured in hundreds and thousands of lives.

The Three Functions of Sacred Space

Although the dialectic nature of the sacred is at the core of this book, we can certainly say more about these sites beyond recognizing their "awesome" nature. One means of reaching beyond Durkheim's rather vague conception of the sacred to arrive at a clearer definition of sacred space is to examine the functions that sacred space fulfills for believers. Mircea Eliade, sociologist of religion and one of the foremost students of the sacred, adopted an interpretivist approach of this sort in his study of sacred places. He took the intuitive experiences of believers as his starting point in attempting to arrive at the essential meaning of sacred space.

According to Eliade, sacred places fulfill three primary functions for believers.[7] First, they act as places in which worshipers can communicate with the divine, whether through prayer, ritual, or contact with an image of the gods. Second, sacred places seem to contain a permanent divine presence. Worshipers thus approach sacred places with the expectation of receiving blessings, healing, forgiveness, spiritual merit, or salvation. Finally, in their layout and design, sacred places provide meaning to the faithful. They evoke passages from history, social structures, or religious precepts and, ultimately, hint at the underlying order of the cosmos by reflecting it, metaphorically, through forms, actions, and objects. The art, architecture, music, and drama that embellish these places represent an ideal of that religion in its purest form.

In identifying these key functions, Eliade and his students focused on three different attributes of sacred places: behaviors attributed to the gods, the behavior of the worshipers at these sites, and the physical design of these sites. These functions combine to form a definition of sacred space: sacred spaces are religious centers at which the heavenly and earthly meet, sites that act as bridges between the human and the divine worlds. They are the locations at which the divine ruptures through the mundane and reveals itself to humans.[8]

The opportunity to communicate with the divine, receive gifts, and gain insight into greater meanings turns all sacred spaces into religious centers for their believers. Mount Meru to Hindus, Mount Gerizim to the Samaritans, and the Temple Mount to Jews are all historical, spiritual, and cosmological centers. Believers often associate these places with the act of creation, the beginning of time, or the end of days. By virtue of providing a two-way channel between the present world and a world removed, the sacred spaces act as the world axis, or *axis mundi* in Eliade's terminology. This axis connects heaven and earth but also functions as a spiritual pivot around which the world revolves.[9]

Pilgrims who journey to sacred places thus travel toward the center, seeking in the sacred space a microcosm both of the universe and of the specific religion it represents. All three sites examined at the outset of this chapter act, or have acted, as destinations for pilgrimage. Native Americans come to the Bighorn Medicine Wheel from across the plains in order to perform fasts and spirit quests, hold councils and sacred dances, offer gifts of thanks to Mother

Earth (often in the form of a buffalo skull placed at the center of the wheel), or pray for healing, atonement, and guidance. Because the wheel is aligned with the stars and represents the lunar calendar, it symbolizes time as well as space. Worshipers enter the wheel to determine the seasons but also to transcend the constraints of time and space by means of prayer and meditation.

The pilgrims who came from across the Roman and Greek empires to consult the Pythia recognized Delphi as the center of their world. According to Greek mythology, two ravens, instructed by Zeus to fly from opposite ends of the earth to its center, met in Delphi. The city's position as the Greek center of the universe was visually represented by means of an *omphalos* or "navel," a decorated stone marker placed inside Apollo's temple. It was said to have been the first place to emerge from the waters after the primordial flood receded.

Similar stones mark different *axis mundi* around the world: Jews pray toward the Temple Mount in Jerusalem and identify the rock at the center of that platform as the former location of the Jewish Temple and "foundation stone" of the world. This stone, too, is associated with the aftermath of a great primordial flood, in this case the flood survived by the biblical patriarch Noah and his family. Muslims pray toward the Black Stone, a meteor embedded in the Ka'ba, the large cuboid structure in the center of the Grand Mosque in Mecca. This stone is said to mark the very first place of prayer, erected by Adam. Once the devout Muslim completes his pilgrimage and arrives in Mecca, his directed prayer is translated into movement as he circumambulates the stone. Orthodox Christians recognize the *omphalos* in the Church of the Holy Sepulcher in Jerusalem as the center of the Christian universe. Located halfway between the site of the crucifixion and the site of the resurrection, it symbolizes the most important moment in Christian history as well as a crucial location, the midway point between death and the conquest of death.

In Amritsar, the representation of sacred space as center takes the form not of a stone but of a sacred text, the Guru Granth Sahib. The book, a collection of poems, prayers, and hymns composed by the first ten gurus of Sikhism, contains the tenets of the faith. The tenth and last leader of the faithful bestowed the title "guru" on the text itself, at which point it became the eternal guide for all Sikhs. Placed in the heart of the Golden Temple, at the center of the Pool of Nectar, which in turn is in the center of the temple complex, the Guru Granth Sahib is sung continuously from dawn to sunset, to the accompaniment of flutes, drums, and strings. Pilgrims can cross the causeway to circumambulate the text or hear the enchanting verses while circling the pool.

In all these cases, the pilgrims' journey to the sacred site is also a journey to the center of the universe, where they can expect to see a representation of their spiritual world and conduct exchanges with the gods. It is toward these centers that *gurdwaras* (Sikh shrines), temples, synagogues, mosques, and churches are oriented and prayer is directed. In cultures across the globe, that journey toward an origin is often represented by a labyrinth, a circuitous route that leads, through twists and turns, to enlightenment. Intended for meditation, the maze also functions as an aid to believers who cannot travel to a sacred site and wish instead to reenact symbolically the arduous pilgrimage toward the center.

The Institutionalization of Sacred Space

Differences in geography, technology, and social structure go a long way toward explaining variation in sacred places across religions and regions. But if all sacred places provide the same three functions for believers, how can we explain variation in sacred places within a given region and religion? The answer has to do with the processes of institutionalization that all sacred spaces undergo over time. Even within one and the same religion, sacred spaces at various stages of institutionalization exhibit different traits, levels of importance, and, as I will argue later in this chapter, different likelihoods of becoming embroiled in conflict.

I have already argued, with Eliade, that sacred sites offer believers a pure and unmediated experience of the sacred. By visiting a sacred place, visitors can witness the divine, converse with the gods, receive blessings or relive an event of historical-religious significance. Given the risk of desecration, however, these visits and experiences must eventually undergo regulation by the community of believers. The community must define the boundaries of the sacred place to delineate where, precisely, the unique rules regarding access and behavior apply. The community must then supervise entrance as well as worship at the site. The rules and definitions then grant the site a social and, as I will show, architectural permanence. I refer to the process by which a religious community gradually assumes control over a sacred site and implements specific rules and restrictions as the *institutionalization* of sacred space.[10]

Before this institutionalization takes place, the sacred place is highly unstable, that is, very much prone to destruction or desecration. Taking some liberty with the work of the German sociologist Max Weber, we can compare such sacred places in their natural state to authority in its natural, or "charismatic," state.[11] Much like sacred space, charisma is a projection of the divine into the human sphere. In the case of charisma, we learn from Weber, the divine manifestation takes the form of the gift of leadership. In both cases, the initial state of the divine presence is unstable because it is unregulated and impermanent. Weber emphasized the difficulties associated with charismatic authority, in particular the problem of succession to the charismatic leader. He argued that processes of legalization and rationalization imbue charisma with a permanence that is less subject to instabilities by transforming it, first, into traditional authority and then, ultimately, into legal authority. Here, I extend and adapt Weber's analytical framework to shed light on the manner in which sacred space is transformed from place to shrine to temple and finally into a local house of worship.

Given the complex rules associated with access and behavior at sacred sites and the extreme dangers associated with desecration, sacred places are likely to undergo a transition from site to shrine. This transition, a parallel of the process of legalization that occurs as charismatic authority is replaced with what Weber termed traditional authority, involves two changes in particular: the construction of a permanent structure and the establishment of a priestly class that is responsible for managing the sacred site. For example, the monastery of St. Catherine in the Sinai, the oldest monastery in Christendom, encloses a shrub claimed to be the burning bush through which God spoke to Moses. Whether or not that is the case, this much is clear: in the absence of the monastery walls protecting it, the bush would not have survived the ravages of time.

Aside from preventing erosion to the underlying site, the construction of a permanent edifice over the sacred site has the purpose of reflecting, in outward appearance, inner design, and detailed ornamentation, the meaning of the sacred site. Its outward appearance is aimed primarily at those prohibited from access to the site. It is likely to represent the host religion at its most splendiferous, all the while hinting at mysteries within that must remain inaccessible to the uninitiated observer. In the design of the shrine, architecture is employed to represent the rules governing behavior and access. The structure channels and constrains movement around the sacred site by means of barriers, gateways, and passageways. It also creates the necessary spaces and facilities for performing rituals such as group worship, ablution, baptism, confession, and sacrifice. The ornate symbols that decorate the shrine recall the founding miracle of the underlying site, retell the movement's myths, and represent its core principles, leaders, and events. Decorations also act as guides to behavior and ritual by designating areas in the shrine according to function or by representing appropriate and prohibited behavior.

In addition to the appearance of a permanent structure, the shift from sacred place to shrine is also accompanied by the formalized presence of religious actors at the site. As public presence and worship take on permanence, such actors are required to control access, supervise behavior, and assist in the performance of ritual. Where believers expect divine favor in exchange for sacrifice, for example, priests collect, administer, and apportion the offering. The shrine structure provides the priestly class with the facilities required for performing their tasks. These may include chambers for storing the implements of ritual and sacred artifacts or sites required for priestly rites. The shrine can also include places at which priests can communicate with worshipers or locations from which they can supervise and guide the behavior of worshipers.

The increase in the religious centrality of a sacred shrine sets off a series of self-enforcing mechanisms. As the number of worshipers attending the site grows, priests will require and demand increasingly elaborate facilities. Increased public attendance will contribute to the expansion and embellishment of the shrine structure, and these, in turn, will enhance the shrine's attraction to worshipers. Once the shrine has superseded competing sacred sites in importance, priestly classes are likely to make it their permanent site of activity or even residence. Shrines that occupy a prominent place in a society's religious landscape are likely to assume a central position in its social, cultural, and even economic and political sphere. Political and economic entrepreneurs drawn to the shrine will strive to associate themselves with the site, contribute to its expansion and decoration, and construct their own centers of activity at the site or in its vicinity, and in so doing they will underscore the centrality of the shrine to the community.

Indeed, once the shrine has been suitably prepared, the gods themselves may choose to make their home in it. Unlike a simple shrine, the construction of which might be initiated and completed by the worshipers themselves, the erection of a divine residence requires levels of planning, supervision, and even execution that can be performed only by religious actors, inspired by divine guidance. This shrine may contain some aspect of the divine presence, as did the Jewish Temple in Jerusalem, or it may act as the actual residence of a god, the place where the god eats, sleeps, bathes, and conjugates, as do Hindu temples.

The product of this process is the temple, grand mosque, or cathedral, a shrine that has expanded to become a social, religious, and political center. Temples and urban population centers are symbiotic, the former often lying at the heart of, giving rise to, and at the same time requiring the existence of the latter.[12] They serve their cities of residence by drawing local worshipers, pilgrims, and powerful actors who wish to incur the favor of the priestly classes or control their activities. The city provides the infrastructure as well as the social capital required for sustaining the temple and the religious elites. At the same time, the city draws its design from the layout of the temple, derives significant financial and political clout from the presence of the sacred site in its midst, and utilizes the temple for a variety of social activities. Temples have doubled as courts, schools, marketplaces, and royal residences.

The construction of the temple completes another process, initiated by the shrine structure, which is the imparting of the site's sanctity to the building above it. The man-made structure can become saturated with the sanctity of the place on which it rests because the sacred is contagious. The transmittable qualities of the sacred make it possible for healers, statues, and relics to cure through contact with the afflicted. The contagiousness of the sacred also explains the power attributed to the souvenirs that pilgrims collect at sacred sites and take home with them. A rock removed from a sacred site, a piece of stone chiseled from a shrine, or a vial of water from a sacred source, all these "capture" some of the sanctity of the original and can transmit it to a different place and time, if appropriately handled and contained.

The contagious qualities of the sacred also create the problem of desecration through inappropriate contact, an issue I discuss at length below. In the case of a shrine and temple, this contagion transmits the sanctity of an underlying site to the structure above it over time, until both come to represent the divine. One difference remains: the sacred place is eternal and indestructible, whereas the structure above it, though important, can be damaged, destroyed, removed, replaced, or repaired. The structure may be of tremendous importance to the community of believers, yet in the end its existence is transitory.

Temples, cathedrals, and grand mosques are institutionalized sacred places, comparable to legalized charismatic authority. Neither of these two forms, however, brings the process of rationalization to its logical conclusion because neither institution is entirely stable. Traditional authority, such as leadership based on patrimony, may degenerate into corruption, while temples are susceptible to a more physical vulnerability: the dangers of foreign conquest and destruction. Indeed, the concentration of religious, political, and economic resources at or near temples creates significant temptations for violence. I will have more to say about the causes and consequences of this violence in the coming chapters. For now it suffices to say that these incidents have disastrous consequences for societies that organize around these religious institutions, as exemplified by the fate of the Jewish people after the destruction of their temple in Jerusalem.

Whether in anticipation of or in response to such catastrophes or other events that may render the temple inaccessible, religious entrepreneurs have initiated the reproduction of temples into local shrines, mosques, churches, or synagogues. The resulting mirror sites, a "bureaucratization" of the original, reflect the design of their source temple yet are significantly more enduring.

In the absence of an underlying sacred place, the likelihood of and risks accompanying desecration are reduced. As a consequence, the rules that govern access to and behavior at these shrines can be partially relaxed and the need for direct priestly supervision is diminished. The multiplicity of small and localized houses of worship pose far less attractive targets for outsiders intent on attacking the financial or political core of a community. Indeed, the mirror site may shed its external structure altogether and become no more than a provisional location for group prayer. Multiple religious movements, including branches of Judaism, Christianity, Islam, and Sikhism, pronounce any site of assembly for worship to be temporary sacred space, thus eliminating the problem of desecration altogether.

Though in appearance and daily administration these mirror sites retain but a faint echo of the original, they continuously invoke the temple, cathedral, or grand mosque that inspired their construction. The house of worship may face toward the temple or its layout and physical components may represent the abstracted design of the temple. Just as the synagogue recalls the design and functions of the Temple in Jerusalem, so the church echoes the Holy Sepulcher, the mosque faces Mecca and derives its layout from the first mosque in Medina, and the gurdwara evokes the Harimandir in Amritsar. The symbols that adorn the house of worship will emulate either the form of the temple, the shape of ritual objects located in the temple, or the very symbols that adorned the temple. Rites performed in the house of worship are stylized variations on rituals performed in the temple, conducted at parallel points in the religious calendar. The link between the two sites is constantly underscored in prayers, rituals, and invocations. In all these, the modern house of prayer constantly conjures up the image of the original temple.

Evaluating the Importance of a Sacred Site: Centrality

The process of institutionalization that sacred sites undergo can explain how sites within one and the same religious movement can differ so dramatically in size, design, and social function. At the same time, institutionalization also drives two important parameters of sacred places, *centrality* and *vulnerability,* that permit an assessment of the importance of a sacred place to believers. The significance of a site can, in turn, indicate the believers' willingness to engage in violence in order to protect or conquer a given site.

The first parameter, *centrality,* locates the space in the spiritual landscape of the group. The centrality of a place to a group depends on its relative ability to fulfill the three crucial functions listed above. The stronger the group's belief that the site provides communication with the divine, divine presence, and meaning, the more important the site is for believers. At the most central of sites, the believer can hope for the clearest and most unmediated exchange with the gods. The Jewish tradition of placing notes with prayers between the stones of the Western Wall in Jerusalem, for example, rests on the belief that this wall, a retaining wall of the former Temple, contains remnants of the *shekhinah,* the divine presence that once resided in the Temple. In other words, some Jews believe that their prayers are more likely to be answered at this site because God's presence is more intense there than it is elsewhere. The Temple in Jerusalem is more central in Judaism than a synagogue, just as the Holy Sepulcher is more central to Christians than a local cathedral and Mecca is more central to Muslims than the largest of city mosques.

Reports of a prior revelation at a site provide the greatest support for the centrality of a shrine, particularly if there is physical evidence for that revelation. Muslims worship at the Dome of the Rock in Jerusalem because they believe that Muhammad prayed on that rock and ascended from it to the heavens. They point to his footprint and head print in the rock as confirmation for that event, a visible manifestation that the rock provides direct access to the heavens. Gaya in India is sacred to devotees of Vishnu because the god is said to have visited the site, as evidenced by the large footprint found there. Similarly, Christians revere the footprint of Christ in the Church of the Ascension in Jerusalem, as do Buddhists who venerate Buddha's footprints across Asia. In all instances, the site takes on a particular importance in the religion's hierarchy of sacred places because the divine presence in it is more immediate.

A second source of evidence for the centrality of a shrine is the record of favors granted to believers at the site. Pilgrims healed of physical afflictions at sacred shrines often leave visible testaments to their miraculous experiences at these sites. These may take the form of *ex votos,* votive offerings such as descriptive plaques, food, or donations. They may assume the shape of *milagros,* casts or miniature copies of the body parts that have been healed or even discarded crutches and braces. These items convey the believer's thanks for a prayer fulfilled and at the same time confirm the value of praying at this specific site for other worshipers.

Healings, miracles, and intercessions of this sort are usually linked either to evidence that a revelation occurred at a sacred place or to the presence of a miraculous relic. The Hazratbal Mosque is the most central Muslim shrine in Kashmir because it holds the Moi-e-Muqqdas, the Sacred Hair of the Prophet Muhammad. The shrines that house the relics of the Buddha (his teeth, hairs, robe, and bowl) are the most central Buddhist shrines in their respective countries and among the most important Buddhist shrines in Asia.

Most religions, then, offer a hierarchy of sacred sites, representing a scale of what I have termed centrality. Although all sacred places are centers, some bring believers closer to the divine than others.[13] Shrines within Japanese homes or the trees and rocks in which local deities reside are inferior to Ise, the central shrine at which the Sun Goddess Amaterasu, protector of the Japanese nation, resides. Christian pilgrimage shrines may attract visitors from nearby villages, the entire region, the country, or the entire globe.[14] In mountainous regions, such as the Himalayas, where villagers are dispersed in small communities, worshipers conduct minor pilgrimages to valley shrines, common to all who reside in the valley. These shrines provide greater contact with the gods than the small shrines in the villages.

Believers will conduct longer and more arduous pilgrimages, at more important occasions, to regional or national shrines. Navadvip attracts Hindus from throughout Bengal, whereas Varanasi draws devotees of Shiva from throughout India.[15] Ayodhya draws over a million pilgrims every year, from across sects and regions, because it is believed to be the birthplace of the god Ram and, according to some, the center of creation.[16] Worshipers from across Mexico are drawn to the Basilica of Nuestra Senora de Guadalupe in Mexico City, just as Polish Catholics travel to Jasna Gora. The miraculous Marian images in these two shrines are said to offer greater access to the divine than any image found in the believers' town or village churches. Some shrines gain such notoriety among believers owing to the magnitude of the miracle or revelation said to have occurred there that they attract believers worldwide. Bodh Gaya, Haifa, and Karbala draw Buddhists, Baha'is, and Shi'a Muslims respectively from around the globe. The ill and afflicted come to the basilicas of Loreto, Compostella, and Fatima from across the Christian world. Lourdes, a French town of eighteen thousand inhabitants, attracts some five million Christian pilgrims every year.[17]

A religious movement's conception of the respective centrality of its sacred sites can be implicit or very explicit. The Mishnah, for example, offers a clear ranking of Jewish sacred places based on their proximity to the center of the Temple Mount.[18] From there, sites radiate out in decreasing importance: the boundaries of the Temple Mount, the boundaries of Jerusalem, the boundaries of Israel, and so on. A Muslim tradition attributed to the Prophet Muhammad assigns the following enhanced values to a single prayer based on its location: in the Holy Land, five hundred prayers; in Jerusalem, a thousand prayers; in Medina, ten thousand prayers; in Mecca, a hundred thousand prayers.[19] Similarly, medieval pilgrims knew that they would earn discrete merits toward a plenary indulgence by visiting sites of differing centrality. A pilgrimage to

Rome, for example, was worth twice that of a visit to a regional shrine, such as St. David's in Pembrokeshire, Wales.[20]

Evaluating the Sensitivity of a Sacred Site: Vulnerability

Though *centrality* offers a good measure for the importance of a site to the body of believers, it does not offer a sufficient estimate of the likelihood of conflict over a site. After all, a site of significant centrality is unlikely to lead to friction between believers if it is inaccessible to believers or, conversely, if it is welcoming to all visitors irrespective of creed, appearance, or behavior.

Mount Kailash, for example, is of utmost sanctity for the members of four religions (Hindus, Buddhists, Jains, and Tibetan Shamans), yet, at twenty-two thousand feet in the Tibetan Himalayas, its peak is one of the least visited sacred sites in the world. St. Peter's Basilica in Rome and Temple Square in Salt Lake City, Utah, on the other hand, while central to the religious beliefs of Catholics and members of the Church of Jesus Christ of Latter Day Saints, respectively, are easily accessible to tourists of all faiths, with few restrictions on access, dress, or behavior within their boundaries. At the same time, there are areas in both St. Peter's and Temple Square that are entirely inaccessible except to a select few. Finally, some marginal sacred sites, such as monasteries or convents, are governed by strict rules that constrain both access and action. The likelihood of friction over rights of access and the free exercise of religion at these sites is therefore relatively high.

To estimate the likelihood of conflict over a site then, we must consider a second parameter in addition to centrality, one that estimates the extent to which access to the site and behavior within it are circumscribed, monitored, and sanctioned. That parameter is the site's *vulnerability*. Members of a religious community are likely to control access to and behavior in their sacred space precisely because of the dangerous aspects of the sacred. To prevent worshipers from offending the divine presence by inappropriate dress or behavior, that is, to prevent sacrilege and ensuing penalties for the offender and the community, those responsible for maintaining the site will want to regulate who enters, how they enter, what they wear, and how they conduct themselves within the shrine.

As a rule, centrality and vulnerability go hand in hand. The more sensitive the site to sacrilege, the greater the restrictions on access and behavior. For example, only Muslims may visit Mecca and Medina, the two sacred cities in Saudi Arabia. Indeed, the Saudi government has paved so-called non-Muslim roads around the cities and enforces a ban on the presence of non-Muslims within fifteen miles of either of those cities. Monasteries and convents, on the other hand, limit access to members of a specific gender. Some sacred sites, such as Mount Athos in Greece, are limited to members of a particular caste. Though Temple Square in Utah is open to all tourists, only members in good standing of the church are permitted into the temple in the center of the square. In rare cases, access to a sacred site is restricted to select individuals at specific times. The Jewish high priest was the only individual allowed into the Holy of Holies in the Temple in Jerusalem, and only on a single day of the year, Yom Kippur.

Beyond limiting access, the rules governing sacred sites may dictate "gestures of approach," actions that must be taken by believers upon approaching and entering the site. In Judaism and Sikhism, these entail covering the head. In Christianity, the head is uncovered, whereas in Islam and Sikhism the shoes are removed. Muslims wash and Hindus bathe before approaching a shrine.[21] At the entrance to Shinto temples, believers are required to rinse out their mouths. Members of certain Maori tribes from southern New Zealand are said to remove their clothes before entering a sacred place.[22] These actions are taken on the threshold of the sacred place and emphasize its distinctiveness. Other religious codes may delineate dress and prohibit a narrow range of activities within the sanctuary or permit only a narrow range of behaviors.

To summarize, the more central the site to the identity of the religious community, the more likely the community is to take action in response to challenges to the integrity of the site. The more vulnerable the site, the greater the risk that foreign presence or conduct will be interpreted as an offensive act.

Predicting Conflict

The institutionalization of sacred places drives both the centrality and the vulnerability of sacred sites. As the site moves from space to shrine and then to temple, it assumes a more central role in the narrative of the religious community. At the same time, with institutions in place to detect and punish transgression, the sensitivity of the community to desecration goes up. Temples, and their parallels in other religions, thus tend to be the most central and most vulnerable sites in any given religion. This process can be uneven across religions and across sites in a particular religion, since institutionalization itself is driven by a variety of social, economic, and political factors.

The escalation of centrality and vulnerability can be even more erratic as mirror sites to the temple are produced, because this shift places the responsibility for maintaining and guarding the new sacred sites in the hands of local communities. Mirror sites, such as city or village churches, mosques, and synagogues, are always less central than the respective temple but they can be even more sensitive to desecration, depending on whether the community chooses to relax or constrain the restrictions on access and behavior at their local site. A community may do so for a host of reasons: because the site is associated with a beloved local saint, because the community relates its identity and history to the site, because the institutions surrounding the site provide crucial economic, political, or social services to the community, or simply because the local community has forged a strong emotional bond with the sacred place.

It is here that political interests, exogenous to religiously motivated concerns about centrality and vulnerability, can complicate matters significantly. As Friedland and Hecht have convincingly argued, actors may wish to enhance the salience of sacred sites in order to fulfill political aspirations, mobilize followers, or subvert the secular foundations of a state.[23] The most central and vulnerable sacred sites offer the most effective tool for such purposes: conflict at these sites provides followers with a powerful religious motivation for action that can supplement and reinforce existing political motivations.

Ambient conflict can also augment the value of sacred sites absent purposive manipulation by political players. Believers are likely to perceive even the most marginal of sacred sites as vulnerable if that site is located in a sectarian conflict zone or near an ethnic fault line. Politically motivated violence, past or present, real or imagined, can thus impinge on religious rationales for valuing a sacred site if the community has reason to fear for the integrity of its sacred site.

In sum, then, we should expect conflict to arise at the sacred places that are the most central and vulnerable of a religious movement. The most conflict-prone sacred sites for any given religion tend to be relatively "legalized" places, such as temples, cathedrals, or grand mosques. That said, the typology suggested here provides a rough heuristic at best. Although the ranking of sacred places within a given religion is often explicit, comparisons of rankings across religious groups or even subgroups are of limited utility, given differences in conceptions of sacred space across religious movements. The importance of sacred space in the system of beliefs and practices and the rewards attached to visiting, or possessing, significant sites vary from religion to religion. Moreover, the religious considerations that determine a site's centrality and vulnerability are not immune to the influence of political actors and interests. Even a mirror site can become the locus of violent conflict if a local community places a high value on the site for political reasons.

All this begs the question: Why do sacred sites, of all sites available, make tempting targets of conflict for sectarian rivals or political entrepreneurs? I examine that question in detail in the next chapter but have already provided the key to the answer. The phenomenon of sacred space concretizes religion, giving it a worldly, material facet. In sacred space, religious ideas become tangible: they can be owned, built upon, dug in, fought over. At the same time, the control exerted by a community over their sacred space assumes political dimensions. It involves defining the boundaries of the sacred space, patrolling those boundaries, and policing behavior within them.

These actions, though derived from religious reasoning, are ultimately political. They call to mind the control by modern society over its most central and vulnerable of secular spaces, the state. Dominion over sacred space, like sovereign control over territory, requires the ability to monitor entry and exit and regulate behavior within clearly defined boundaries. "Ritual rights," as Friedland and Hecht aptly put it, "require property rights."[24] In sacred space, religiously motivated actors translate the inherent characteristics of the sacred into political, and often violent, action.

5. The Borobudur Temple complex in Java, Indonesia, consists of nine platforms, decorated with 2,672 relief panels and surmounted by 504 Buddha statues. Photo copyright Luca Tettoni/Corbis.

Chapter Three

The Indivisibility Problem

Sacred spaces are replete with paradoxes. Religious movements embrace the unity and sanctity of all creation but also recognize that some sites are more sacred than others. Believers regard the divine as omnipresent but consider its presence at these sites to be somehow more intense. Earth-bound and confined in material dimensions, these sacred sites are nevertheless capable of revealing the sacred order of the entire universe to the believer, capturing both micro- and macrocosmos at the same time. Pilgrims will endure great travails to reach these places, only to learn that their pilgrimage was an inward journey to a place not of this world. And, most troubling of all, the sacred places at which they arrive are sites that unite splendor and amazement, on the one hand, with terror and violence on the other.

In the preceding chapter, I relied on the study of sacred places by sociologists of religion to introduce some order into these contradictions. I now turn to political science for insight into why sacred places should become contested in the first place.

I begin with a discussion of the notion of indivisibility. Ever since King Solomon rudely suggested cutting a child in half, indivisibility has become linked in our minds with babies. But why should babies be indivisible, whereas cakes or pieces of land are not? The question itself is, of course, misleading. Children are perfectly divisible. But they are perceived as indivisible by humans, especially parents. Because indivisibility is a quality attributed to an object or issue by an agent, I begin this chapter with an interpretivist definition of indivisibility, that is, a definition that accepts the beliefs of agents at face value. I contrast this intuitive three-part definition with existing approaches to indivisibility in the political science literature.

In a concurrence that is perhaps best described as a cruel twist of fate, the tripartite definition of indivisibility matches perfectly with the three functions of sacred space. The second part of this chapter thus proceeds through the qualities of sacred places to show why all sacred places are necessarily indivisible.

What is Indivisibility?

1 Kings 3 tells the story of Solomon's judgment. The incident is designed to exemplify the king's exceptional wisdom as he resolves a seemingly intractable dispute between two women, both staking claim to the same child. It transpires that one of the women accidentally smothered her newborn child to death during the night and swapped the dead child with the living child of her neighbor. Each woman now claims to be the true mother of the living child and accuses the other of having killed her own. Solomon, to unmask the identity of the true mother, gives the facetious order to slice the child in half. The woman who intercedes to stop this cruel exercise, even at risk of losing the child entirely, is thus revealed to be the child's true mother.

Solomon's judgment has come to symbolize innovative conflict resolution approaches and exemplifies how identity can be revealed through expressed preferences.[1] At the same time, the episode has interesting implications for understanding a specific type of dispute, namely, disputes over indivisible goods. The indivisible good in this particular case is the body of a living child. This is not a paternity suit: the women are not disputing their rights to the child or negotiating visitation rights, in which case the object of dispute would have been entirely divisible. Rather, they are in conflict over ownership of the child's body. Both wish to possess it whole and alive. Nevertheless, as the biblical story demonstrates, a true mother is willing to give up ownership of her child altogether in order to avoid the violent division of her child.

Mothers perceive children to be indivisible, but what exactly does this mean? The political science literature defines indivisible conflicts as situations in which actors prefer conflict to any compromise settlement.[2] Scholars have suggested several actor-oriented accounts of indivisibility. James Fearon has argued that indivisibility should be a rare situation in political disputes because the multidimensional issues over which states usually bargain can always be linked to other issues or resolved by means of side payments. Issues may seem inherently indivisible, but "the cause of this indivisibility lies in the domestic political and other mechanisms rather than in the nature of the issues themselves."[3] In the end, Fearon finds explanations based on indivisibility interesting in theory but neither compelling nor convincing in practice.

Barbara Walter and Monica Toft have examined the problem of indivisibility in civil wars and have concluded that certain disputes do exhibit indivisibility.[4] This indivisibility is traced not to the economic, strategic, or "psychological" value of a territory but to the issue of reputation: a government that expects future separatist challenges to arise has incentives to create a reputation for toughness in territorial negotiations, even if the territory currently negotiated is of little value to it. Like Fearon, Walter, and Toft, Stacie Goddard believes that "there is no inherent property of an issue that determines its divisibility; rather, indivisibility is produced by dynamics internal to interaction."[5] Goddard has used network theory to show how claims made by actors during the negotiation process create increasingly narrow social coalitions and restrict bargaining positions. Indivisibility arises when the actors adopt positions that are incommensurable with all other claims to an issue, removing all possible mechanisms of distribution.

These studies draw on strong analytical tools to set the foundation for an understanding of indivisibility. At the same time, the approach to indivisibility adopted in these analyses is somewhat counterintuitive: rather than describe indivisibility as a characteristic attributed to a substance or issue, they describe indivisibility as the outcome of a strategic interaction. Were we to apply their interpretation to the case of Solomon's judgment, we would be led to conclude that Solomon's suggestion of slicing the child in half was problematic not because human babies are perceived as inherently indivisible but because the specific litigants in that case were engaged in an exchange of signals, alliances, and side-payments, or suffered failures of commitment, that made cutting that specific baby in half difficult. Clearly, one should not reject a model on the basis of its inconsistency with a biblical parable. But one might aim at supplementing it by means of a more intuitive account of indivisibility that would be easier to operationalize, test, and apply to a wider range of cases, from disputed territory to babies. The interpretivist definition of indivisibility I offer below seeks to complement this actor-oriented view by offering an understanding of indivisibility that is attuned to social facts. Such an approach can shed light on indivisibility in those instances in which an issue has been constructed as indivisible long before the onset of a dispute.

In part, prevailing views on indivisibility are counterintuitive because they take the social construction of reality too far. Fearon, Toft, Walter, and

Goddard all argue that indivisibility is the creation of actors involved in disputes. In Fearon's view, mistrust between parties in anarchy prevents credible commitment that should be able to solve any indivisibility problem with ease. In Toft and Walter's case, claims that there can be no compromise over territory are ploys designed by crafty negotiators who seek to dissuade future separatist challengers. In Goddard's account indivisibility is an unfortunate side effect of a negotiation in which coalitions have become too restricted. These accounts seem to imply an "ideas all the way down" sociology of indivisible issues: agents create and destroy the indivisibility of issues unremittingly, often unwittingly.[6] It should thus be impossible to identify indivisible issue ex ante, because they will not exist prior to interaction. This all but postmodern approach has the consequence of diverting the research agenda away from the question of the resolution of indivisible disputes. The implied assumption is that the very same entrepreneurs that create indivisibility are capable of mitigating indivisibility.

These studies give insufficient credence to the existence of fundamental social facts, those types of issues that actors cannot easily define and redefine. Some beliefs constitute the identity of agents and create the structural constraints within which they act. These include analytical truths but also certain beliefs about reality, basic human needs, or embedded intersubjective beliefs.[7] One example of the latter type of belief is the benevolent predisposition that humans have toward their own progeny. As I will argue presently, another example is the inviolability of places central to the religious beliefs of a community. It is our confidence in social facts such as the intense attachment between mothers and their infants that enables us to identify one of the litigants in Solomon's trial, the woman who supports cutting the child in half, as an impostor. A human who can contemplate cutting up his or her own baby is either a lunatic—meaning someone outside our intersubjective network—or not a parent, that is, someone whose identity is not constituted by that social fact.

Contrary to Fearon's claim about the dearth of indivisible issues, we can think of several categories of indivisible issues.[8] James Rosenau, pioneer of the issue-area typology in the study of international relations, has argued that status issues, involving both intangible means and intangible ends, create persistent contention and intractable disputes.[9] Edward Mansbach and John Vasquez developed this notion further and argued that issues characterized by transcendent stakes posed the greatest difficulties for dispute resolution because they were both intangible and indivisible, often equated with fundamental values, norms, and rules of the game.[10] Roy Licklider has argued that culturally grounded and deeply held beliefs, such as ethnic identities, give rise to indivisible disputes.[11] Fred Ikle has claimed that indivisibility problems occur in civil wars whenever "partition is not a feasible outcome because belligerents are not geographically separable, one side has to get all, or nearly so, since there cannot be two governments ruling over one country."[12] Paul Pillar agrees that disputes over sovereignty in civil war pose indivisibility problems if "neither side can get most of what it wants without depriving the other of most of what it wants."[13] In separate papers, Cecilia Albin and Ian Lustick have examined how perceptions of indivisibility, linked to core needs and values, have created obstacles to the resolution of the Jerusalem dispute.[14] I argue here that sacred places form a coherent set of cases that are perceived as inherently indivisible.

It seems, then, that while in some cases indivisibility is the creation of actors or a product of the construction of identities, alliances, and preferences during a dispute, in other cases it is a characteristic of the disputed issue that precedes the dispute. Actors may possess the skill to redefine issues in certain cases, but not in other cases, such as the case of sacred space. I will bring the social construction of sacred space back into the picture in the second half of this book to suggest some very limited conditions under which certain actors can shift the meaning of sacred space to mitigate indivisible disputes.

An Interpretivist Definition of Indivisibility

My goal is to arrive at an intuitive definition of indivisibility, yet the simplest definition as found in the Oxford English Dictionary, "incapable of being divided," seems to miss the point entirely. What we are concerned with here is not the viability of the task but the perceptions and preferences of the parties to the undertaking. Economists and game theorists take us a step closer to actor preferences by defining indivisible goods as "goods whose value is destroyed if they are divided."[15] This works for economists, because they assume that goods are both fungible and discrete. In politics, however, many of the issues at stake are not "goods" at all and can be nonfungible as well as overlapping or hazy in demarcation. Thus a definition of indivisibility that seeks to shed light on political disputes needs to make these two assumptions, issue boundaries and nonfungibility, explicit.

The result is a simple three-part definition of indivisibility: First, as in the economic definition, the parties must hold that the issue cannot be parceled out or subdivided without significantly diminishing its subjective value (*cohesion*). Second, the parties must mean the same thing when they refer to the issue they are bargaining over (*boundaries*). If there is no overlap between the issue boundaries as they perceive them then the issue is, at least in part, divisible. Finally, the parties must believe that the issue cannot be substituted for or exchanged for something of equal value (*uniqueness*).[16] Each of these three conditions is necessary, but not by itself sufficient, for achieving indivisibility. Combined, they offer the necessary and sufficient conditions for an interpretivist definition of indivisibility. This is an interpretivist definition because it focuses not on the objective characteristics of a good or issue but on its qualities as perceived subjectively by parties to a dispute. What matters is not whether the good can in fact be divided physically but whether the parties perceive it as the kind of good that can be divided.

Given these three conditions, it becomes clear why Solomon's judgment strikes us intuitively as an indivisibility scenario. The infant cannot be divided without diminishing its value to the mother. The litigants are arguing over a single clearly defined issue, namely, ownership of the child's body, leaving no room for negotiation over parts of the issue. Neither mother will accept a side payment in return for relinquishing her child.

Whereas the first two elements of the definition, cohesion and boundaries, are sufficient for defining an indivisible *issue,* uniqueness is necessary for defining an indivisible *dispute.* Indivisibility is problematic only when it coincides with multiple claims to ownership: it is the need of more than one party to possess, or hold sovereignty over, an indivisible good that creates an indivisibility dispute. Thus, in effect, indivisible disputes are indivisible in two distinct ways. First, parties in these disputes view the issue as indivisible in and of itself, meaning that it cannot be taken apart, and second, they consider the issue indivisible from themselves, signifying that they will not tolerate parting with it.

There is a tension between the twin meanings of the term. Parties to an indivisibility dispute, torn between their wish to preserve the unity of the issue or good and their desire to possess it, wish to have their proverbial cake whole and eat it too. Solomon's judgment builds on this tension: the child's true mother is torn between the desire to possess her child, on the one hand, and the desire to maintain the integrity of her child, its body and life, on the other. Curiously, any act taken by a party to enhance indivisibility in one sense necessarily diminishes indivisibility in the other sense. This is the *indivisibility conundrum:* The more each side acts to take possession of its part of the disputed good, the more divided the good becomes. The stronger the claims made by the parties regarding the indivisibility of the good, the clearer it becomes to each party that it does not possess the good in its entirety.

There are only two possible solutions to an indivisible dispute. In one outcome preferences are reordered and both parties forgo cohesion for ownership.

This is the outcome supported by the false mother during the trial: "It shall be neither yours nor mine; cut it in two." The other possibility is suggested by the true mother: "Please, my lord, give her the live child; only don't kill it."[17] In this solution both parties insist on maintaining the cohesion of the good, but the preferences of one party are reordered and it agrees to forgo ownership.

Indivisibility and Sacred Places

Most plots of land are easily divisible. Indeed, it is difficult to think of a piece of land that fulfills even one of the three necessary conditions for indivisibility. It is rare to find territory that is perfectly integrated: this would require it to be evenly populated, developed in its entirety, rich in resources throughout, or consistently valued for historical or nationalist reasons. Since no disputed territory is homogeneous in value, there are always some segments that disputants will be more willing to bargain over or even cede. Similarly, it is unusual for the boundaries of a piece of land to be so clearly and precisely defined as to preclude any ambiguity about its size and location. Finally, most territories are entirely replaceable. Parties can be compensated for their willingness to engage in compromises resulting in loss of property, real estate, natural resources, or access to trade routes. Even the strategic value of territory can be offset by means of third-party presence, confidence-building measures, or the compensatory transfer of weapons technology or military intelligence.

Sacred spaces are unique in this regard because all sacred spaces fulfill the three conditions for indivisibility. Sacred places are integrated monolithic spaces that cannot be subdivided; they have clearly defined and inflexible boundaries; they are unique sites for which no material or spiritual substitute is available. Each of these characteristics is a necessary but insufficient component in the creation of the indivisibility of sacred space. Unfortunately perhaps, these three dimensions are present wherever space has been defined as sacred.

The inherent indivisibility of sacred spaces arises from the three core functions that these places provide to believers: because various elements of a sacred site combine to represent the believer's spiritual cosmos, any division of a sacred site undermines its symbolic coherence; because it is a site at which believers can expect to communicate directly with the divine, an encounter that entails promise as well as danger, the site must be separated from the surrounding secular space by means of precisely delimited boundaries; because revelations and miracles occur at a site it is rendered irreplaceable in the eyes of believers.

The Cohesion of Sacred Space

Sacred shrines are often large and complicated structures composed of multiple elements. They may contain numerous stations, subdivisions, and even areas with varying degrees of sanctity relative to the core of the sacred space. Even the simplest Christian church or Hindu temple is composed of multiple interlocking parts. The different components of a sacred site may vary in material, design, and location, but they serve a combined purpose: to convey a message of religious order to the believers. If any part of a sacred site is removed or destroyed, the site is rendered meaningless. The division of sacred space, in other words, is tantamount to desecration.

Consider the manner in which disparate elements in Buddhist, Christian, and Hindu sacred sites combine to form a cohesive whole. The great Buddhist temple in Borobudur, Indonesia, for example, consists of eight terraces crowned with 72 *stupas* (bell-shaped relic shrines) and 504 Buddha statues.[18] All these elements unite to form a giant *mandala,* a map of the Buddhist cosmos. The temple's two-hundred-square-yard base symbolizes the mundane world. Each of the square terraces above it depicts an obstacle that needs to be overcome on the path to enlightenment. These are surmounted by circular terraces that represent the spiritual world. The bottom two are slightly misaligned to symbolize the progress toward spiritual perfection as one ascends toward ultimate truth, represented by the topmost terrace. The number of levels, statues, and relic shrines on the Borobudur temple plays on the number 9, the sacred number in Buddhism. Indeed, even the particular design of the seventy-two *stupas* carries meaning: as one ascends the temple, the latticed openings in these shrines become smaller. This makes it harder for the pilgrim to touch the Buddha statues placed in their center, denoting the increased challenge of achieving true enlightenment. The largest and topmost *stupa,* perfectly centered, is empty to signify the emptiness of all sensual appearances.

Similarly, traditional churches represent both the cross and the divine body of Christ. The aisle and transept symbolize the vertical and horizontal beams of the cross. Were the body of Christ symbolically superimposed on this cross, it would rest with its arms over the transept and the body over the congregation, so that the head would coincide with the location of the altar, where the Eucharist is performed. Thus the body of Christ and the congregation as living church are symbolically united through the architecture of the church. At the same time, the church building serves to recall the most significant event and location in Christian history and geography, namely, the crucifixion and resurrection of Jesus Christ in Jerusalem. The crucifixion is recalled not only in the cruciform design of the building but also in the fourteen Stations of the Cross that are marked on the walls around some churches, recalling episodes that occurred on the path to the crucifixion. The church also echoes in its layout the design of the Church of the Holy Sepulcher in Jerusalem, with the altar representing the site of sacrifice, Mount Calvary, and the sanctuary behind it representing the site of the resurrection, the Holy Tomb.

The design of every Hindu temple, on the other hand, is based on a *yantra,* the Hindu equivalent of a *mandala.*[19] Its square plot is dissected by a grid into smaller squares, the central of which is usually occupied by the image of a deity associated with creation. This sanctuary is often designed to symbolize a cave, and the overall structure of the temple is shaped to resemble a sacred mountain. The peak of this mountain, aligned above the sanctuary, represents the enlightenment that emanates upward from the deity. Surrounding the sanctuary, representations of deities with various cosmic responsibilities symbolize the order emanating from creation.

A similar logic unites panels, steps, platforms, and intricate carvings of the Temple of Kukulcan in Chichen Itza, Mexico; the elements, forms, and colors of the Altar of Heaven in Beijing; the components of the Stupa of a Thousand Images in Gyantse, Tibet; and even various parts of the Meenakshi Temple in India, with sixteen towers and hundreds of rooms sprawling over fifteen acres. It is through architecture, symbol, and practice that these different components become integrated into a single, cohesive whole.

This unity is buttressed through the rituals performed by believers in the sacred space. By walking around the interior of the church, Catholics symbolically reenact the last hours in the life of Jesus and tie the fourteen points in the church interior into one. Hindu worshipers will enter a temple from the east, perform clockwise circumambulation of the temple interior, and only then enter the sanctuary. Similar circumambulations are performed by Muslim, Buddhist, and Sikh worshipers. By walking along the borders of the site, believers confirm its boundaries and unite its disparate elements. Indeed, the act of circumambulation is often employed in the ceremonies that serve to dedicate and consecrate these sites in the first place.

Any attempt at dismembering a sacred place would thus be tantamount to symbolically dissecting the universe that the sacred place represents. In the eyes of believers, such an act would deprive the sacred space of its function and the world of its meaning. The cohesion of a sacred site can also be thought of in terms of Mircea Eliade's *axis mundi.* As world axis, the sacred place is not the three-dimensional space that it appears to be but a pivot, both connecting the earth to the heavens and acting as center for the rest of the universe. Metaphorically, a sacred place can be thought of as a two-dimensional vertical line and not a space with physical breadth and depth.[20] Imagining a sacred space as an axis helps explain, in part, why the design of so many shrines is based on concentric circles radiating from single point and why the rituals practiced by believers often involve circumambulation of that point. Conceived as an axis, a sacred place cannot be sliced on the vertical plane. Cutting it across the horizontal plain is tantamount to severing the link it establishes between the heavens and the earth.

The Boundaries of Sacred Space

Because the sacred is defined as that which is set apart from and contrasted with the profane, strict regulations circumscribe the difference in behavior inside and outside this space and restrict entrance to the sacred place. This is the same dichotomy that, according to Emile Durkheim, is at the core of all religious belief: "Since the idea of the sacred is always and everywhere separated from the idea of the profane in the thought of men, and since we picture a sort of logical chasm between the two, the mind irresistibly refuses to allow the two corresponding things to be confounded, or even put in contact with each other."[21] This distinction is also captured in the Sanskrit term for a site of pilgrimage: *tirtha* means both "ford," in the sense that many sacred Hindu sites are placed near water, and also a symbolic crossing point, marking the stark transition from the mundane to the spiritual.[22]

Any act that blurs this sharp distinction is an act of desecration. Desecration poses a direct danger to the violator who, by entering a forbidden place or by failing to adapt his behavior to a sacred environment, incurs the anger of the gods.[23] The Bible is replete with example of individuals struck down by the hand of God for entering prohibited sacred space or performing prohibited acts in sacred space.[24] In Leviticus 10:9, for example, God issues the following warning to the high priest Aaron regarding behavior inside the sanctuary: "Wine and strong drink you shall not drink, you and your sons with you, when you come into the Tent of Meeting, lest you die—a perpetual statute for your generations, to divide between the holy and the profane, and between the unclean and the clean."[25] The warning could not have been phrased more clearly, particularly in light of the fact that, eight verses prior to this warning, Aaron's two sons were devoured by divine fire for burning the wrong type of incense in the sanctuary.

Desecration also poses an indirect danger to the community of believers who, through carelessness, permitted the violation to take place. The community is thus likely to confront the violator in order to prevent desecration or to exact punishment for a violation that has taken place. To avoid accidental desecration, religious communities take extreme measures to define the boundaries of their sacred places clearly and to demarcate them in a manner that is unambiguous and easily recognizable. In the Jewish Temple in Jerusalem, for example, a stone balustrade, the *soreg,* separated the parts of the shrine accessible to all from those accessible only to Jews in a state of purity. Archaeologists have uncovered one of several stone plaques, placed along that barrier, inscribed in Latin and Greek, that warned foreigners to stay away on pain of death.[26] A modern variant of these signs, printed in Hebrew, Arabic, and English, is now mounted on the tourists' entrance to the Temple Mount, proclaiming the sanctity of the site and listing prohibited behavior.

Religious leaders responsible for institutionalizing the site and supervising worship at the site can consult sacred sources and rely on a religious logic in determining its boundaries. Buddhist priests, for example, will align the square plot on which a shrine is to be constructed with the cardinal directions.[27] They will then mark the corners and boundaries of that plot by means of sharp wooden pegs, summoning the four Great Kings of the North, South, East, and West to consecrate and protect the site and uttering curses to ward off all demons. In other religions, founders have limited visitor access to specific pathways by surrounding the site with fences, walls, cliffs, trenches, or water. Bridges, gates, stairways, and other markers on these paths signal the moment at which the path crosses into the sacred site. Visitors can rely on these visual clues to determine where they may go and what gestures of approach they must adopt.

These gestures of approach perform two functions in relation to the boundaries of the sacred site. They affirm and entrench the recognized borders of the sacred place but also provide visual signals to uninitiated observers that a threshold is about to be crossed. Worshipers visiting a Japanese Shinto shrine, for example, will walk a sacred path to the *torii,* the gateway that marks the transition into sacred space.[28] There they wash their hands at a source of flowing water, rinse their mouths, and may change into white robes. They then proceed onto a raised platform, the *haiden,* where they make offerings, drink rice wine in honor of the gods, and strike a gong and clap twice to announce their presence to the gods. Beyond that lies the *honden,* the inner shrine in which the spirit of the shrine resides and which only the priests may enter.

The rigid demarcation of sacred space creates boundaries that are unequivocal and inflexible. This leaves no doubt as to the precise location and dimensions of the site. Of course, there are always exceptions to this pattern. Because the constructed boundaries of a sacred site have a depth of their own, they produce liminal space along the edges of every site that is neither sacred nor profane. The walls, bridges, or stairways that surround a sacred place or lead directly up to it are therefore ambiguous in status. Boundaries will be even more ambiguous when the sacred site is not constructed at all but rather a natural site. Whereas rivers and lakes might have clear boundaries, mountains, caves, or forests do not. Finally, determining the boundaries of a sacred place is problematic when the space is mobile. Buddhists, Hindus, and Christians worship at some shrines that, while large and elaborate, can be mounted on platforms and moved around, particularly on feast days. The Tabernacle, the Jewish sanctuary that preceded the Temple in Jerusalem, was an array of tents and concentric courts, demarcated by barriers of wood and cloth, that followed the Israelites in their journey through the wilderness for forty years.

These exceptions bolster the more general rule regarding the precision and permanence of sacred boundaries and its connection with conflict. There are no cases of disputes, indivisible or otherwise, over mobile shrines or the narrow liminal areas immediately adjacent to sacred sites. Disputes over natural sacred places do occur, particularly around Native American holy places in the Americas, but these focus on the parts of the site that are unambiguously sacred and not on its margins. When Native Americans and U.S. authorities clash over sacred mountains, such as Mount Shasta, Devil's Tower, or Mount Rushmore, it is the bulk of the mountain, and in particular its peak, that are in dispute and not the low foothills that surround it.

Indeed, disputes over mountains are few and far between because most sacred mountains are revered from afar. There are no shrines on the peaks of Mount Olympus, Kailash, or Kilauea, if only because they are very difficult or dangerous to access. Natural sites that can be accessed, on the other hand, are often clearly delimited: Waterfalls sacred to Shintoists are frequently surrounded by the same markers that signify the entrance to a Shinto shrine. Mountains sacred to Buddhists are often divided, visibly, into ten segments. Ascending pilgrims are required to perform particular rites at the transition points between one section and the next.[29]

The Uniqueness of Sacred Space

Sacred places that are constructed in response to a divine sign or to commemorate a religious event are unique: it is impossible to place a value on, let alone substitute for, these locations. The crucifixion and resurrection occurred in Jerusalem and nowhere else. Pilgrims who wish to experience Christ's suffering in the most unmediated manner do so by following in his precise footsteps, as many do by carrying large crosses along the Via Dolorosa. Because Muhammad was born in Mecca, ascended to heaven from Jerusalem, and was buried in Medina, it is only at the shrines in these three cities that worshipers can revere the authentic locations of his birth, ascension, and death. By worshiping in the actual place at which a divine revelation occurred, rather than a site that mirrors that place, believers can expect a more immediate and intense interaction with the gods and consequently clearer communication, greater gifts, and a deeper understanding. This explains, in part, why pilgrims are willing to assume substantial risks and costs in traveling to a site that is higher in centrality than the shrines near their homes.

But even man-made sacred places, from cemeteries and village mosques to parish churches or gurdwaras, provide an authentic link with the divine once they have been consecrated. The act of consecration, discussed at length in chapter 6, elevates the site from its initial mundane state so as to make it worthy of a divine presence. Once complete, the consecration ceremony transforms the place into a sacred place in which previously impossible acts may be performed and in which other acts previously permitted will no longer be tolerated. Adopting an interpretivist stance, Joel Brereton has argued that this transformation is so extreme as to suggest to the believer that the gods themselves were responsible for the creation of the sacred site. Such a place "is not a place of wholly human creation or choice...its significance is grounded in its unique character, a character that no purely human action can confer on it."[30]

Once a sacred place has been constructed or identified, it provides unique functions that no other site can provide. For example, because members of the Church of Jesus Christ of Latter Day Saints consider their temples to exist outside time, they can perform ceremonies there that they cannot perform in their churches. Mormons may undergo baptism or weddings at any Mormon church, but only in a temple can they be baptized on behalf of the dead or seal marriages that will last for all eternity (that is, beyond "death do us part"). Only Later Day Saints married in this manner will encounter God fully in the highest level of heaven, the Celestial Kingdom.[31] Shintoists, on the other hand, need not marry at a shrine, but weddings performed at Shinto shrines are considered more auspicious, and those performed at the shrine of Izumo Taisha, the spirit god of matrimony and relationships, are considered the most fortunate of all. Catholic Christians can obtain plenary indulgences, and thus avoid purgatory, by completing pilgrimages to certain shrines but not others. Only in the Holy Temple in Jerusalem could Jews perform the animal offerings commanded in the Hebrew Bible. As a result of the destruction of that space, Judaism has had to dispense with its priestly classes, sacrificial rituals, and ceremonial implements proscribed, with excruciating detail, in Leviticus.

The more central the space in the religious landscape of the community, the greater the divine power vested in the place and the greater the obligation of the community to defend the sanctity of the space. This obligation is owed, not only to all members of the community, but to future generations, deceased ancestors, and the gods themselves, leaving the community with no ability or desire to bargain over the space with rivals. Asked about Jewish claims to the Noble Sanctuary, the director of the Islamic Trust in Jerusalem summed up the uniqueness of the site to Muslims as follows: "This is a mosque. It is not subject to any negotiations.... We can't deal in details in such a place. This is God's will that there be a mosque here. We can't say, 'Let's change God's will.'"[32]

Thus, the cohesion, boundaries, and uniqueness of sacred space create the conditions for an indivisible dispute at each and every sacred space. This indivisibility need not, in and of itself, pose a direct problem. Just as parents are not normally troubled by the indivisibility of their children unless a divorce is at hand, believers need not worry about the indivisibility of their sacred places unless they find themselves in situations of conflict over these sites.

Sadly, causes for disputes over sacred places abound. As I show in the next chapter, five widespread historical trends create rivalry over sacred spaces, either among religious groups or between religious and secular forces. These five trends transform the abstract problem of indivisibility into a tangible concern: once sacred places come to stand at the heart of disputes, their indivisibility renders resolution of these disputes difficult if not impossible.

6. The Selimiye Mosque in Nicosia, Cyprus, originally the thirteenth-century Cathedral of St. Sophia. After the Ottoman conquest of Cyprus in 1570, the cathedral was converted into a mosque and minarets were added to its gothic exterior. Photo copyright Jonathan Blair/Corbis.

Chapter Four

CONFLICT OVER SACRED PLACES

Five widespread historical trends convert the potential difficulty posed by the indivisibility of sacred space into concrete rivalry over such space, either among religious groups or between religious and secular forces. Disputes stem from the splitting of religions into rival factions; the fusion of opposed beliefs through syncretism; competition over sacred space as real estate; the use of sacred space as force multiplier; or the vulnerability of sacred space as a social symbol. The resulting disputes need not be indivisible in the sense of concerning sovereign right to a shrine. They may involve access to the site, maintenance of its integrity, conduct within it, or political factors complicated by the centrality and vulnerability of the site.

Is conflict at contested sites inevitable? In brief: yes. Because of the indivisibility challenge, cases of peaceful coexistence at sacred places claimed by multiple parties are few and far between. Two exceptions to this pattern bear scrutiny: believers from competing religious groups can worship peacefully in the same space if that space is of exceedingly low centrality and vulnerability or if a third party is willing to invest significant resources to regulate access and monitor behavior. This last scenario, while common, offers a partial solution at best to the conflict between the parties.

Intrareligious Rivalry

When religious traditions split into rival branches, they tend to engage in competition over what was once their common sacred space. Religious movements may separate because of disagreements over doctrine and practice, differences over leadership, or, most often, some combination of both. Each of the movements emerging from this separation faces the twin challenges of establishing its own legitimacy and preserving its constituency.

The possession of an important sacred site can serve both of these goals. By staking claim to a sacred site that once served the religious movement as a whole, each rival can assert its claim as inheritor of the true faith. Insofar as the control over the site is political, entailing jurisdiction over access and behavior within, it enables the faction that governs the site to exclude its rivals from the sacred space. This deprives the opposing movement and its followers of the many benefits of accessing the sacred place. It also allows the movement that now dominates the site to accentuate the doctrinal and ritual aspects unique to itself by introducing unilateral changes to the site, its appearance, and the rules that govern it. Only rarely will one of the factions opt for the more difficult maneuver and establish a new sacred site elsewhere, declaring it more authentic than the original.

At its most extreme, the fragmentation of a religious movement leads to the emergence of completely distinct religions. Although there is much overlap between the historical origins of Judaism and Islam, for example, they have diverged significantly in theology, doctrine, and ritual. Nevertheless, they continue to exhibit a shared reverence for some of the same sacred sites, a reverence that stems from their common veneration of shared figures and events. Thus both Jews and Muslims worship at the tombs of Abraham, Sarah, Isaac, Rebecca, Jacob, and Leah in Hebron, because these are patriarchs and matriarchs common to both religious movements. At the same time, differences in belief and practice render common worship at these sites extremely difficult. In the absence of a way to divide the site, conflict is the most common outcome.

When religious disagreements are less extreme or when the fragmentation of a religious movement occurred relatively recently, the factions may agree significantly on matters of ritual and doctrine. It is not uncommon to find different Protestant denominations, for example, sharing the facilities at a local church as long as the church is of sufficiently low centrality and vulnerability and doctrinal differences between the worshiping groups are minimal. Yet where differences in practice between the groups exist, each group's desire to assert its right as the true religion by controlling the space to the exclusion of others can lead to virulent conflicts. In the Church of the Holy Sepulcher in Jerusalem and the Church of the Nativity in Bethlehem, for example, the Greek Orthodox, Catholic, Armenian, Coptic, Syrian, and Ethiopian Churches all compete over control. In these particular cases, no faction has been able to assert its sovereignty over the entire site, with the result that all groups are in constant conflict over every stone, step, pillar, and door. Similarly, conflict between two Jewish groups has halted repairs at a major pilgrimage site in the Galilee, the tomb of Rabbi Shimon bar Yohai, credited with composing the central text of the Kabbalah. The Ashkenazi and Sepharadi groups, representing Jews from Europe and the Middle East, respectively, vie over the right to develop the site in the hope of securing prestige, donations from pilgrims, and the favors of the miracle-working rabbi.[1]

Even young religious factions that share strong doctrinal commonalities will compete over a sacred place if that place is of sufficient centrality and vulnerability to merit conflict. Two churches that seceded from the Church of Jesus Christ of Latter Day Saints, the Reorganized Church of Jesus Christ of Latter Day Saints (RLDS) and the Church of Christ (Temple Lot), have conducted a legal battle with each other and with the dominant Utah-based church over an empty lot at the intersection of River and Walnut Streets in Independence, Missouri.[2] According to Mormon revelation, this vacant lot was the site of the Garden of Eden and will be the site of the future Temple of Christ, to be established upon the Second Coming. When the Church of Christ came in possession of the lot, the RLDS placed its headquarters and world conference auditorium at the two adjacent corners of this street intersection, whereas the Utah-based Church of Jesus Christ of Latter Day Saints opened a small visitor center on the fourth corner of the intersection. In January 1990 a member of the Church of Christ who converted to the mainstream church burned the Church of Christ structure adjacent to the lot. He reported that "God had ordered him to cleanse the church site."[3]

Interreligious Rivalry

Because sanctity rests in a location, as well as in the structure that marks the location, sacred places are difficult to erase. The physical destruction of a sacred structure does not diminish the sanctity or centrality of the underlying sacred site and may, indeed, act to increase its importance. Shrewd conquerors who wished to displace local religious traditions with their own have thus often resorted to integrating existing sites into their own traditions instead of trying to obliterate the sacred structure. To appropriate the site, they rededicated the shrine to their own religion or constructed a different shrine on the same site. Such action fulfills a dual purpose: by utilizing an existing focal point, the new shrine gains immediate prominence as a symbol of the new religion; at the same time, by symbolizing the new religion, it can gradually displace the old shrine.

Readers will be familiar with the implications of this practice for sacred time as well as space. In the Christian calendar, for example, Christmas is timed so as to subsume several of the traditions previously associated with pagan winter solstice celebrations, and Easter is placed so as to coincide with and displace the Jewish Passover.[4] Such processes are best described, perhaps, as "forced syncretism." Syncretism is the process by which religious movements incorporate the beliefs and practices of other religions into their traditions. When forced syncretism is applied to sacred places, rather than sacred time, the outcome is the layering of sacred sites on top of one another.

As a result, many sacred sites resemble a layer cake or, to draw a more poetic parallel, a palimpsest, a manuscript in which a new text is written on top of an older text that has been partially scraped away.[5] As with a palimpsest, the purpose tends to be the destruction of the original by utilizing its underlying materials to produce the substitute. In sacred space this occurs wherever a site has suffered conquest by a force allied with an alien religion. The new religion constructs its sacred shrines on top of the vanquished shrines, a process that is repeated with each successive wave of conquest. The result is a series of competing claims to strata along the sacred axis, demanding different and often conflicting rites from members of opposed religious affiliations. In wars over these sacred sites, the shovel can prove as potent a weapon as the gun.

The epitome of the layering process that sacred space often undergoes is the Noble Sanctuary or Temple Mount in Jerusalem. This is not surprising, given the fact that Jerusalem is perhaps the site with the longest record of continuous worship in the world, while at the same time having served as the battleground for as many as 118 distinct conflicts in the last four millennia.[6] The Dome of the Rock and al-Aqsa Mosque are located atop the ruins of three successive Jewish Temples, the same site having been occupied at various points in history by a Templar church, a temple of Zeus, and possibly a temple of Jupiter and a Jebusite shrine.[7] Each successive conqueror in the history of the city succeeded in weaving the Temple Mount into its religious traditions: the Jews by identifying the location of the Jebusite shrine with Mount Moriah, on which Abraham had prepared to sacrifice Isaac, and by building their most sacred temple on it; the Muslims by claiming that Muhammad had visited this same mountaintop in the miraculous journey described in the opening lines of sura 17 of the Qur'an. When, in the late Middle Ages, Jews were barred from the Mount itself and transferred their rituals to its exterior Western Wall, Muslims followed suit by declaring that wall the location to which Muhammad had tied his steed upon arriving in Jerusalem.

Similarly, the dispute over the Babri Masjid in Ayodhya, India, leading to the destruction of the mosque in 1992 and ensuing sectarian riots, was rooted in the belief that the Muslim emperor Babar had destroyed a Hindu temple marking the birthplace of the god Ram in order to construct a mosque on the same location. This religious-historical claim, while erroneous, was not unreasonable given the frequency with which Mughal rulers replaced Hindu shrines with mosques, often incorporating building materials from destroyed shrines to construct the new ones. Hindu nationalists argue that three mosques in particular, in addition to the Ayodhya mosque, bear evidence of construction on top of desecrated Hindu temples, and they have claimed the right to conduct Hindu rituals in these mosques. These mosques, now all guarded by Indian military troops, are the Krishna Janmasthan in Mathura, the Kashi Vishwanath Temple/Gyanvapi Mosque in Varanasi, and the Quwwat-ul-Islam Mosque in Delhi.[8] Ironically, Hindu claims to the Babri Masjid in Ayodhya emerged initially in 1855 as a backlash against Muslim claims to a Hindu site in Ayodhya. Muslims had argued that the Hanumangarhi, the temple dedicated to Hanuman, had been built atop a destroyed mosque.[9]

Examples of forced syncretism are plentiful. The adoption of Christianity as the official religion of the Roman Empire prompted the conversion of Rome's pagan temples into churches, such as the transformation of the Pantheon, a temple the emperor Agrippa had dedicated to all pagan gods, into a church dedicated to Mary and the martyrs, or the appropriation of the Coliseum, the great Roman amphitheater, for ceremonies commemorating the crucifixion. Similarly, several Spanish churches are built on the site of, or even into the structure of, Moorish mosques. Most famous among these is the Mezquite (from the Arabic *masjid,* meaning mosque) in Cordoba, the site of which served as a pagan Roman temple, then a cathedral, then a mosque, only to be reconsecrated as a cathedral with the Reconquista. The Hagia Sophia in Istanbul was a Byzantine church before it was converted into a Roman Catholic cathedral by crusaders, then into a mosque by the Ottoman Turks, and finally into a museum under Kemal Ataturk's secularization program. Synagogues-turned-churches in Israel and Jordan, Egyptian temples converted into early Christian churches, Christianized Sun Dance lodges in the American Midwest, and the synthesis of Shiite and Zoroastrian practices in central Iranian shrines all bear witness to processes of voluntary or forced syncretism in sacred spaces.[10]

Complicating matters further, from both the believer's and the archaeologist's point of view, is the fact that many of the recent incarnations of these shrines are constructed out of the remnants of the shrines they supersede. Throughout the Roman Empire, stone, columns, and even obelisks from demolished pagan shrines were incorporated into the structure of new churches to signify the triumph of the new religion over the old. In the sixth century, the Roman emperor Justinian used stones from the Jewish Temple, demolished in the second century, to build his New Church in Jerusalem, a structure that was destroyed during the Persian conquest in the early seventh century, its stones in turn reused by Muslim conquerors to build the shrines on the Temple Mount starting in the late seventh century.[11] The Quwwat-ul-Islam Mosque in Delhi is said to have been constructed out of the ruins of twenty-seven Jain and Hindu temples.[12] This recycling of sacred materials creates allegiances in members of one faith to the very stones from which a foreign religious shrine is constructed.

Claims to specific strata in layered sacred space can be the product of conquest or the figment of a fertile imagination. In the former case, the vanquished find their sacred sites appropriated by religious traditions with conflicting practices. In the latter case, sectarian forces seek to undermine rival groups by introducing revisionist readings of the archaeology of their sacred sites. In either case, the vertical overlap between sacred sites combines with the indivisibility problem to create direct and intractable conflict between the adherents of different faiths.

One need not stray far to find examples for this type of interreligious competition. Northern Arizona provides one startling example of the difficulties caused by conflicting practices in overlapping sacred space. As result of Navajo territorial expansion and tribal relocations, Hopi, Navajo, and Paiute Native Americans have come to lay claims to the same land, the 1934 Act Arizona Navajo Reservation.[13] The Echo Cliffs, located in the center of this contested land, are sacred to all three tribes. Since 1934, the tribes have been involved in a federal lawsuit to have the Arizona Navajo Reservation divided, each trying, so far unsuccessfully, to gain exclusive rights over the Echo Cliffs.

This state of affairs has led to significant friction between the Paiute and the Hopi, both of whom worship the eagles who nest in the Echo Cliffs. The Paiute consider these eagles to be their special guardians, and they communicate with the eagles in their dreams. The Hopi, on the other hand, regard the eagles as messengers to the gods and use eaglets from the Echo Cliffs in the *niman* ceremony, designed to enable the eagles to return to the gods and report about the tribe. Regrettably, these competing beliefs lead to conflicting practices: while the Paiute revere the eagles by protecting their aeries from harm, the Hopi revere them by smothering them to death at the climax of the *niman* ceremony.[14]

Sacred Space as Real Estate

The land on which a sacred place is located may hold value other than the religious. Secular forces may wish to use the same land for development, exploration, or tourism. This gives rise to a type of dispute that has religious repercussions for only one of the parties involved. Often, these disputes will include a disenfranchised religious party on the one hand and a party motivated by material interests on the other. Insofar as this asymmetry mitigates the indivisibility problem, such disputes can be resolved by means of compromise and are usually conducted beneath the threshold of violent confrontation.

Orthodox Jews routinely protest against road construction or archaeological excavations that risk desecration of presumed ancient Jewish graves.[15] In 2006, for example, Orthodox Jews supported Muslim protesters in halting a $150 million construction project on the site of a Muslim cemetery in Jerusalem designed, ironically enough, to house Jerusalem's new Museum of Tolerance.[16]

Native Hawaiians have protested the desecration of their sacred sites by tourists, vendors, and developers.[17] Across the Americas, Native Americans are rallying to protect sacred mountains from development.[18] These include claims by the Northern Wintu and the Yurok of California to Mount Shasta, the Blackfoot and Cree to Chief Mountain in Montana, Arizona tribes to Mount Graham, the New Mexico Navajo to Shiprock (*Tsé Bit' A'i*) and the Pueblos of New Mexico to the Sandias and Medicine Deer Rock in Montana.[19]

In Australia, the Anangu protest the desecration of the Uluru monolith, also known as Ayers Rock, by tourists who climb the sacred sandstone formation and even take fragments of the rock home with them as souvenirs. The Anangu are also concerned that tourist photographs will expose tribe members to images of particular Uluru areas prohibited to them. The belief that stolen pieces of Uluru rock can bring curses upon their owners has, however, led international tourists plagued by misfortune to desperately attempt to mail their fragments back to Australia.[20]

As we would expect, these disputes rise above the threshold of violence if the site at stake is particularly central or vulnerable. Conflicts between the Lakota Sioux and gold prospectors over the Black Hills, regarded by the

Sioux as the very center of the world, culminated in the Indian Wars of the 1870s. It was thus a dispute over sacred space as real estate that stood behind the fatal encounter between George Armstrong Custer and Crazy Horse at Little Bighorn in 1876. Lakota Native Americans continue to protest the desecration of their sacred hills, in particular the defacement of Mount Rushmore. In 1971, members of the American Indian Movement expressed their contempt by occupying the monument and by perilously forming a human chain to urinate on George Washington's head.[21]

Sacred Space as a Force Multiplier

Sacred places have served as targets of attack even when the cause of the conflict was only indirectly related to the space at hand. This type of violence at a sacred site tends to occur whenever one party to a conflict expects a tactical gain from drawing the fighting toward a sacred site. Insurgents, in particular, have recognized the "home court advantage" that their own sacred sites can offer when facing an adversary of a different faith. Although the core concern of this volume is conflicts over the ownership of sacred sites and not conflicts set in sacred sites, several of the arguments proposed in the previous pages have direct implications for the conduct of warfare at sacred sites.

Sacred sites make for good insurgent strongholds because they constrain the ability of counterinsurgency forces to act with impunity, particularly when the insurgents share a religious affinity with the community that worships at a shrine and the counterinsurgents do not. In this scenario, common in the Second Gulf War, for example, counterinsurgency forces are likely to hesitate before attacking, entering, or damaging a site sacred to a local community. The insurgents, on the other hand, can fight with vigor and confidence under the pretext of defending their sacred place from an intruder.

Insurgents seeking protection in a sacred structure also enjoy the architectural advantages offered by many of these sites. Often, these are the largest and most massive structures erected by a community. Many temples, mosques, churches, and monasteries were designed to protect a community's most valuable treasures and relics. At the same time, the priests and monks who established these structures in remote areas often sought a measure of defense from a hostile environment. Consequently, many shrines, such as the Greek Orthodox monasteries atop the steep cliffs of Meteora, Byzantine churches in the Holy Land, and Buddhist monasteries in the Himalayas, look more like fortresses than sanctuaries. When warriors withdraw into the safety of structures such as these, the double standard that applies penalties for transgression and desecration only to the counterinsurgents can correct asymmetries of power.

The three Shi'a shrines in the cities of Najaf and Karbala in Iraq, for example, have repeatedly occupied center stage in power struggles between the Shi'a community and Iraq's Sunni rulers. These mosques became not only centers of agitation against Sunni rule but fortified strongholds into which Shi'a rebels could withdraw at times of unrest. The Mosque of Hussein in Karbala was the site of the lynching of seventy-one Saddam loyalists that started the 1991 Shi'a uprising. Repression of this uprising, at a cost of some three hundred thousand Shi'a lives, involved dynamiting Shi'a mosques and desecrating their cemeteries across Iraq.[22] The uprising ended with an Iraqi siege against rebel strongholds in the two great mosques of Karbala and the Mosque of Ali in Najaf. After the shrines had been pounded with tank shells, artillery shells, and Scud missiles, the area within a five-hundred-yard radius was said to resemble London at the height of the German blitz.[23]

Shi'a insurgents sought refuge from American troops in those same mosques during the Second Gulf War. In April 2004, for example, Shi'a cleric Moktada al-Sadr successfully avoided capture by U.S. troops by seeking refuge in a mosque in Kufa, guarded by militiamen armed with heavy machine guns and rocket-propelled grenades.[24] He then moved to the most sacred Shi'a shrine in Iraq, the Imam Ali Shrine in Najaf, and continued to call for war against U.S. forces. Although U.S. military helicopters and jets targeted houses around the mosque and U.S. Marines conducted intense combat in the adjacent cemetery, the Marines received explicit instructions not to fire at the shrine. Predictably, the insurgents eventually withdrew into the shrine itself. After eight days, U.S. forces withdrew completely from the site in response to intense pressure from Arab and Muslim leaders worldwide. They were replaced by Iraqi policemen who, thanks to intervention by Grand Ayatollah Ali al-Sistani, were able to enter the shrine and disarm al-Sadr's men.

It was Iraq's Sunni Muslims who made the most extensive use of Iraqi mosques as insurgency strongholds during the Second Gulf War. They did so by turning the largest of these mosques into centers for rallying public support for the insurgency. Other mosques throughout Baghdad, Karbala, Kufa, and Mosul were used to store ammunition, including explosives and bomb-making materials, rifles, machine guns, bullets, mortars and rounds, and rocket-propelled grenades and launchers. The use of mosques for weapons storage was most apparent in Falluja where, according to one U.S. military report, more than 20 of the city's 133 mosques contained caches of weapons or were used as bases for insurgency operations.[25]

The greatest challenge to U.S. operations in Iraq was posed by enemy fire directed at American troops from inside mosques. In most cases, insurgents used rifles or rocket-propelled grenades to target soldiers from inside mosques or from the mosques' minarets. Often, conflicts between soldiers and insurgents that began elsewhere ended with the latter's retreat into the apparent safety of the mosque and a final clash at the site. The U.S. military has responded with an uneasy compromise, often sacrificing the success of a mission for the integrity of a sacred site, but just as often arresting or killing insurgents and incurring the wrath of the Iraqi population for the destruction of a venerated local shrine.[26]

Sacred sites have also functioned as insurgent strongholds in the Muslim uprising against the Indian government in Kashmir, in the Palestinian uprising against Israel, during a hostage crisis in Mecca designed to challenge the Saudi monarchy (which I examine at length in chapter 8), in the Malay-Muslim uprising against the government of Thailand, and in the Sikh secessionist movement in the Punjab.[27] In all these cases the conflict was sparked not by a party's wish to conquer a shrine but rather by the execution of military operations that culminated at or near sacred shrines. The characteristics of the shrine, however, add a complicating element to otherwise standard military operations. Whereas the insurgents, posing as the defenders of the shrine, can act with relative autonomy, the counterinsurgents face the difficult choice between restraining the use of force against the insurgents and risking offense to the sensibilities of a local religious community.

Sacred Space as a Social Symbol

A final common trend typifying the history of conflicts over sacred spaces is the manipulation of these spaces in order to punish or reward religious groups, usually ethnic or sectarian minorities. Actors have targeted their opponents' sacred sites in military strikes and terrorist attacks with the intention of sowing fear, panic, or discord. Leaders have destroyed and embellished sacred sites or constricted access to these sites in order to enhance their control over a community and exert influence over its affairs. These strategies are effective, in part, because sacred sites fulfill three functions in addition to their religious functions: they serve as symbols of a religious community; they function as social centers and thus offer convenient targets for mass casualty attacks; and they attract pilgrims from a range of political communities, both near and far.

By representing a religious movement at its most splendorous, sacred sites become potent social symbols of a targeted group to outsiders. Their design and ornamentation capture key elements of the religious tradition in a symbolic form that is immediately recognizable to others. Many of the world's great religious shrines, such as the Grand Mosque in Mecca, the Western Wall in Jerusalem, the Church of Saint Peter in Rome, or the Shinto shrine in Ise, have become synonymous in popular perception with the religions they represent.

This parallelism between the religious group and its sacred space makes that space vulnerable to attack from those seeking to harm the group. By targeting or damaging the shrine most sacred to a group, its rivals hope to strike at the heart of the group's values, heritage, and pride. Such an attack carries unmistakable significance: it is not merely an act of violence but a challenge to the core of the religious group and all it represent. Assaults on sacred sites are attempts by one group to undermine the foundations on which their opponent's identity and faith rest.

Muslim rulers in India of the twelfth to eighteenth century, for example, desecrated Hindu temples, either as punishment of rebellious communities or in order to remove, and thus symbolically disable, the gods that functioned as patrons of rival Hindu rulers.[28] Iraq's repressive eighth- and ninth-century rulers, such as al-Mansur, al-Rashid, and Mutawakkil, sought to control the Shi'a community by demolishing the mosques in Najaf and Karbala. Their successors sought to curry favor with their Shi'a subjects by repairing the damage done by their predecessors or by embellishing the mosques with brass, bronze, and gold. Seeking to pacify the Shi'a community after the 1991 revolt, Saddam ordered the mosques of Najaf and Karbala restored and donated four hundred pounds of gold and six hundred pounds of silver for decoration of the domes of the sacred shrines.[29]

Because sacred places are visible representations of an ethnic or sectarian group, they have often borne the brunt of attacks by rival groups. During the war in the former Yugoslavia, for example, Croat mosques were a common target of Serbian attack. Over six hundred mosques were destroyed in the course of this ethnic war.[30] Mosques and Hindu shrines routinely attract sectarian conflict in the Indian subcontinent. In the Western Hemisphere, synagogues and Jewish cemeteries have offered a convenient target for anti-Semites who wished to intimidate a local Jewish community. The aftermath of the al-Aqsa Intifada in 2001, for example, saw a 400 percent leap in worldwide attacks on synagogues, totaling more than 130 attacks on synagogues in Australia, Tunisia, Bosnia, Italy, Spain, Germany, France, Belgium, Sweden, Britain, Canada, Russia, Brazil, and the United States.[31]

Rather than attempt to exert influence by means of destruction alone, shrewd rulers have understood that extending favorable treatment to sacred sites may incur the worshipers' gratitude as well as establish the ruler's legitimacy as a patron of sacred places. In third-century BCE India, the emperor Asoka constructed hundreds of stupas throughout his realm into which he then dispersed relics of the Buddha in order to legitimate his right to rule. The population understood that the king's protection of the relics assured him the support of these relics in governing his subjects with wisdom and justice.[32] The monarchs of Saudi Arabia, Morocco, and Jordan have sought to mark their status as leaders of the Muslim world by founding monumental mosques in their capitals, by enlarging and embellishing existing shrines, and by vying over the honor of funding clergy and restoring the shrines in the Noble Sanctuary in Jerusalem.

In addition to acting as the visual representation of a community, sacred places make tempting targets for a second reason: they tend to teem with religious adherents. Believers are drawn to sacred places not only because of the religious functions these sites perform but also because they fulfill a variety of social roles. Because sacred places can fulfill a range of political, legal, and financial functions, they draw powerful actors from all walks of life into their orbit. Often the largest public structure at the center of a village or town, they become the primary locus of societal interaction. Rivals striking at these structures can thus expect to exact significant casualties from the target community.

Exceptionally violent attacks on sacred shrines have occurred in the aftermath of the U.S. occupation of Iraq in 2003. Assaults timed to coincide with peak attendance at religious services have resulted in massive casualties, particularly in the attacks of August 2003, March and December 2004, February, March, July, and November 2005, January, February, April, and July 2006, and January 2008. The most extreme of these attacks, on March 2, 2004, coincided with the observance of the Shi'a holy day of Ashura. Over 180 Shi'a worshipers lost their lives in separate attacks in Baghdad and Karbala that day, making this the deadliest day in Iraq since the U.S. invasion of 2003.[33] The bombing of February 22, 2006, demolished one of the most revered and beautiful shrines in Iraq, the Askari Mosque in Samarra. It ended the lives of over one hundred worshipers and led to a series of revenge attacks on Sunni mosques with mounting casualty figures. The intensification of sectarian violence that followed has led some analysts to view the attack on the Askari Mosque as the symbolic starting point of an Iraqi civil war.[34]

Sacred places function as a social symbol in a third important way: they often attract masses of pilgrims from a variety of political communities. This renders control over these shrines crucial for local leaders who wish to extend their influence beyond their immediate realm. Rulers who fail to capitalize on their control of a pilgrimage shrine may find their power undermined by rivals outside their sovereign sphere, employing pilgrims to spread ideology and dissent. It is for this reason that Hellenic and Roman rulers over Jerusalem placed their garrisons at the boundaries of the Jewish Temple, a site that proved time and again a focal point for unrest. Pilgrimage offers the host regime opportunities for sanctioning rival regimes or demonstrating exceptional generosity and hospitality. To opponents of the host regime, these mass events offer a forum for organized protests and subversive activities.

The presence of potentially hostile pilgrims is most likely to cause conflict at sites already disputed because of sectarian rivalry, such as the Muslim shrines in Saudi Arabia and Iraq. Saudi Arabia controls the shrines in Mecca and Medina, the two most sacred mosques in Islam, and Iraq controls multiple shrines and burial sites of central importance to Shi'a Muslims, yet both states were ruled by Sunni regimes. Consequently, Saudi Arabia and Iraq often placed restrictions on the numbers of Shi'a pilgrims from Iran, or barred pilgrimage altogether during the Iran-Iraq war or after the Iranian revolution. Iran's Shi'a regime, on the other hand, has exploited the presence of Shi'a pilgrims at these sites to spread its revolutionary message and incite unrest.

The Possibility of Peaceful Coexistence

Groups arrive at conflicts over sacred sites through multiple pathways. Many sacred sites are holy to more than one sect or religious movement and thus subject to intra- or interreligious conflict. Others are located on land valued for reasons other than religious or offer tempting venues for insurgents seeking to even the odds in their clash with pursuers. Finally, because sacred space holds economic, political, and cultural value to communities, it offers a tempting target for rulers or opponents.

The characteristics and functions of sacred sites lead to frequent conflicts over these sites. The resolution of these conflicts is hampered by the indivisibility problem. Should we take this to mean that violent conflicts at contested sacred places are inevitable? Several scholars studying sacred sites in the Middle East and South Asia have argued otherwise. They have enthusiastically pointed to interfaith harmony at the Cave of Elijah in Haifa, the Tomb of Samuel (Nebi Samwil) north of Jerusalem, and, in the nineteenth century, the Cave of Simon the Just in Jerusalem.[35] An expert on the sharing of Sufi shrines by Hindus and Muslims in the Punjab, India, has highlighted "the reality of peaceful interaction that counters the stereotype of perennial Hindu-Muslim antagonism."[36] Another student of shared sacred sites, in the Middle East in this case, concludes that although worship excludes plurality, "it would be misleading to conclude that for this reason there cannot be sharing among distinct religions."[37]

Hopeful outlooks such as these form part of a larger backlash against the pessimistic stance that has dominated the study of religion and politics since the publication of Samuel Huntington's *Clash of Civilizations* and the disproportionate focus on fundamentalism and extremism in the wake of September 11.[38] Authors defying the tragic implications of Huntington's deterministic view have taken pains to point to the benevolent potential inherent in all religious traditions and have lauded the peacemaking capabilities of religious actors. Religious conflicts, these scholars argue, are not inevitable but rather the result of failure to implement widely available conflict resolution measures.

Given the empirical record on conflicts at sacred sites, the optimistic attitude that characterizes current research on sacred places is nothing short of baffling. It is also dangerously misguided. Conflicts at contested sacred sites are inevitable and, owing to the very nature of these sites, exceedingly difficult to manage. Students of religion and politics who have reached alternative conclusions have done so by unduly focusing on one of two types of exceptions.

First, temporary concord is possible in cases in which third parties have intervened to force coexistence on the groups vying over a sacred site. For this to occur, a powerful actor, usually a state, must be willing to employ or threaten force to keep the peace at a sacred site. Such cases are rare enough: not only are the contending parties required to be weak in relation to the enforcer but the enforcer is required to be relatively neutral to the dispute. I discuss these cases at length in the next chapter to show that the management of sacred places by fiat, far from resolving disputes, actually serves to increase tensions and eventually leads to the inevitable outbreak of hostilities. The presence of an enforcer merely constrains the groups' ability to immediately satisfy their ambitions by means of violent action. The top-down imposition of cooperation produces tensions that seethe under the surface, threatening to erupt as soon as one party perceives a change in the balance of power.

A second category of cases in which peaceful coexistence is possible relates to sacred sites of particularly low centrality and vulnerability, such as "mirror" sites: local churches, mosques, temples, synagogues, or shrines that occupy a marginal role in the religious landscape. "Folk sites," like the tombs and caves mentioned above, also fall into this category if they have not been fully institutionalized into the formal framework of the relevant religious movements.

Muslim-Jewish coexistence is possible at sites like the Cave of Elijah because restrictive rules that delimit access and behavior have not been implemented. Indeed, worshipers may not even agree on the identity of the saint to be revered at the site.[39]

The possession of such sites confers little to no legitimacy on one religious community or the other. Because they are relatively insignificant they make for a poor symbol of the religious movement to outsiders and a poor target for mass attack by adversaries. Should sites like these ascend in importance, owing to a miracle or a divine apparition, for example, their vulnerability to conflict is certain to grow as well. At significant sacred sites that are claimed by more than one religious group, conflict is inevitable. Peaceful coexistence is possible only where it matters least.

7. A VHP activist agitates for the construction of a Hindu temple for Ram in Ayodhya, in place of the destroyed Babri Masjid. He is wearing a photograph of the proposed temple. Photo copyright Deshakalyan Chowdhury/AFP/Getty Images.

Chapter Five

Mismanaging Conflicts
over Sacred Places

A combination of spiritual, political, and historical factors creates conditions for indivisible conflict over sacred space. Owing to religious requirements, examined in chapters 2 and 3, sacred places are irreplaceable and cohesive sites with inflexible and highly visible boundaries. The benefits that accrue from controlling sacred sites create competition between disparate religious communities or between religious and secular actors. Because disputes about sacred space involve religious ideals, divine presence, and absolute and transcendent values, there is no room for compromise and no substitute for the disputed space.

Absent any one of these components, conflict over sacred space would be as easily resolvable as common territorial disputes, where flexible border definitions, the availability of substitutes, and the possibility of division allow for a variety of conflict resolution approaches. If history did not create competition or overlap of sacred spaces, the indivisibility of those spaces would be a moot issue. If the spaces overlapped but had boundaries that were flexible, indivisibility could be overcome by manipulating the dimensions of the disputed space. Even with rigid boundaries and overlapping claims, territory that can be parceled out or exchanged need not lead to indivisible disputes. The coming together of these factors, combined with the need for political control that arises from the centrality and vulnerability of sacred space, creates a combustible combination: territory of supreme value, disputed and indivisible.

If conflicts over sacred places are inevitable and divisions of sacred space are untenable, how have decision makers attempted to deal with disputes over sacred space? The simple answer to this question is "not well." The most common policy responses to conflicts at sacred space can be represented as one of two ideal types. At one extreme, *Hobbesian pragmatists* reject the importance of the symbolic dimension of these disputes and treat them as standard territorial disputes. At the other extreme, *Huntingtonian pessimists* accept the intractability of these disputes as the product of religious forces beyond the influence of political actors.

The combined effect of these preconceptions has been to lead decision makers toward strategies, such as forced partition or exclusion, that completely sidestep the religious components of these disputes. Yet both the forced division of a space that parties perceive as indivisible, and the exclusion by fiat of actors from space they perceive as vital, tend to be unsatisfactory to either side involved in a dispute. Such arrangements are highly unstable, routinely violent, and generally short-lived. Indeed, rather than resolve or ameliorate a dispute, these partitions of space by fiat repress the conflict, creating tensions that seethe under the surface and threaten to erupt as soon as one party perceives changes in the balance of power.

This chapter attempts to explain failures to resolve conflicts over sacred places, as exemplified by cases from India and Israel. Past analyses of these cases have focused on the manner in which political actors and interests have influenced these disputes. My emphasis here is on the manner in which religious principles and interests, grounded in the characteristics of sacred space, impeded political attempts at conflict resolution.

Policy Responses to Disputes over Sacred Space

Policy making in response to conflicts at sacred space has been informed by two theoretical traditions, the Hobbesian and the Huntingtonian. The former is the product of a Western political tradition, running from Machiavelli through Hobbes, that rejects the distinction between religious and political interests. Instead, this approach seeks to strip conflicts of their symbolic pretenses to expose underlying material interests. Deferring to the symbolic coating of these disputes, argue proponents, will create unnecessary difficulties by expanding the set of actors and issues in what would otherwise be a fundamentally political enterprise. Hobbesian pragmatists dismiss the likelihood of indivisible conflicts and reject the possibility that indivisibility is inherent in disputed territory. They argue, to paraphrase George Bernard Shaw's quip, that the crucial question to be addressed in resolving these disputes has little to do with the identity of the space; it is merely a question of bargaining over its price.

If the independent impact of authentic religious interests on political processes catches the Hobbesian pragmatist off guard, his counterpart, the Huntingtonian pessimist, accepts this force at face value. Drawing on Huntington's theory of religious identity as inextricably associated with conflict,[1] this approach accepts religion as a mysterious, irrational, and disruptive force inexorably interfering with the conduct of politics. Here, the indivisibility of sacred space is accepted as a factor beyond the control of decision makers. Again, no attempt is made to critically examine the meaning of sacred space, not, in this instance, because the significance of sacredness is dismissed, but because it is accepted axiomatically as a dead end in negotiations.

Both schools of thought have led policy makers toward the same set of conclusions. If the religious dimension of conflicts over sacred space is uninteresting or inaccessible to decision makers and if indivisibility is irrelevant or insurmountable, then disputes over sacred places can and should be approached with the same repertoire of tools as all other territorial disputes: negotiation or arbitration, leading to exchange, partition, compensation, or compromise. Peacemakers have thus faced the challenge of conflicts over sacred places with defiance, adopting a variety of approaches for managing coexistence at sacred sites. These tools tend to fall into two broad categories: partition and exclusion.

In the first conflict resolution approach, the sacred space is divided so as to permit two or more religious groups to worship at a sacred site at the same time. When this division is applied across space (as opposed to across time), it establishes restrictions on access to specific parts of a shrine or merely indicates spheres of jurisdiction without restricting access. The former is the approach adopted in several Indian mosques that have been constructed on top of, and with materials recycled from, destroyed Hindu temples. At the Krishna Janmasthan in Mathura, the Kashi Vishwanath Temple/Gyanvapi Mosque in Varanasi, and the Quwwat-ul-Islam Mosque in Delhi, Hindu and Muslim worshipers pray in distinct areas, separated by barriers.[2] Jurisdictional division was implemented in the Church of the Holy Sepulcher in Jerusalem and the Church of the Nativity in Bethlehem, where members of the different Christian sects are free to move about the entire shrine most of the time but are limited in their right to clean, maintain, or decorate sectors other than their own.

Partition can also occur across time rather than space. In this scenario, a detailed schedule establishes the times at which different groups have access to the site. Such an agreement might permit only one group to access the site at one time or establish periods of common versus separate worship. Thus only Muslims are permitted to access the Noble Sanctuary platform in Jerusalem on Fridays but both Muslims and non-Muslims are permitted there at all other times. In most cases, these two approaches are combined, so as to further reduce friction between the groups. In the Church of the Holy Sepulcher, for example, parts that are in the public domain most of the year are reserved for the exclusive use of one sect or another at specific times of the year at which members of the sect perform significant rituals.

A strategy of exclusion, on the other hand, seeks to resolve conflict over a sacred site by barring one or all religious groups from worshiping in a shrine altogether. This can be achieved by secularizing the sacred place, conferring historical or archaeological status on the site, or simply locking its gates to worshipers. The Hagia Sophia in Istanbul, for example, could have formed the backdrop for significant Christian-Muslim tension. Once the spiritual center for Orthodox Christianity, it was converted into a mosque after the Muslim conquest of Constantinople. The Turkish government has prevented conflict at this site by declaring the shrine a national museum in which neither Muslim nor Christian worship is permitted.

Although strategies of partition and exclusion are routinely practiced at contentious sacred sites worldwide, their record of success is disappointing at best. The reason why common conflict resolution methods have proven unsuccessful lies in their failure to address the root causes of violence at sacred sites. Partition does not obviate the desire by multiple parties to control access and behavior over an entire sacred space. Indeed, it deprives either party to the dispute of the ability to prevent what it considers sacrilege in half of the sacred place all the time or in the entire sacred space half of the time. Similarly, partition fails to resolve or even suspend the looming question of legitimacy. Instead, sharing space and time among the rival groups establishes the basis for increased competition, as each group attempts to control more space and more time to establish its authority and authenticity.

The second approach, exclusion, does address the problems posed by a sacred place's vulnerability as social symbol and community center, by barring some or all worshipers from the site altogether. Yet this is a blunt tool indeed. Because it is likely to antagonize all religious groups involved, only the strongest of states can afford to adopt a risky strategy of this sort. Moreover, only a government neutral to the interests of all religious rivals involved would be likely to desire exclusion as an outcome. The secular Turkish regime's handling of the Hagia Sophia offers one exception that proves this rule.

Forced Partition in Hebron and Jerusalem

Two ongoing conflicts in Israel and the Palestinian Territories offer compelling evidence for the inadequacy of partition as a conflict resolution measure. The first is the continuing conflict in the heart of Hebron at a site known to Jews as the Machpela Cave and to Muslims as the Ibrahimi Mosque. This site is considered by Jews and Muslims to be the location of the tombs of Adam and Eve, as well as the patriarchs Abraham, Isaac, and Jacob and the matriarchs Sarah, Rebecca, and Leah. These tombs, covered by cenotaphs, are contained within a first-century BCE structure.

Muslim rulers prohibited Jewish access to this sanctuary starting in the thirteenth century. The conquest of Hebron in 1967 thus enabled Jewish access to the tombs of the patriarchs for the first time in seven hundred years. Upon his first visit to the Tomb of the Patriarchs in Hebron, in June 1967, Israeli Minister of Defense Moshe Dayan recognized the combustible potential of common Jewish-Muslim prayer in this shrine.[3] On August 1, 1967, he negotiated an elaborate system of timetables with Muslim representatives that set out separate prayer times for members of both faiths. This schedule, which had to take into account daily, monthly, and seasonal changes in prayer duration and attendance, is so complex as to take up three entire pages in Dayan's autobiography.[4] The arrangement could not, however, resolve the underlying contradictions resulting from common prayer at this single site. Dayan's edict did not, and presumably could not, instruct Jews to remove their shoes before entering the site, nor could it prevent the noise from one praying congregations from disturbing the services of the other congregation.

Less than a year after the war, in April 1968, Israeli settlers, unhindered by the military administration over the West Bank, reestablished a Jewish presence in Hebron.[5] Since that date, the route linking the Jewish stronghold to the tombs has seen more rioting, terrorist strikes (by both parties), random shootings, army raids, and assassinations than any other Jewish outpost in the West Bank. In August 1975, the Israeli government bowed to pressure and permitted Jewish prayer in the main hall of the tomb, which previously served as a mosque only. This decision sparked violent protest by hundreds of Muslim worshipers emerging from the tomb, causing damage to property in Hebron, and stirred riots in all major cities in the West Bank.[6]

A year later rumors of desecration touched off renewed violence and acts of retaliation as Jews were found beating a Muslim clergyman and tearing up a copy of the Qur'an, while Muslims stole the cloth covering the Jewish sanctuary and tore up Bible scrolls. The 1976 riots led to the shooting of six Arab youths and one Arab girl, wounding fifty-five others, and led to sixty arrests and seventy-four charges of desecration of religious artifacts. Hebron was placed under military curfew for two weeks.[7] In both cases the issue was brought before the UN General Assembly and Security Council by Pakistan and Egypt, who accused Israel of destroying the mosque and condoning desecration.[8]

In 1979, a first Palestinian attempt to plant a bomb near the tomb failed, wounding both assailants.[9] The next attack, a year later, killed five Jewish students and wounded seventeen as they were walking from Sabbath prayers at the tomb. Authorities termed the attack, executed by means of gunfire and hand grenades, "the worst Arab attack on Israelis in the 13-year occupation of the West Bank."[10] A precursor of the escalated violence of the intifada, this attack preceded similar acts of force by five to ten years. In the first fifteen years of occupation the tomb had already witnessed three grenade and shooting attacks.[11]

The site underwent appropriate change: twenty-four-hour surveillance cameras were installed to keep watch over worshipers inside the shrine; head-high aluminum barricades were placed between the praying groups; soldiers were placed on folding chairs between the congregations; an army post was placed nearby, making this "the only house of worship anywhere with its own army commander"; the Ark of the Law in which Torah scrolls are placed was replaced with a fireproof iron safe.[12]

These measures did nothing to prevent further bloodshed. The tomb became an epicenter of riots by Jews and Muslims in the late 1980s, instigated whenever Muslims tried to pray in the Jewish section and vice versa.[13] Individual attacks left Palestinian residents and Muslim and Jewish worshipers, as well as Israeli soldiers, dead and wounded.[14] In all cases the attacks took place in the tomb itself or on routes leading worshipers to prayer at the tomb. Assaults took place at dates of religious significance: Jewish or Muslim high holidays and Friday or Saturday prayer services. Such was also the case on February 25, 1994, when a Jewish settler emptied three magazines from an automatic rifle on Muslim worshipers conducting Ramadan services at the tomb. This attack and subsequent violence killed 55 Palestinians and wounded 170 others, setting the Arab-Israeli peace process back by months.[15]

Conditions at the Church of the Holy Sepulcher in Jerusalem, revered as the site of Christ's crucifixion and resurrection, are slightly more placid, but the arrangement is infinitely more complicated. It is based on the status quo enforced by the Ottoman Empire in 1757, confirmed in 1852 and enforced by the State of Israel today. It divides the church into minute segments and subsegments with clearly delineated areas of responsibility for the competing religious groups: Greek Orthodox, Latin (Catholic), Armenian, Coptic,

Syrian, and Ethiopian. Pillars have been numbered, walkways divided tile by tile, doors halved, and candelabras dissected, with each party zealously guarding its rights to own, clean, and decorate the segments allotted to it, while maintaining its claim to the entire church. These claims are no mere demands for the exercise of ritual. They are private property claims, pure and simple. Diane Herbert reports:

> Bishop Kapikian of the Armenian Orthodox Church asserts that the three major sects are "owners of the Holy Places, and when I say 'owners,' it is their property." Father Basileos, Metropolitan of Caesarea for the Greek Orthodox Church, corroborates this statement. He claims rights of "possession, ownership and usage" of the Holy Places as their "private property." Archbishop Yacoub of the Syrian Orthodox Church concurred that Christian groups "own" the Holy Places and were not simply inhabiting them. Asked if it were possible to own sacred as well as secular space, Bishop Kapikian replied, "Of course."[16]

The relatively peaceful status quo at the Holy Sepulcher is possible only because the claimants are more or less equal in power, whereas a third party, the State of Israel, enjoys power preponderance over all. The status quo was instituted by Saladin under similar conditions—power preponderance by a party neutral to the dispute—and could be enforced under Ottoman, British, and Jordanian rule for the same reasons. Given this state of affairs, the sects have chosen to place a wide range of decision-making capabilities in non-Christian hands, rather than see themselves exploited by their Christian rivals. At the suggestion of Saladin, it is said, the Christian sects placed the keys of the only entrance to the church in the trustworthy hands of a Muslim family because they were unable to agree on who would control entrance and exit to the shrine. The keys remain in Muslim hands to this day.

The status quo is nonetheless fragile, for multiple reasons. For one, each group considers some aspect of the arrangement to be unjust. Thus all groups have the short-term goal of constantly trying to adjust the status quo, in addition to their long-term desire to overthrow it altogether in order to become sole proprietor. Second, no authoritative version of the status quo exists. Each community thus has its own version or interpretation of the status quo.[17] Third, new challenges continue to arise that the centuries-old status quo was not designed to address. For example, when increased crowding created the need for a new opening to the church, no party was willing to cede the space required to create such a common area and no door was constructed. Fourth, the State of Israel's ability and willingness to enforce the status quo have depended on the waxing and waning of Israeli influence in Jerusalem. As both the Kingdom of Jordan and the Palestinian Authority vie for influence over religious institutions in Jerusalem, Israel's ability to keep the peace in the church fluctuates. This, combined with Israel's hesitation to intervene in what it considers an internal Christian matter, erodes the Christian rivals' confidence both in Israel's abilities to arbitrate disputes and in the status quo altogether.

As a result several areas of the church remain contested, and the entire structure is in a grave state of disrepair, since disagreements have stalled repair procedures for decades.[18] One dispute pertained to the rebuilding of a wall torn down in 1982, because the reconstruction had created a three-inch-wide band of new, and thus disputed, floor area. The wall was eventually constructed by the Israeli government in 1998, in response to a request for intervention by the wrangling churches.[19] As Raymond Cohen has shown, in the most comprehensive documentation of the struggle over the Holy Sepulcher, brawls over jurisdiction inside the church are common. Coptic monks have attacked the Armenian bishop with pickaxes for knocking over a lectern holding their Bible, which they had placed two inches into a common area of the church.[20] A Greek Orthodox monk stabbed an Armenian monk in the arm for refilling a small oil lamp in an area allegedly owned by the Greek Orthodox community.[21] Several Armenian monks nearly beat the senior Greek Orthodox priest to death because he was trying to fix a sewage cover located, they claimed, in their part of the church.[22] In 2003, the Greek Patriarch forcibly prevented the Syrian Orthodox bishop from ascending Calvary in formal vestments, breaking the bishop's staff in the process.[23] In 2004, Greek Orthodox monks, Franciscans, and worshipers scuffled over a door that had been accidentally left open during an important ceremony.[24] Conflict continues between the Armenians and the Syrians over rights to the Chapel of Nicodemus. Whereas the Copts have been known to throw stones at Ethiopian religious processions, the Ethiopians exploited the preoccupation of the Copts with the ceremony of the Holy Fire, the climax of the Coptic religious calendar, in order to exchange the locks on the disputed Chapel of Michael.[25] "The ecumenical spirit may be active elsewhere," summarized a young Armenian monk, "but here in this church we're the last to know about it. We fight for our corner as we've always done."[26]

Partition and Exclusion in Ayodhya

The Indian government's failure to manage the Ayodhya crisis demonstrates the dangers of attempting conflict resolution at sacred sites in the absence of strict neutrality and overwhelming power preponderance. This case is worth dwelling on because the two strategies of partition and exclusion were implemented, at some point or another, in the recent history of the conflict. Yet both approaches, as well as attempts to combine the two, failed to prevent a tragic outcome in 1992.

The dispute over the Babri Masjid (Mosque of Babur) in Ayodhya is rooted in the belief that the Muslim emperor Babur constructed this mosque on the site of the Ramjanmabhumi, an earlier Hindu temple marking the birthplace of the god Ram.[27] The mosque was constructed by the Mughal emperor in the sixteenth century. Until the mid-nineteenth century, the site was a popular folk shrine, revered for its miraculous drinking water. Muslims and Hindus shared access to the well in the central courtyard, whereas the rest of the shrine was divided into Muslim and Hindu sectors.[28] This state of harmonious coexistence was interrupted in the mid-nineteenth century by the onset of direct British rule over India, which led to a rise in sectarian tensions that affected Hindu-Muslim relations in Ayodhya as well.

Consequently, a low railing was installed to keep Hindu worshipers out of the inner courtyard. Hindu believers responded by constructing a *chabootra* (prayer platform) in the outer courtyard and by making offerings there, but their exclusion, while convenient for Muslim worshipers, was unacceptable to the Hindus, who appealed to the courts on several occasions. The instability of the situation was further underscored in Hindu attacks on the mosque and the railing during communal riots in the 1930s.[29]

In 1949, Hindu worshipers escalated the situation further when they demanded the right to worship idols of the gods Ram, Sita, and Hanuman that had "mysteriously" appeared inside the mosque. A violent attempt by crowds to storm the mosque resulted in an order by Prime Minister Jawaharlal Nehru to remove the idols. This order was never executed by local police, who feared mob retaliation. Instead, the mosque was placed under lock and key, barring worshipers of all faiths.[30] A year later, however, Hindu worshipers received permission to worship the idols, once a year, inside the mosque. Soon, Hindus established regular worship routines outside the mosque's gates.[31] At the same time, Hindu worshipers continued to appeal to the courts and founded the Ramjanmabhumi Mukti Yajna Samiti (Organization for Sacrifice to Liberate the Birthplace of the God Ram). Its efforts were ultimately successful: in 1986 the locks were removed and exclusive Hindu worship began in the mosque courtyard. Muslims responded by founding the All India Babri Masjid Action Committee, a movement that led their protests in the years to come.

As far as extremist Hindu worshipers were concerned, Hindu prayer in the mosque was merely the first step toward the construction of a Hindu temple in place of the mosque. The foundation for such a temple was laid in 1989, two hundred feet from the entrance to the mosque. Hundreds of nationalist processions bearing consecrated bricks arrived in Ayodhya from across India, unleashing riots along the way.[32] Once three hundred thousand bricks had been assembled at the temple site, the plot was consecrated with waters from all of India's sacred rivers and earth from all of India's sacred sites.[33] This ceremony prompted anti-Hindu riots and the destruction of over four hundred temples in Pakistan and Bangladesh. Nevertheless, the World Hindu Council (VHP) and the Indian People's Party (BJP) continued in their campaign for the construction of a temple for Ram. In 1990, dozens of Hindu devotees, known as *kar sevaks* (volunteers in service to the god Ram), died in clashes with the police in Ayodhya. The mosque was surrounded by barbed wire and protected by paramilitary troops. An Indian supreme court ruling ordered that no temple be built and that the mosque should remain unharmed.[34]

Two years later, on December 6, 1992, thousands of *kar sevaks,* using their bare hands, pickaxes, iron pipes, and sticks, attacked and demolished the Babri Masjid in under fourteen hours and constructed a shrine for Ram among the ruins.[35] This incident, instigated by the VHP and BJP, provoked riots across India in which an estimated twenty thousand Hindus and Muslims died. The backlash was felt in Pakistan, where Hindus and Muslims attacked one another's shrines.[36] Hundreds more died the next year in a series of bombings in Mumbai, said to have occurred in response to the destruction of the mosque. The violence also led to the looting and destruction of hundreds of thousands of homes, businesses, and offices. Ayodhya had unleashed the worst sectarian violence on the Indian subcontinent since partition.[37]

Since 1992, the ruins of the mosque are under lock and key. Visitors must pass a steel barricade, half a kilometer from the site, then a metal detector, then a second metal detector at which they must abandon all personal items.[38] The area is protected by a force of three thousand policemen, bearing automatic weapons and employing closed-circuit cameras. Predictably, this attempt at exclusion has not resolved the conflict. Hindu extremists continue planning in earnest for the construction of a temple, the plans and construction materials for which have already been assembled and consecrated. Muslim radicals, in turn, attacked Hindu worshipers returning from Ayodhya in 2002 and the mosque site itself in 2005.

The Temple Mount Issue at Camp David

Like the Ayodhya dispute, the conflict over Jerusalem has both reflected and triggered regional sectarian tensions. Indeed, scholars have noted intriguing

8. December 6, 1992: Hindu extremists overrun and demolish the Babri Masjid in Ayodhya with their bare hands. Photo copyright Reuters/Corbis.

parallels between these two cases.[39] Both disputes involve a "layered" sacred site at which a shrine valued by one religious group is alleged to have been constructed on the ruins of a shrine valued by a competing group. In both cases, entrepreneurs have exploited tensions over rights to access and to perform rituals at the contested site in order to mobilize their followers to take political and even violent action. Both disputes have also had a direct impact on regional politics.

The failure of Israelis and Palestinians to agree on the status of the sacred site in Jerusalem was by most accounts a principal cause, if not the primary cause, for the failure of the Israeli-Palestinian negotiations in Camp David in July 2000.[40] Although records of what precisely happened at Camp David remain contentious, there is broad consensus among participants and analysts on the Israeli side about the singular importance of this issue in preventing agreement at Camp David.[41]

Israeli prime minister Ehud Barak instructed his delegates to treat the Temple Mount dispute as "the central issue that will decide the destiny of the negotiations" and confessed: "I have no idea how this will end, but I am sure that we will face the world united if it turns out that this agreement failed over the question of our sovereignty over the First and Second Temple. That is the Archimedean point of our existence, the anchor point of the Zionist struggle...we are at the moment of truth."[42] Barak later explained Israel's negotiation position to George W. Bush, successor to U.S. president Bill Clinton: "The Temple Mount is the cradle of Jewish history and there is no way I will sign a document that transfers sovereignty over the Temple Mount to the Palestinians. For Israel that would be a betrayal of its Holy of Holies."[43]

Similarly, Palestinian Authority president Yasser Arafat encouraged his delegation to demonstrate flexibility, "but do not budge on this one thing: the Haram [al-Sharif] is more precious to me than everything else."[44] Egyptian president Hosni Mubarak had warned that "any compromise over Jerusalem will cause the region to explode in a way that cannot be put under control.... No single person in the Arab or Islamic world can squander East Jerusalem or the al-Aqsa Mosque."[45] At the climax of the negotiations, Arafat reportedly broke off a discussion with U.S. Secretary of State Madeleine Albright in anger, because Albright mistakenly referred to the site by its Judeo-Christian name.[46] To Clinton he said: "I can't betray my people. Do you want to come to my funeral? I'd rather die than agree to Israeli sovereignty over the Haram al-Sharif."[47] One negotiator recalled Arafat's parting words to Clinton: "To tell me that I have to admit that there is a temple below the mosque? I will never do that."[48]

Israeli delegate Amnon Shahak described this dispute as "the issue that is stuck, that is holding back everything else," while chief Israeli negotiator on Jerusalem Shlomo Ben-Ami defined Israel's position on the Temple Mount as a "taboo" and recognized that it had become "the make or break issue of the entire negotiations."[49] Contrary to claims that various issues had hampered agreement at Camp David, Ben-Ami stated that there had been "a breakthrough that could have led to an agreement on all issues, aside from Jerusalem."[50] When the summit collapsed, Barak similarly admitted to the press that the Jerusalem issue had been the cause.[51]

Negotiators had reached some common ground on security issues, on Palestinian refugees, on Israeli withdrawal from Palestinian areas, even on dividing the modern city of Jerusalem, but reached an impasse on the issue of sovereignty over the sacred site at the heart of the old city. Political scientist Menahem Klein, who advised the Israeli government during the negotiations, confirmed that "Jerusalem [turned] into the benchmark issue. Jerusalem was not the last subject on which the entire compact would stand or fall.... On the contrary: Jerusalem blocked all progress on the other subjects. The failure to reach agreement on the Temple Mount and the Old City affected the agreements that emerged at Camp David on the other issues on the agenda."[52] "The Camp David summit," confessed government advisor Moshe Amirav, "became a 'Jerusalem summit,' perhaps even a 'Temple Mount summit,'" with all three leaders dedicating "hundreds of hours to discussions on Jerusalem in general and the Temple Mount in particular."[53]

In many ways, the negotiations over the Temple Mount at Camp David exemplified Hobbesian thinking at its very worst. Both parties seem to have assumed that the religious dimensions of the dispute could be ignored. As a result, neither party had prepared seriously for the possibility that the Temple Mount issue would come to stand at the heart of the negotiations. In the weeks of preparations leading up to the summit, the Mount had been treated as a secondary issue. Insofar as religious issues were discussed in preparations for the conference, they were treated as standard political problems, to be addressed by conventional political tools. Jerusalem was handled as a demographic, administrative, municipal, and legal problem, not as a religious problem. Reporting on the preparations by the Israeli team, Klein writes: "The professional back channels did not sufficiently treat Jerusalem as a religious city. They treated the sacred city with respect but at a distance and with some fear. It was easier to conduct discussions about preservation of historical structures in the old city than to discuss the link between the political sanctity and the religious sanctity at the historical and religious heart of the city. A small number of meetings dealt with the religious issue and few religious leaders participated in those."[54]

Before Camp David the Israeli team consulted security experts, lawyers, political scientists, sociologists, engineers, and architects but met few religious experts or religious leaders.[55] Barak went as far as to block observant members of his own party from becoming involved in the negotiations, despite their willingness to contribute, lest their initiation of a religious discourse restrict his bargaining freedom.[56] In hindsight, Klein identifies this failure to communicate with religious actors as the Achilles' heel of the negotiations:

> Whereas the dialogue between experts and politicians had been going on for years, the dialogue with religious actors was in its infancy. Too few back channels were opened between experts and religious actors, and between Jewish-Israeli religious actors and Muslim or Christian Palestinian actors.... The absence of a comprehensive and intensive religious dialogue at two levels— within each of the relevant religious movements and between them—was to have negative consequences at Camp David. There the religious-nationalist issue arose suddenly and came to stand at the heart of the dispute.[57]

The failure to incorporate religious actors and experts in preparing for the negotiations had two direct consequences: both parties were caught off guard by the demands concerning sacred space raised by their opponents, and the religious leaders excluded from the process succeeded in hampering progress from without.

Palestinians confessed as much surprise at Israeli demands concerning the Temple Mount as at the religious rationale that accompanied these demands. They rejected the Israeli claim that the Jewish Temple had stood at the site as unsubstantiated and irrelevant, even though, unbeknownst to them, the Jewish heritage of the site was openly embraced by most Muslim scholars as a justification for its importance in early Islam. The Palestinian delegates also misinterpreted the Jewish desire to pray at the site as signaling a desire to construct a Jewish Temple on the ruins of the Muslim holy places, an extremist goal espoused by a fanatical fringe in Judaism only.

The secular makeup of the Israeli team, on the other hand, prevented the Israeli delegates from familiarizing themselves with the complexities of the Jewish legal position on Jerusalem. Instead, they perceived the most radical Jewish stance on the issue as the most authentic position and turned it into a matter of stiff principle in the negotiations.[58] So ignorant was Israeli prime minister Barak of the Jewish history at issue that he began referring to the entire Mount, including the mosque, as the "Holy of Holies," a term reserved for the four-meter-square sanctuary at the heart of the former Jewish Temple.[59] The single meeting between Israeli delegates and rabbinical leaders on record is said to have taken place mere hours before the Israeli team departed for Camp David. Rather than meet with a panel of religious experts or influential rabbis, a single delegate met with the two Chief Rabbis of Israel to hear their position on concessions over Jerusalem. Because the Chief Rabbis, as the official rabbis of the State of Israel and heads of the religious bureaucracy, neither represent nor influence the Orthodox community the meeting provided no insights into public opinion or tools for shaping such opinion. The rabbis, presumably slighted by the very timing of the meeting, adopted the most conservative stance available: they informed the delegate that the entire city of Jerusalem was indivisible and nonnegotiable.[60]

Meanwhile, outside Camp David, the very religious leaders who had been excluded from the process issued rulings to block compromise over Jerusalem. An American proposal to divide the four quarters of the old city equally between the two parties was scuttled by the leaders of the Catholic, Greek Orthodox, and Armenian Orthodox Churches in Jerusalem. They argued that the proposal would separate the Christians of the Armenian quarter from those residing in the Christian quarter.[61] The Chief Rabbis of Israel published a legal ruling prohibiting absolutely the "transferring to foreigners, indirectly or directly, any sovereignty or ownership on the Temple Mount," adding that "the very discussion of such a [step] constitutes the desecration of God's name."[62] The foremost Muslim authority in Jerusalem, the Mufti Sheikh Ekrima Sabri, issued a ruling denying Jewish rights to the Western Wall at the foot of the Temple Mount.[63] Mocking American attempts at dividing the sacred sites at the heart of the dispute, Sabri scoffed: "Does al-Aksa belong to the Americans? Is it a cake, that Clinton can divide? Al-Aksa belongs to the Muslims alone, and we will not accept any compromise."[64]

And yet political leaders continued to cling obstinately to real-political assumptions even when confronted with evidence of the obstructive power of religious actors and despite the collapse of Camp David over the Temple Mount issue. This dismissive attitude toward religion was demonstrated by the chief Israeli negotiator for Jerusalem, Shlomo Ben-Ami, in an interview one month after the collapse of the negotiations: "Indeed, a discussion about the sanctity of the Temple Mount did take place. It is interesting that you go into negotiations on a political issue, or almost a real estate issue, as it were, and it becomes a theological discussion.... But we are not going to turn this conflict or this process, which is essentially political, into a religious war."[65]

Political scientists who analyzed the negotiations proffered similar views, arguing that Camp David had failed because religion had been allowed to play too great a role in the proceedings. Shibley Telhami, a senior fellow at the Brookings Institution, recognized the crucial role played by the Temple Mount issue in the negotiations yet at the same time argued that negotiations had failed because the issues had, mistakenly, been framed in religious terms. "For American diplomats," he went on to recommend, "the priority must be preserving the nationalist framing of the conflict and separating the religious status from the issue of political sovereignty."[66] Klein has argued that "sanctity does not require sovereignty" and expressed astonishment at the fact that "while, from a philosophical and theological standpoint, it is correct to separate holy sites from worldly political sovereignty, that is apparently not possible in Jerusalem."[67]

The media, on the other hand, adopted a Huntingtonian stance, in which religion was perceived as a destructive force beyond the control of political actors. One news analysis, under the headline "Jerusalem, City of Faith, Defies Rational Solution," vacillated between expressions of awe at the Jerusalem phenomenon, "resisting rational analysis and seemingly impervious to creative compromise" and resignation. "When the subject is Jerusalem," exclaimed one Israeli columnist, "pragmatism is replaced by anxiety and rational interests are replaced by slogans. It is as if some 'force majeur' has decided that Jerusalem must remain a city that defies all solutions."[68] An American editorial reinforced this point: "It may be that this is one of those historical conflicts that cannot be settled by mutual agreements, that survive until a new relation of force obliges an end."[69]

The Limits of Innovative Conflict Resolution Measures

Tempting as it may be to attribute the failure of the negotiations over Jerusalem to a lack of creative thinking on the negotiators' part, this much is clear: the parties at Camp David suffered no shortage of innovative solutions to the problems at hand. Over sixty different solutions, proposed by international organizations, world leaders, academics, and activists throughout the twentieth century, were available to the delegates at Camp David.[70] Of these solutions, twenty-six had been discussed within the Israeli delegation before the negotiations, and, of those, several were floated with their Palestinian counterparts, including offers to share, divide, suspend, or internationalize sovereignty over the Temple Mount.[71] One account of the negotiations has the American delegates spending "countless hours seeking imaginative formulations to finesse the issue of which party would enjoy sovereignty over this sacred place—a coalition of nations, the United Nations Security Council, even God himself was proposed."[72]

Bill Clinton, who compared his frustrating attempts at resolving the Jerusalem dispute to "going to the dentist without having your gums deadened,"[73] offered one of the most original solutions for resolving the Temple Mount dispute. The American president proposed dividing the Temple Mount horizontally rather than vertically, granting the Palestinians the "top" of the Mount and the Israelis the "bottom."[74] This was not merely a creative but also a sensible solution that offered each party what it wanted most: Palestinians would continue to control the platform and use it for accessing the Muslim shrines, whereas Israelis would control the Mount under the platform, where the remnants of the Jewish Temple were located.

As promising as Clinton's solution seemed, it suffered from a fundamental flaw: it contradicted basic Jewish understandings of the sanctity of the Temple Mount. Rabbinical consensus required Jews to respect the sanctity of the Temple Mount, even though the Jewish Temple that once stood on it had been destroyed. Because the Mount maintained its sacred status, rabbis argued, ancient rules delimiting access to various parts of the Mount remained intact. These rules restricted Jewish access but prohibited non-Jewish access altogether. More important, whereas the boundaries of the Mount delimited these restrictions on the horizontal plane, they extended infinitely on the vertical plain. In other words, the air above the former Temple was as sacred as the ground below it.[75]

This fine point of halachic trivia continues to pose problems to observant Jews wishing to fly above Jerusalem, a subject of much contention among Orthodox rabbis. It goes without saying that this religious-legal position precluded any arrangement in which Muslims would be permitted to walk "above" the remnants of the Temple. Clinton's solution, while ingenious, thus typifies the overall malaise of the negotiations. Like his Israeli and Palestinian counterparts, Clinton had not met or consulted with religious experts before Camp David. His proposal was thus doomed to failure, despite making sense from a geometric or pragmatic point of view, because it made no sense from a religious point of view.[76]

Clinton's was a political solution uninformed by religious considerations. The more troubling, then, that the Israeli delegation, equally ignorant of the Jewish position on the matter, gave conditional approval to the idea of horizontally dividing sovereignty over the Temple Mount toward the conclusion of the negotiations.[77] Had their Palestinian counterparts agreed to the proposal, the accord would have collapsed upon publication in Israel. The Palestinian delegation managed to avert that embarrassing scenario by rejecting outright any compromise that recognized as legitimate a Jewish attachment to the Temple Mount. "Boiling mad," Arafat is said to have asked Clinton "if he would ever agree for someone else to be sovereign over territory beneath the streets of Washington."[78]

A second and no less ingenious solution was proposed by Ruth Lapidoth, professor of international law at the Hebrew University of Jerusalem, who suggested that the parties resolve their dispute by relegating all sovereignty over the Temple Mount to God. Borrowing the concept of "functional sovereignty" from the international law of the sea, she argued that multiple parties could enjoy sovereignty over one and the same territory provided they executed different aspects of that sovereignty.[79] Her solution to the Temple Mount dispute was to divide sovereignty over the site into functional components, such as the physical and the spiritual. Thus one party to the dispute might gain political sovereignty over the Mount, including such rights as controlling access or policing, while the other gained spiritual sovereignty, involving the rights to determine prayers and rituals.

Better yet, because the spiritual component was the more contested of the two, Lapidoth proposed that the parties to the dispute agree to a formula that attributed spiritual sovereignty over the Temple Mount "to God." Not only did this approach muddy the waters surrounding the sovereignty question, an issue of excessive complexity and insufficient importance, in her opinion, but it also provided a formula that audiences on both sides of the conflict would be forced to accept, if grudgingly. After all, she explained in an interview with the *Jerusalem Post,* "sovereignty can belong to God, the whole world belongs to God, so no one has a problem with that. But we have to take religion and sovereignty out of the negotiations. We have to negotiate over responsibility, authority, rights and such. I prefer not to discuss sovereignty at all."[80]

Like Clinton's proposal, Lapidoth's proposal failed the test of religious feasibility. Contrary to Lapidoth's perception, spiritual sovereignty over sacred sites cannot be separated from political sovereignty. Because the safeguarding of spiritual resources requires the ability to police access to sacred space and behavior within that space, spiritual sovereignty *is* political in sacred places. To maintain the distinction between sacred and profane and thus prevent desecration, believers must be able to monitor and police who enters the space and what actions are taken within the space. This requirement, though driven by religious principles, is tantamount to political control over territory. Aspiring to this type of political control amounts to striving for sovereignty.

Indeed, confrontations between Jewish and Muslim worshipers on the Mount have consistently revolved around the twin issues of access and freedom of worship.[81] Muslim and Palestinian activists have tried to restrict non-Muslim access to the platform, or the two shrines, by locking the gates, charging tourists a fee, or simply blocking the way to visitors, moves that have led to confrontations with Israeli authorities. The Israeli military, on the other hand, has asserted its authority by controlling access routes to the gates of the Mount, confiscating keys to the gates from the Muslim authorities, or blocking all worshipers from entering the Mount in periods of high tension. Jewish and Israeli activists have tried to gain access to the site on religiously significant dates and have appealed to the Israeli Supreme Court to protect their right to conduct prayer sessions and rituals on the Mount, a privilege the court has refused to grant thus far.

Sectarian competition over access and control of the Temple Mount, in the years leading up to the Camp David summit and in the years since, has run the gamut from court battles to physical altercations. Given this context, any solution to the Temple Mount dispute that seeks to separate political from religious sovereignty seems divorced from reality. In sacred space, God's sovereignty has very real mundane implications.

Two months after the collapse of the Camp David negotiations, on September 28, 2000, then Israeli opposition leader Ariel Sharon visited Jerusalem to assert Israeli sovereignty over the sacred site. Although the visit had been coordinated with Palestinian security authorities and although Sharon did not set foot inside the Muslim shrines on the Mount, his visit was regarded by Palestinians as a callous provocation. The Palestinian uprising in response to this visit signaled the collapse of the Israeli-Palestinian peace process and the resurgence of violence at unprecedented levels. Palestinians named this confrontation "the al-Aksa Intifada" in honor of the shrine in Jerusalem.

That most recent round of Middle East violence was sparked by sensitivities toward sacred space, but increased hostility also played itself out through acts of reciprocal desecration of sacred space. One week after Sharon's visit to Jerusalem, Palestinian rioters targeted the tomb of the patriarch Joseph in nearby Nablus. The Jewish seminary at the site was burned to the ground, its library desecrated, and the dome of the tomb was painted green, to symbolize its conversion into a mosque.[82] In Jericho, Palestinian security forces failed to prevent a Palestinian mob from torching a seventh-century synagogue.[83] Reports of the events at Joseph's Tomb led to Jewish vandalism of three mosques in Tiberias and Jaffa, cities in which Jews and Muslims live side by side.[84] Muslims in mixed communities retaliated: synagogues in Jaffa, Haifa, Ramla, and Shfaram were firebombed, the tombs of Jewish saints in several Galilean towns were defaced, and the walls of a synagogue in a Jewish settlement were spray-painted with swastikas and anti-Semitic slogans.[85] To express his outrage over Israeli tactics against Palestinians, an American tourist from Los Angeles used red paint to deface the Western Wall, where the violence had originated.[86] From that point on, confrontations snowballed from isolated acts of vandalism to armed clashes between Israeli and Palestinian forces. By December 2007, the al-Aksa Intifada had cost the lives of some six thousand Palestinians and Israelis.[87]

Perhaps, had the correct formula for a compromise over the Temple Mount surfaced at Camp David, the ensuing crisis in Israeli-Palestinian relations could have been averted. Yet all the proposals considered over the course of negotiations, like many solutions discussed since, have walked the same Hobbesian and Huntingtonian line: they strive to ignore the troublesome religious facets of conflicts over sacred sites or subsume them under political aspects that are deemed manageable by means of division and exclusion.

Proposals such as these must ultimately fall short, not only because they fail to comply with the logic of religious consequences but also because they fail the test of appropriateness.[88] As I argue in the next chapter, the reconfiguration of ideas about sacred space for the purposes of resolving conflicts must come from religious authorities, not political actors. Religious leaders are uniquely suited for shaping and reshaping ideas about sacred space, not only because they are experts in the religious laws that manage access to and behavior in sacred space but also because they enjoy charismatic authority over their followers. This expertise and authority have their constraints, and consequently the abilities of these actors to shape the parameters of sacred space are not without limit. Yet one cannot help but wonder how Israeli-Palestinian negotiations would have fared had the proposal to divide the Temple Mount horizontally, or defer its sovereignty to God, come from authoritative Jewish and Muslim figures rather than from an American president and an Israeli law professor.

PART II

Managing Conflicts over Sacred Spaces

9. Pope John Paul II sits with Chief Rabbi Israel Lau (*left*) and Palestinian Muslim cleric Sheikh Tatzir Tamimi (*right*) under a mural of Jerusalem during an interfaith meeting in Jerusalem on March 23, 2000. Photo copyright Gabriel Bouys/AFP/Getty Images.

Chapter Six

THE FOUNDATIONS AND LIMITS
OF RELIGIOUS AUTHORITY

The papal bull "Antiquorum Fida Relatio," issued by Pope Boniface VIII in the year 1300, turned on its head the relative positions held by Rome and Jerusalem since the fourth century as Christian pilgrimage destinations. Prior to the bull, a plenary indulgence, the formal remission of punishment for sins already forgiven, required a pilgrimage to the Holy Land.[1] Such a pilgrimage, with all the risks it entailed, was considered a supreme act of devotion by the Church. Boniface's declaration of 1300 was revolutionary in establishing a cyclical jubilee year, to recur once a century, during which plenary indulgences could be obtained in Rome. Rather than risk life and limb to visit the great churches in Bethlehem, Nazareth, or Jerusalem, pilgrims could obtain remission for their sins by worshiping at two great basilicas in Rome: St. Peter's in the Vatican and St. Paul Outside the Walls.

Boniface's substitution of Rome for Jerusalem met with resounding success. A contemporary witness to the first jubilee reports that "a great part of the Christians which were living at that time, women as well as men, made the said pilgrimage from distant and diverse countries, both from far and near. And it was the most marvelous thing that was ever seen, for throughout the year, without break, there were in Rome, besides the inhabitants of the city, 200,000 pilgrims, not counting those who were coming and going on their journeys."[2] The event inspired Dante Alighieri's description of the souls trapped in the eighth circle of hell:

> The nearer half came toward us as they walked,
> The rest went with us, at a swifter pace—
> Just as the Romans, for the multitude
> Thronging the bridge, the year of Jubilee,
> Devised a method for the folk to pass,
> So that all those upon the hither side
> Faced toward the castle, going to St. Peter's,
> While those beyond the barrier faced the mount.[3]

Dante, who may have witnessed the jubilee in Rome firsthand, is describing the first traffic regulations in modern history, an arrangement necessitated by the immense volume of pilgrims arriving in Rome in response to Boniface's proclamation. Owing to popular demand, subsequent popes reduced the time between jubilees to fifty years, then forty years, and eventually twenty-five years, but the popularity of the practice seemed only to grow. During the jubilee of 1450, two hundred pilgrims died when the Sant'Angelo bridge collapsed under the weight of the multitude. Roman authorities concluded that overcrowding had reached intolerable levels and began constructing new roads into the city as well as opening additional gates in its walls. The pontiffs also expanded the number of locations in Rome in which indulgences could be obtained from the initial two to three, then four, then seven, to the current number of nine.[4]

Crowd control became a chief concern among the organizers of the Grand Jubilee in the year 2000 as well, with twenty-six million worshipers expected to visit Rome on the occasion of the second millennium since the birth of Christ. It is for this reason, perhaps, that Pope John Paul II issued an unusual proclamation in the months leading up to the jubilee, in which he permitted the chapel at Fiumicino airport to be used as one of the sites at which pilgrims could obtain a remission of sins over the course of the year.[5] A visit to the small chapel, located halfway between the Alitalia counter and the VIP lounge at the airport, could now function as a proxy for pilgrimage to Rome, which, in turn, was already a substitute for pilgrimage to the Holy Land. One journalist could not resist quipping: "Can drive-through be far behind?"[6]

The popes' ability to redefine the meaning and function of Christianity's most sacred sites raises two obvious questions. The first, regarding the popes' motivations, is easily addressed. Concern for the safety of pilgrims offered one incentive. If in the year 2000 the worry was overcrowding in the streets and churches of Rome, the concern in 1300 CE was for the very lives of pil-grims. The fortress of Acre, the last crusader stronghold in the Holy Land, had fallen to the Muslim Mamelukes in 1291, signifying the dissolution of the Crusader Kingdom of Jerusalem. Without the knights to protect the pilgrims on their perilous journey to the shrines in the Holy Land, pilgrimages trickled to a halt. The bull "Antiquorum Fida Relatio" offered a safe substitute.

Beyond protecting the lives of believers, the elevation of Rome also stood to benefit the Church financially. Giovanni Villani, who chronicled the surge of pilgrims in response to Boniface's proclamation, also noted how "from the offerings made by the pilgrims much treasure was added to the Church, and all the Romans were enriched by the trade."[7] Eventually, the Church would come to abandon the pilgrimage requirement altogether and enjoy a steady income from the sale of indulgences.

The second question, regarding the pilgrims' unwavering acceptance of the two papal declarations, is somewhat more difficult to explain. After all, the two popes were radically redefining the importance of Christianity's most sacred sites. Believers could have protested or simply ignored these guidelines. Why, instead, were these redefinitions so enthusiastically embraced? Several possible explanations come to mind. First among these is convenience. A visit to Rome was cheaper, safer, and easier than the perilous journey to Muslim Palestine. The temporary nature of the edicts, affecting the status of the sacred sites for yearlong periods separated by several decades, must also have allayed some of the concerns that these changes might have provoked. The first of the two proclamations also resolved a difficult dilemma at a time of great uncer-tainty for the Christian community in Europe: How should the pilgrim walk in the footsteps of Christ without access to the actual places in which Jesus had lived? Boniface's bull offered a symbolic solution to that problem by propos-ing that pilgrims reenact key moments from the life of Jesus by performing appropriate rituals in the Roman basilicas.

Finally, the strictly hierarchical nature of the Catholic Church and the popes' position at the summit of that hierarchy must have left little doubt in the believers' minds that both Boniface's and John Paul's proclamations were to be taken seriously. These were no mere proclamations, after all, but veritable "speech acts": upon being uttered by the pope, the bull transformed Rome, ipso facto, into a proxy for Jerusalem, just as the tiny chapel at Fiumi-cino airport would, by virtue of John Paul's declaration, become an authentic stand-in for the basilicas of Rome.

In this chapter, I investigate the abilities of religious leaders to shape and reshape sacred space. I begin by introducing a social constructivist view on sacred space that contrasts with the interpretivist view that has dominated this volume so far. Instead of focusing on the meaning of sacred space as perceived by believers, this approach explores the processes through which agents and societies construct space as sacred. This shifts the focus of the analysis onto religious entrepreneurs, the actors who utilize their expertise and their charisma to consecrate, convert, or secularize sacred space. Whereas great religious leaders have executed some of these transformations under extraordinary circumstances, less dramatic variations are performed by religious officials on a routine basis. I examine several historical cases in which leaders have attempted, successfully or otherwise, to reconfigure the status of sacred sites.

Religious actors' ability to change the value or configuration of sacred space or shift the rules that regulate access to such space and activities within it is limited by what their audience will accept. The religious community is thus the second set of actors directly involved in the construction of sacred space. The response of believers to proposed change in the status of sacred space, in turn, is influenced by variables already alluded to, such as the importance of the sacred site involved, the nature and timing of the change, and the position of the leader in the religious hierarchy. If religious leaders are to assist in the management of contested sacred sites, then the range and interaction between these variables should be of some interest to students of religion and conflict.

The last piece missing in this puzzle is the process by which religious leaders are persuaded to cooperate in the management of conflicts over sacred places. Unlike Popes Boniface VIII and John Paul II, religious authorities may have no incentives of their own to change the meaning and value of a contested sacred site. Under restricted conditions, they can be induced or coerced to do so by a third set of actors, the political leadership, on behalf of whom the sacred space is to be manipulated. The successful reconfiguration of sacred space in a manner conducive to conflict resolution is thus dependent not only on the relationship between religious actors and their audiences but also on the relationship between the religious and the secular leadership.

The Social Construction of Sacred Space

On November 19, 1863, Abraham Lincoln delivered a speech at the dedication of the Soldiers' National Cemetery in Gettysburg that attracted little attention. Indeed, when he concluded his remarks, after speaking for less than three minutes, few among the fifteen thousand assembled as much as applauded.[8] The Gettysburg Address, now accepted as one of the great speeches in the American canon, offered a terse interpretation of American history and the ongoing civil war focused on the theme of equality. At the

same time, Lincoln's "few appropriate remarks" successfully captured a crucial ambiguity inherent in all sacred spaces: they are both divinely instituted
and socially constructed.

At Gettysburg, the sacred space in question was a civil-religious sacred space,
a military cemetery. Speaking of this setting, Lincoln declared: "We have come
to dedicate a portion of that field, as a final resting place for those who here
gave their lives that that nation might live." Two sentences later, he offered
this famous qualifier: "But, in a larger sense, we can not dedicate—we can not
consecrate—we can not hallow—this ground. The brave men, living and dead,
who struggled here, have consecrated it, far above our poor power to add or
detract."

Lincoln's words reflect two fundamentally different ways of thinking
about sacred space. This volume, thus far, has focused exclusively on the view
articulated in Lincoln's qualifier, a reading in which humans are consumers
of sacred space rather than producers of such space. This is the interpretivist
view, adopted by students of sacred space such as Mircea Eliade and Harold
Turner. "Neither natural nor human agency makes a place sacred," Turner
writes, "but only the action of the gods."[9]

It is the other interpretation, the first of the two referenced in the Gettysburg Address, to which I now turn. In this variant, Lincoln and his audience do dedicate the sacred site through their own speech and actions. This
interpretation exemplifies a constructivist understanding of sacred space. It
recognizes that the concept of sacred space is an intersubjective idea, an
understanding shared by multiple individuals who, as members of a religious
congregation, form a society. Their shared understanding of a space as sacred
is a social construct, produced and sustained by interaction between members
of the society. As a social construct, sacred space can be compared to other
institutions, such as marriage, currency, or the national flag, that manifest
themselves through laws, symbols, and recurring social practices.

What makes space sacred, then, is not merely a divine pronouncement
but the social response to that pronouncement, the rituals, interpretations,
and symbolic maneuvers that characterize a society's attitudes toward sacred
space. As Roger Friedland and Richard Hecht write: "There is an intimate
connection, then, between the organization of sacred space and the material
and cultural organization of power. Sacred space is socially constructed. Its
meaning is made, and that meaning has implications for the doctrines which
motivate those who claim it as their own."[10] This is not to say that the meaning of sacred space is perfectly flexible or constantly open to interpretation.
A social constructivist analysis stops short of the poststructuralist rejection of
the inherent essence of the sacred. Instead, constructivists observe that social

meaning, once initiated, undergoes institutionalization. Through repetition and routine, social practice embeds ideas about sacred space until these ideas take on a permanence and life of their own. They become "social facts."[11] With the passage of time, these ideas become entrenched and increasingly resistant to change. Any shift in the perception of sacred space now occurs gradually through gentle adjustments in social practice.

This process, which Anthony Giddens calls "structuration," in which social agents constrain and shape a structure that in turn constrains and shapes the agents, is at the core of the constructivist understanding of meaning.[12] The structuration process explains well how identities can become institutionalized over time and how change can gradually emerge as agent and structure respond to one another. It is a theory less well suited for explaining radical change and entirely unsuitable for explaining innovation. New ideas are exogenous to this theory: it can explore the preconditions and setting for new ideas or suggest how ideas spread and morph, but it cannot illuminate how ideas germinate in the minds of individuals.

In the case of sacred space, social constructivism can provide an explanation for changes in the manner in which society thinks about and perceives its sacred space, but it cannot explain radical changes in the identity or parameters of such space. Such extreme changes in the status of sacred space for purposes of dispute management, discussed below, must originate with an individual, the "idea entrepreneur."[13] Primary among these radical changes is the moment at which the sacred site is founded.

Although social constructivism cannot shed much light on the moment of consecration, it can explain the next step in the process, the phase in which society translates innovation into enduring structures to construct "permanent" sacred spaces. Indeed, social constructivism can do more than that: it can define the limits of innovation acceptable to society. New ideas that do not fit into existing social frameworks will be rejected. In that sense, true innovation is impossible because the truly new is unintelligible. Change in the status of a sacred site, including its initial construction, has to be presented in terms that society can understand and implement.

The key to religious innovation, then, is to convince believers that no innovation has taken place.[14] Religious actors rely on established language, rituals, law, and symbol to justify their actions, even when these actions diverge from traditional precedents. To wit, neither Boniface VIII nor John Paul II presented his decision regarding the jubilee year as a groundbreaking revolution. Boniface's bull made reference to "ancient customs" and, in naming the event "jubilee," drew on his audience's familiarity with the eponymous biblical custom.[15] Similarly, John Paul could rely on his audience's familiarity with previous extensions of the right to grant plenary indulgences outside Rome, particularly to significant churches in remoter corners of the world. Although such extensions were not commonly applied to airport chapels, they were not entirely without precedent.

A change in the status of a sacred site, then, requires the presence of an individual with significant social influence who at the same time is proficient in the traditions, rituals, and religious-legal precedents of a religious movement. The successful shaper and mover of sacred space enjoys both a prominent position in the social network and a technical expertise in matters sacred. Enter the religious leader. The greater his sway among his followers, either because of his formal status in the religious hierarchy or because of what one might loosely term "charisma," the greater his ability to persuade the religious community to accept changes to their sacred space, the rules governing access to it, or the rules governing behavior inside it. Members of society can and do participate in decisions about the value, cohesion, and boundaries of secular territory. Yet in defining sacred space, the community is entirely dependent on religious actors who have a monopoly over the interpretation and manipulation of sacred parameters.

It is worth noting that there is an interpretivist "version" to this social constructivist account of the power vested in religious leaders. In this variant, believers perceive religious actors as capable of shaping sacred space not because they possess social ties and technical savvy but because they possess the unique ability to communicate with the divine and represent it on earth. That is, religious leaders are perceived as enjoying "charisma" in its traditional usage, a divine gift. Religious movements tend to restrict the right to consecrate sacred sites to those rare individuals who have been graced with that gift, charismatic individuals who can in their words and actions invoke divine intentions.

It is in this capacity that a priest can utter the phrase "those whom God hath joined together let no man put asunder" even when it is he, and not God, who is conducting a marriage ceremony. In a church, during the course of such a ceremony, the priest's actions *are* God's actions. A Catholic priest is said to act "in the person of Christ" (*in persona Christi*), to become the vessel through which God is present and acting. From the community's point of view, these actions are of such complexity and religious intensity that nobody but the designated religious leader could perform them.

In the interpretivist account, religious actors are capable of shaping religious institutions because of the divine power vested in them. In the social constructivist account, they may do so because of the social power vested in them. The two accounts are complementary: An interpretivist account in which religious power is exclusively the function of divine intervention threatens to lead us down the *Huntingtonian* path to the conclusion that religion is isolated from political influence. A social constructivist account in which religious power is exclusively the function of status and expertise threatens to lead us down the *Hobbesian* path to the conclusion that religious power is nothing more than political power in disguise. Combining both views opens a middle path in which religious power can serve political ends and political power can serve divine ends.

Creating Sacred Space

The consecration of sacred space, in either one of the accounts presented here, requires human agency. In both a religious and a secular framework, this places a paradox at the heart of sacred sites: divinely inspired though they may be, they depend for their instigation on mundane acts. The sanctity of Bethel manifested itself to Jacob in his dream of the ladder, mentioned in the prologue to this book. But Jacob had to consecrate it himself by anointing the stone on which he had slept and, later, by constructing an altar next to it. The angels in his dream did not step off that ladder to consecrate the site on his behalf. And retract as he might, Lincoln did, by uttering the very words "we cannot dedicate," contribute to the dedication of the Soldiers' National Cemetery at Gettysburg.

The consecration ceremonies developed by religious traditions mediate between the requirements for the creation of new sacred space and the unique capabilities of religious actors. As a result, these rituals tend to be characterized by religious-legal complexity and require the kind of divine invocation that only a religious leader is capable of providing. The Roman Catholic rite for the consecration of a church exemplifies these two aspects well.[16] The ritual begins, after a solemn day of fasting, with the consecration of the church's altar. The officiating bishop places the relic of a saint within the altar.[17] He then anoints the twelve crosses on the inside walls of the church with sacred oil, affixes or paints twelve permanent crosses on its outside walls, circumambulates the church three times while symbolically baptizing the building with holy water, traces the letters of the Greek and Latin alphabet on the church floor in the form of a cross, and so forth. The community accompanies these procedures with liturgy, prayer, and song.

Because of the dangers implicit in desecration (or is it because religious leaders strive to maintain their monopoly over the performance of consecrations?) the rules governing these rituals are not merely precise but also complex. Deviation from the exact conditions under which consecration takes place, as dictated by tradition and religious law, invalidates the process. In the Roman Catholic case, for example, a site, once consecrated, cannot be reconsecrated because the initial act is deemed permanent and irreversible. However, if a church has been destroyed or if its walls are "in greater part *simultaneously* demolished," then the church is considered desecrated and the consecration ceremony has to be repeated in its entirety. The range of individuals who may perform particular acts of consecration is defined with similar meticulousness, restricting actors by rank, location, or mandate. A Roman Catholic priest can bless a church using holy water, but only a bishop may consecrate a church using holy oil; a diocesan bishop can consecrate a church, but he cannot do so outside his own diocese; yet the simplest priest can consecrate a church, regardless of location, if appointed to do so by the pope.

There are, in sum, two types of constraints on a religious actor's ability to create new sacred space: religious constraints as dictated by law and tradition and social constraints as exercised by the religious community. To the extent that religious precepts are socially constructed, these two constraints interact: the community will not accept sacred space that has not been appropriately consecrated, and consecrations that deviate from socially accepted ritual are, by definition, null and void.

The power wielded by religious leaders over sacred space is nonetheless significant. Their ability to create sacred space ex nihilo raises an important question: Can these actors redefine existing sacred space in a manner supportive of dispute management or resolution? Could religious leaders reduce the significance of contested sacred sites or relax the rules constraining worship so that groups in conflict might coexist peacefully at these sites? Constraints imposed on these actors by the religious tradition they represent and by the community that worships in the sacred space must limit their ability to shift the status of existing sacred sites. How then might we go about assessing the likelihood of the successful reconfiguration of sacred space at times of conflict?

Religious Constraints on the Reconfiguration of Sacred Space

I would like to suggest three parameters that influence a religious leader's freedom to reformulate the status of a sacred site. Two of these parameters are constraining. They are the ex ante importance of the site and the type of change attempted. The greater the significance of the sacred place in the eyes of believers, the smaller the change that religious leaders can successfully implement and the more important it is that the change be justified in terms acceptable to the religious community. The third parameter, the status of the religious leader initiating the change, is enabling. The greater the influence wielded by a particular religious leader, the greater his freedom of action in implementing significant change at significant sites.

The Importance of the Site

The first and most obvious parameter that constrains the reconfiguration of a sacred site is the value of that site to believers. In chapter 2, I suggested two means of estimating this value, centrality and vulnerability. I defined centrality as the relative ability of a space to provide crucial religious functions to a group, such as communication with the divine, divine presence, and religious meaning. The better a site is at providing these functions, the more central it is in the religious landscape of a community. I defined vulnerability as the measure of a site's sensitivity to sacrilege. The greater the vulnerability of a site, the greater the extent to which access to a site and behavior within it need to be circumscribed, monitored, and sanctioned.

Centrality and vulnerability form a two-dimensional continuum that defines a sacred site's importance. Some sites, such as roadside chapels, can be both peripheral to a group's religious beliefs and require little monitoring of access and activity. If a site enjoys high centrality but low vulnerability, as would a folk shrine that has not undergone institutionalization, the community is likely to notice changes in its parameters but it is not likely to protest these changes. On the other hand, the religious community might express concern over changes to a site characterized by high vulnerability, such as a monastery or convent, but in the absence of constant presence at such a site the change may well elude observation. At the extreme of the continuum lie the religious centers of the major religious movements. Any proposed change to these sites runs the danger of sacrilege and is unlikely to escape the attention of the religious community.

The centrality and vulnerability of the Grand Mosque in Mecca, for example, provides the background to an unusual ninth-century report of a failed reconfiguration of sacred space, told by the Muslim historian Ya'qubi.[18] In 692 CE, so Ya'qubi, the caliph Abd al-Malik faced a challenge to his authority from a rebel leader, Ibn al-Zubayr, who had gained control of Mecca and demanded tribute from all pilgrims to the city. Abd al-Malik, so the story goes, chose to resolve this dilemma by attempting to create an ersatz religious center in Jerusalem designed to replace Mecca:

> Then Abd al-Malik forbade the people of Syria to make the pilgrimage [to Mecca], and by this reason that Abdullah ibn Zubayr was wont to seize on them

during the time of the pilgrimage and force them to pay him allegiance.... But the people murmured thereat, saying "How do you forbid us to make the pilgrimage to God's house, seeing that the same is a commandment of God upon us?" But the caliph answered them, "Has not Ibn Shihab al-Zuhri told you how the Apostle of God did say 'Men shall journey to but three mosques, the Holy Shrine (at Mecca), my mosque (at Medina) and the mosque of the Holy City (of Jerusalem)'? So this last is now appointed to you (as a place of worship) in place of the Holy Shrine of Mecca. And this Rock, of which it is reported that the Apostle of God set his foot when he ascended into heaven, shall be to you in the place of the Ka'ba." Then Abd al-Malik built above the rock a dome and hung it around with curtains and brocade, and he instituted doorkeepers for the same, and the people took up the custom of circumambulating the rock, even as they had paced around the Ka'ba, and the usage continued thus all the remaining days of the Umayyads [from 692 to 750 CE].[19]

Ya'qubi's tale, a "Just-So Story" designed to explain the unusual layout of the Dome of the Rock in Jerusalem, fails the most basic tests of history.[20] Ya'qubi may well have invented the story out of whole cloth, since it amounts to slander against Abd-al Malik, a caliph from a dynasty that rivaled Ya'qubi's rulers'. Yet several elements woven by Ya'qubi into the tale are instructive. Despite Abd al-Malik's supreme status as successor of Muhammad and chief commander of the faithful, and despite the significance of the site offered as substitute, Ya'qubi recognized that the alleged ruse was ultimately doomed to failure.

The justifications that Ya'qubi attributes to the caliph are equally interesting: he has Abd al-Malik framing the change as consistent with previous practices and beliefs. The circular design of the dome built by the caliph constitutes a feeble attempt to emulate the structure of the Grand Mosque in Mecca and to encourage rituals similar to those practiced at the more important of the two sites. Despite all these efforts, the enterprise is short-lived. Indeed, had any such attempt to challenge the position of Mecca actually taken place, it would have likely endangered the stability of the caliphate itself.

Ya'qubi's account illustrates the challenges posed by sites of high centrality and exclusivity. The more embedded a sacred site is in preexisting social practice, enshrined in commonly understood rules, and delimited by clearly visible symbols, the less room religious leaders have for maneuvering rules, symbols, and practices. Tragically, but not surprisingly, sites that are characterized by high centrality and exclusivity are also the most conflict prone, a connection I elaborated in chapter 3. Thus, religious actors may well find themselves most constrained in reshaping sacred space at the very sites where their intervention would be needed most.

The Magnitude of Change and Its Justification

In Ya'qubi's account of the construction of the Dome of the Rock, the failure to replace Mecca with Jerusalem can be traced not only to the importance of the site targeted and the magnitude of change proposed but also to the caliph's weak justification for the proposed change. Concerned as Abd al-Malik may have been about the threat posed by his rival, the faithful could not have accepted such rivalry as sufficient cause for abrogating the status of their most sacred site.

In contrast, routine amendments and updates to the status of lesser sacred sites, what for lack of a better term might be called "religious maintenance," require a modicum of authority and are likely to encounter little communal resistance. Religious actors regularly consecrate, reconsecrate, and deconsecrate sites characterized by low centrality or vulnerability. Whenever new churches need to be dedicated, cemeteries relocated, or temples torn down, religious leaders play their part. Expanding communities, the need to vacate lots for newer construction, destruction caused by natural disasters and the ravages of time, or acts of desecration that cause irreparable damage to sites of worship, all these create a need for rituals that only select religious functionaries can perform. Often, these leaders will act in an advisory capacity, supervising the construction or destruction of shrines and recommending location or design for new sites.

Challenges arise when the community perceives the functions performed by the religious leader to be out of the ordinary. Such extreme changes in the status of sacred places require more significant windows of opportunity. In such instances, several factors must conspire to persuade the religious community that a significant shift is justified: a threat to the sacred site or perhaps even the religious movement itself, an unbearable status quo, and the realization that the change is a necessary act of last resort. If we conceive of social perceptions of sacred space as hegemonic ideas, along Antonio Gramsci's lines, the parallels become obvious: dramatic shifts in dominant ideas are possible at times of crisis, when old ideas are no longer capable of fulfilling social needs and new ideas are available that can fill these gaps.[21]

One such crisis, and the most fundamental reconfiguration of sacred space in Jewish history that accompanied it, illustrates the potential for dramatic changes in social perceptions and practices surrounding sacred space. Its protagonist was Yochanan ben Zakkai, a student of the great sage Hillel, who was the only member of Jerusalem's religious elite to survive the Roman razing of the city and its Temple in 70 CE.[22] Smuggled out of Jerusalem in a coffin just prior to the final Roman assault, ben Zakkai managed to avoid the fate that befell the priests, the members of the supreme council (the *Sanhedrin*), and the leading rabbis of his era, all killed by the Romans in the ensuing massacre.

Ben Zakkai and his students escaped to the town of Yavneh where they grappled with the existential predicament facing their community in light of the destruction of its religious, political, and economic center. Absent a Temple and a priestly caste, unable to fulfill core ritual and spiritual obligations, the Jewish community threatened to disintegrate. Ben Zakkai addressed this crisis by creating rabbinical Judaism, shifting the focus of Jewish practices from animal sacrifice in the Temple to prayer in synagogues, with rabbis replacing the functions previously performed by priests.[23]

He did so, in part, through a series of formal proclamations (*takkanot*) that established Yavneh as the new academic, religious, and judicial capital of Israel and that prescribed how religious requirements that had previously centered in Jerusalem could now be performed in synagogues everywhere. He also began the task of preserving existing oral legal traditions by accumulating, synthesizing, and organizing these traditions into what would later be known as the Mishnah, which in turn would set the foundation for the Talmud. More surprisingly, ben Zakkai overturned traditional Jewish practices regarding sacred space through a series of faits accomplis.

The Mishnah reports one particularly audacious moment in which both ben Zakkai's extraordinary confidence and his eclectic personality come to the fore. The event is significant: for the first time since the destruction of the Temple, the ram's horn (*shofar*) needed to be sounded on a Sabbath, an act previously performed only in the confines of the Temple. How was this ritual to be completed in the absence of the Temple? The Mishnah reports on ben Zakkai's solution to the dilemma: "Once it happened that Rosh Hashanah fell on the Sabbath, and all the villagers gathered in Yavneh to hear the shofar. Rabban Yohanan ben Zakkai said to the men of Bathyra: 'Let us sound the shofar!' They said to him: 'Let us discuss whether it is proper to do so or not.' He said to them: 'Let us sound the shofar, and afterward, let us discuss.' After they blew the shofar, they said to him: 'Let us discuss!' He said to them: 'Already the shofar has been heard in Yavneh, and one does not discuss after the fact.'"[24]

What is peculiar about this dramatic rule shift, aside from ben Zakkai's extraordinary chutzpa, is the stark contrast between ben Zakkai's formally low ranking in the religious hierarchy and the extreme value of the religious site whose status he was challenging. His reconfiguration of the very meaning of sacred space in Judaism succeeded because it fulfilled a dire need at a particularly precarious historical juncture. At moments of uncertainty such as these, when the religious community is completely dependent on its leader for the adaptation and application of rules to new circumstances, religious authorities are the only actors capable of updating codes and enforcing subsequent behavior.

The Identity of the Religious Leader

Yochanan ben Zakkai's transformation of Judaism, from a religion centered on a Temple to a religion organized into synagogue communities, is the exception that proves the rule. Although he was a mere scholar, ben Zakkai commanded the authority of the dwindling Jewish community in Palestine because he was the only authority figure who had survived the destruction of Jerusalem. Other things being held equal, greater charismatic presence and legal expertise are required to induce changes in sites of greater importance. The average religious actor is thus limited in his abilities to shape and reshape sacred space, but extraordinary religious leaders have employed their charismatic influence to enact extraordinary changes in the status of sacred places.

Religious leaders have often resorted to identifying and consecrating sacred places in order to mark critical junctures in the development of a religious movement and consolidate their status within that movement. The Hebrew patriarchs do so repeatedly throughout the events described in Genesis, as does Moses at Sinai. Israel's kings define and redefine biblical Judaism's religious center through acts of dedication and consecration and place themselves within those centers: King David elevates Jerusalem over competing religious centers, such as Shiloh and Bethel, by moving the Ark of the Covenant into the city; his son, Solomon, constructs a permanent abode for the Ark, a temple, to function as the religious hub of his kingdom. When this kingdom is torn apart by rivalry for Solomon's throne, one of the contenders, Jeroboam, consecrates altars in Bethel and Dan to divert his subjects from worshiping in Jerusalem.

At their most dramatic, these reconfigurations occur when the founders of new religious movements overthrow existing conceptions of sacred space in order to set themselves and their followers apart from their predecessors. Examples relating to the subversion of Jerusalem as Judaism's sacred center, for instance, are legion.

Less than three centuries after the sack of Jerusalem by Rome, the Roman Empire aligned itself with Christianity, and it was left to Constantine, the first Christian Roman emperor, to implement this transition by constructing a new sacred center for Christianity in Jerusalem. To define the new religion in opposition to its Jewish roots, Constantine rejected the Jewish sacred center in Jerusalem, the former site of the Temple, and constructed a competing site across from it, on the other side of the city. His biographer, Eusebius of Caesarea, describes the new Church of the Holy Sepulcher in a manner that clearly emphasizes the antagonism between the two sites and the two religions: "On the monument of salvation itself was the new Jerusalem built, over against the one so famous of old which, after the pollution caused by the murder of the Lord, experienced the last extremity of desolation and paid the penalty for the crime of its inhabitants. Opposite this the emperor raised, at great and lavish expense, the trophy of the Savior's victory over death."[25]

This decision of Constantine's explains why the conflict over the Temple Mount today involves two and not three religious groups. It was a remarkable shift, given the place occupied by the Jewish Temple in seminal events in the lives of Jesus Christ and other Christian figures. But it was not a decision without parallel. Similar reasoning serves to explain why Islam is not a party to the dispute over the Church of the Holy Sepulcher. According to one tradition, when the caliph Umar ibn al-Khattab conquered Jerusalem for Islam in the seventh century, he was taken on a tour of Jerusalem that included a visit to the Church of the Holy Sepulcher. Halfway through the visit, the call for prayer resounded through the city, so Sophornius, the patriarch of Jerusalem and guide to Umar, invited the caliph to conduct his prayers inside the church. Karen Armstrong, citing the ninth-century *Annals* of Eutychius, recounts what happened next:

> Umar courteously refused; neither would he pray in Constantine's Martyrium. Instead he went outside and prayed on the steps beside the busy thoroughfare of the Cardo Maximus. He explained to the patriarch that had he prayed inside the Christian shrines, the Muslims would have confiscated them and converted them into an Islamic place of worship to commemorate the caliph's prayer.[26]

If this account is to be believed, the lack of Muslim-Christian conflict over the Church of the Holy Sepulcher, like the absence of Muslim-Christian and Jewish-Christian conflict over the Temple Mount, has its roots in a conscious decision made by a charismatic leader at a critical time in the history of a religious-political movement. Constantine, first Roman-Christian emperor, chose to position Christianity's sacred center in Jerusalem away from the city's sacred site for Jews. Umar ibn al-Khattab, successor to the Prophet Muhammad, placed the Muslim sacred site in Jerusalem apart from the Christian site but on top of the Jewish site, thus dooming Islam to conflict with Judaism but not with Christianity in the city.

There is, then, an alternative to conflicts at sacred places. At crucial historical junctures, leaders have proven capable of drawing believers to new sacred sites without destroying or appropriating existing sacred sites. This, as Arthur Conan Doyle would have put it, shifts the attention to "the dog that did not bark": whereas the divergence of Jewish, Christian, and Muslim beliefs and practices has led to conflict at certain sites, it has also averted conflicts at other sites. Often lost in the litany of conflicts is the catalog of replica sites that enable rival religious groups to commemorate the same person or event separately and peacefully. There is no Jewish-Muslim conflict over the tomb of Moses, no Christian-Muslim conflict over the tomb of John the Baptist, and no Christian-Jewish conflict over the tomb of Adam, despite the shared reverence for these figures, because their tombs exist in duplicate, one for each rival movement.[27]

Sadly, such founding moments are few and far between.[28] The extent of religious influence required to accomplish such feats is extraordinary, since founders must satisfy the needs of their followers while at the same time dramatically severing the ties with the original religious movements from which these followers are drawn. The creation of a new religious movement can both create and avoid overlapping claims to sacred sites, but only rarely do these founding moments afford opportunities for resolving preexisting conflicts.

Founding moments are nonetheless instructive because they illustrate the extreme case in which actors wielding a maximum of religious authority revolutionize preexisting conceptions of sacred space. *Ceteris paribus,* the higher the position a religious actor occupies in a religious hierarchy, the greater his leeway in reconfiguring significant sacred space. In the case of strictly hierarchical religious organizations, such as Catholicism, Orthodox Christianity, Shi'a Islam, or Mormonism, this calculus is relatively straightforward: religious influence peaks in the office of the Holy Father, Patriarch, Grand Ayatollah, or President, respectively, and declines with vertical distance from that office. In religious movements that are less hierarchical, such as Judaism, Hinduism, Sunni Islam, or mainstream Protestant movements, the absence of leaders who can dominate the religious decision-making process is compensated for by means of consensus or majority rule. In these cases, religious leaders assemble in sufficiently large numbers to provide "cumulative" authority. As I demonstrate in the chapters that follow, the more representative and authoritative these groups, the greater their ability to persuade believers to accept significant changes at important sacred sites.

One can envision the set of religious constraints on the reconfiguration of sacred space as a bargaining range between religious leaders and the community loyal to a sacred space. The religious actor's authority, a composite of his expertise and his charisma, usually captured by the actor's formal ranking in a religious hierarchy, broadens the range of possible reconfigurations. The range is narrowed, on the other hand, by the value of the sacred site that stands to be reshaped and by the ambitiousness of the change attempted. The greater the centrality and vulnerability of the site, the greater the change attempted, and the feebler the pretext for the change, the smaller the possibilities of a successful reconfiguration of sacred space.

Political Constraints on the Reconfiguration of Sacred Space

The ability of religious leaders to reshape sacred space depends on their relationship with two sets of actors: their religious constituency and the political elite. So far I have focused on the conditions under which a community of believers might accept or dismiss a religious ruling that seeks to change the status of a sacred space. Religious actors who diverge too far from the parameters acceptable to their audience, relative to the significance of the site targeted, the type of change attempted, and the status of the actor issuing the ruling, may find their rulings ignored or, worse, may find themselves without a job.

The relationship between a religious group that holds particular sets of beliefs regarding a sacred site and its leaders who are potentially capable of restructuring those beliefs is complicated by the presence of a political leadership on whose behalf these changes are to take place. Political elites might wish to see an increase in the religious value of a sacred site or a constraining of rules regarding access and freedom of action inside a sacred site as a device to rally the support of a sectarian audience in preparation for conflict or political competition. They could also profit from such a change as a means of tying their own hands or bolstering their bargaining position in negotiations with ethnic or sectarian opponents over the sacred site.

In other cases, political elites may wish to see the value of a sacred site diminished and rules constraining access and freedom of action inside the site relaxed. This is likely to occur where political leaders wish to deescalate sectarian conflicts or resolve disputes over sacred sites. In either case, the ability of political elites to coerce or persuade religious actors is constrained both directly and indirectly: directly, because religious actors can ignore pressure applied by political elites and even retaliate against such pressure, if need be; indirectly, because even the most compliant of religious leaders are constrained, as aforementioned, by what their constituency will bear.

We can thus imagine a range of scenarios bounded by two extremes. On one extreme lie cases in which the religious leadership is impervious to the wills of the political elite. This is particularly likely when religious and political leaders draw on discrete resources and aim for antithetical goals, as elites representing rival and relatively powerful constituencies. For example, in the Babri Masjid/Ramjanmabhumi dispute, examined in the previous chapter, the government of India found itself unable to prevent Hindu priests from initiating the consecration ceremonies for a temple at the site of the Ayodhya mosque, sparking deadly sectarian riots throughout South Asia. Indeed, even Prime Minister Rajiv Gandhi's pleas that the temple be constructed several feet away fell on deaf ears, in part because the priests involved had allied themselves with the World Hindu Council (VHP) and the Indian People's Party (BJP). Similarly, the Israeli government is unlikely to elicit the cooperation of Muslim clerics in seeking to address tensions with the Palestinian Authority over the Temple Mount issue.

At the other extreme lie cases in which the political leadership is impervious to counterpressures by the religious leadership and is thus able to achieve change in the status of a sacred place without the cooperation of religious actors. Such scenarios are likely to occur when the interests of religious and political constituencies are opposed yet all power is concentrated in the hands of the latter. Such was the case during the great iconoclastic revolutions of the modern era: the English Reformation under Henry VIII in its annihilation of English monasticism in the scope of four years; the French Revolution and its desecration of the churches of France; and the all-out assault on religious structures, institutions, and clergy during the communist revolutions in Russia and China. More recently, the Taliban have tried to assert the absolute rule of Islam in Afghanistan by destroying fifteen-hundred-year-old statues of the Buddha in Bamiyan, once the largest standing Buddha carvings in existence.[29] In none of these cases could religious leaders prevent the desecration or threaten the perpetrators with sanctions.

Political leaders can also enact unilateral changes of this sort when they are willing to incur the wrath of religious actors, costly as this may be. Pope Pius IX threatened King Victor Emmanuel II with excommunication when he heard of his "sacrilegious" intention to annex the Papal States.[30] Victor Emmanuel ignored the warning and was promptly excommunicated, along with his councilors, soldiers, and subjects, past and present. Though he continued to plead for the pope's understanding until his death, the act of excommunication did not affect Victor Emmanuel's popularity or policies. He engaged the papal forces at Castelfidardo, entered Rome, and conquered the Vatican by force, accompanied by the pope's public outrage and condemnations but also by the unanimous support of the Italian people.

Between these two extremes lies the interesting range of cases in which political elites depend on religious leaders to reconfigure the meaning or significance of sacred space but also have the ability to influence those leaders. The extent of this range is determined by the power balance between the religious and the political leadership: If the former enjoys power preponderance and is able to retaliate against political coercion, the range shrinks. If the political leadership enjoys the upper hand, the range expands. Within this bargaining range lies a narrower range, in which social understandings of the rules constraining a sacred site leave religious actors with sufficient leeway to attempt reshaping that space.

The resulting scope of possibilities is very narrow indeed. It circumscribes a universe of cases in which the interests of a society, its religious leadership, and its political leadership are sufficiently aligned so as to allow for the successful reconfiguration of sacred space in support of a political effort to reduce or enhance violence at such space. Given the correlation between the centrality and the vulnerability of a sacred site and the proclivity for conflict at such a site, the existence of an opportunity for reconfiguration in support of conflict resolution at an important sacred site necessitates the following components: religious actor(s) powerful enough to change the status of the relevant sacred space, a change of reasonably modest extent, a compelling need for change, and a political elite capable of motivating the religious actors to induce the change.

In this chapter, I offered a complement to the preceding interpretivist analysis of sacred space: a social constructivist analysis in which religious leaders, equipped with religious expertise and religious authority, are able to shape and reshape sacred space. Religious leaders may wish to do so of their own volition, or they may be induced to do so by political leaders capable of compelling their cooperation. In so doing, religious leaders are constrained by an audience that places limits on their ability to manipulate the value and meaning of sacred space.

Their expectation of how this audience might respond to an attempt at the reconfiguration of a sacred site will influence how religious actors respond to sanctions from the political elite urging them to participate in the reconfiguration of sacred space. This is particularly bad news for those who place their faith in religious authority as the panacea for managing religiously motivated conflict, since religious actors are not immune to the sway of political motivations. The very fact that a site valued by their constituents is an object of contention with a rival community may suffice to discourage religious actors from meddling with it.

The resulting range of opportunities for cooperation along the lines suggested here is very narrow but very real. In the next chapter I demonstrate how cooperation between the Israeli government and the leading rabbis in Israel led to the reconfiguration of Jewish practices on the Temple Mount in 1967 in a manner both acceptable to the Jewish Orthodox population in Israel and conducive to the maintenance of peace and order on the Mount. Whereas sacred sites of lesser importance throughout the West Bank erupted into violence soon after the War of 1967, the Temple Mount in Jerusalem saw no violence until the mid-1980s, when a powerful group of opposing rabbis issued their counterruling. In chapter 8, I illustrate the same principles at work in the reconfiguration of Muslim sacred space. Cooperation between the Saudi monarchy and the religious elite in Saudi Arabia, the ulema, permitted the resolution of a hostage crisis in the heart of the Grand Mosque in Mecca in 1979. Owing to an unprecedented religious ruling by the Saudi ulema, Saudi forces were able to use armed force inside the most sacred space in Islam and thus subdue the insurgents, without immediate repercussions from the Muslim community.

10. A sign at the entrance to the Temple Mount bars Jews from entry. The controversial rabbinical ruling of October 1967 reduced Jewish-Muslim conflict at this sacred site by proclaiming that accessing the site amounted to desecration. Photo copyright Richard T. Nowitz/Corbis.

Chapter Seven

Successful Conflict Management

Jerusalem, 1967

The Temple Mount is a trapezoid plateau, thirty-five acres in area, occupying the southeastern quadrant of the Old City of Jerusalem. It is called Har Habayit (the Temple Mount) by Jews and Haram al-Sharif (the Noble Sanctuary) by Muslims. For members of both religious movements it is a sacred space of the utmost centrality and vulnerability, located at the epicenter of the Arab-Israeli conflict. Ehud Sprinzak, an Israeli political scientist who specialized in radical Jewish movements, referred to the Temple Mount as "the most volatile spot in the Middle East, perhaps on the planet."[1] The *New York Times* has referred to it as "the single most explosive piece of real estate on the planet."[2]

For Muslims and Jews alike this is the foundation stone of creation and the site of the last judgment. Jews revere it as the site of a succession of temples, all of which marked the religious, social, political, and geographical center of pre-Diaspora Judaism. Muslims revere it as the "Remotest Mosque," the destination of the Prophet Muhammad's miraculous Night Journey and the site of his ascension to heaven. For well over a millennium, two Muslim shrines have adorned the plateau: al-Aqsa Mosque and the Dome of the Rock. The mosque commemorates the site of Muhammad's prayer, whereas the Dome marks the location of his ascension.

The history of both faiths is inextricably linked to the city of Jerusalem and its spiritual core, the Mount. Tragically, though not coincidentally, there is an overlap between the sites sacred to both faiths on the Mount. Successive conquerors, Babylonian, Greek, Roman, Muslim, and Christian, have placed their temples on the former site of the Jewish Temple, which was in all likelihood placed on a prior Jebusite sacred site. Complicating matters further, Islam and Judaism respect mutually exclusive rules regarding access to the site and behavior in it.

Muslim tradition prohibits all non-Muslims from entering the compound. It prohibits acts of violence on the platform, designated a sanctuary (*haram*), and requires Muslim gestures of approach, such as ablution and the removal of shoes, before entering the shrines. In Temple times, Jewish law limited access to various sections of the plateau according to their proximity to the Holy of Holies, the center of the Temple. There is broad consensus among contemporary rabbinical interpreters that some, if not all, of these prohibitions still apply to the site, even in the absence of the Temple structure. Non-Jews may access the boundaries of the plateau only. Jewish women in a state of purity may advance further into the center of the compound. Jewish men may approach the former location of the Temple structure but may not enter its courtyard or interior. Priests and Levites could enter the court and structure but only the High Priest was permitted into the Holy of Holies. Jewish tradition locates this epicenter of the Temple compound on the very rock revered by Muslims. Jews also require gestures of approach that are distinct from Muslim requirements, including complicated ablution ceremonies and restrictions on access for pregnant and menstruating women, the handicapped, diseased, and so on. Those Jews who wish to rebuild the Temple expect the renewal of animal sacrifices at the site as mandated in the Hebrew Bible. This scenario contrasts rudely with Muslim prohibitions on the shedding of blood in a haram.

The conquest of Jerusalem by Israel in 1967 turned these hypothetical religious disagreements into a very real political crisis. Jerusalem and the sacred sites at its heart were immediately seized upon by religious and political entrepreneurs from all parties to the conflict. Israelis rejoiced in their ability to regain access and worship at sites, in Jerusalem and elsewhere in the West Bank, from which Jews had been barred for centuries. Arab and Muslim elites protested the threat to the status quo and underscored the menace of sacrilege. The Israeli government realized that here, as in other sacred sites revered by both Jews and Muslims in the West Bank, a legal prohibition on Jewish access was politically unfeasible and therefore physical confrontations, and eventually violence, were unavoidable.

And yet, to the immense relief of the Israeli government, no interfaith hostilities broke out on the Temple Mount in the first nineteen years after its liberation. Whereas Jerusalem itself and other sacred sites shared by Jews and

Muslims in the West Bank, such as the Tomb of the Patriarchs in Hebron or the Tomb of Rachel in Bethlehem, were constantly plagued by acts of violence, the Temple Mount saw no violence until the mid-1980s.

This outcome was particularly unexpected, for several reasons. For one, the Temple Mount supersedes in religious significance all other shrines conquered by Israel in 1967. Given its centrality and vulnerability in both Islam and Judaism and the role it plays in Israeli, Palestinian, and Arab nationalist rhetoric, the Mount should have become the locus of immediate violent confrontations between the contending parties to the Arab-Israeli dispute. It did indeed become the focus of violence, but only after two decades of Israeli rule over Jerusalem.

A second reason why the initial period of peace on the Mount is surprising is that the Temple Mount poses extensive security challenges unlike any the Israeli military had to face at the smaller shrines in the West Bank. The Temple Mount compound covers dozens of acres and has nine entrances all of which can be accessed through the narrow alleys of the Old City of Jerusalem. The compound contains some twenty independent sites of religious importance to Jews and Muslims, all of which would make suitable targets for violent attack. It should have been easier for police and military to keep the peace at the smaller tombs in Bethlehem and Hebron. These are single buildings limited in size, with single entrances and single access routes that can be easily surveyed. Yet the extensive steps taken by Israeli security forces to contain violence at these smaller shrines failed to prevent a constant escalation of violent incidents. In the same period, Israeli security forces rarely entered the Temple Mount compound and guarded only one of its nine entrances. How can we explain the Temple Mount anomaly?

West Bank Sacred Sites after 1967

The tomb of the biblical matriarch Rachel lies on the road to Bethlehem, one kilometer south of the Gilo suburb of Jerusalem. A minor shrine until the early twentieth century, it gained in popularity in periods of rapid social and political transformation in the 1940s and after 1967. Dominant political themes were linked to the image of the matriarch and reexplored through the use of new rituals at her tomb.[3] The tomb has become a central place of prayer on the traditional anniversary of the matriarch's death and on the anniversary of the destruction of the Temple, when up to twenty-five thousand Jewish pilgrims visit this shrine.[4] A mosque and Muslim graveyard are at the same site, flanked by the Palestinian city of Bethlehem and two refugee camps.

Since 1967 the tomb has been an epicenter of Jewish-Muslim and Israeli-Palestinian violence.[5] Locals have attacked pilgrims, thrown Molotov cocktails and fired at Israeli soldiers, rioted, and even attempted to blow up the tomb.[6] The Israeli military has responded with rubber bullets, live fire, and tear gas. Strikes and protests have occurred on a weekly basis.[7] Acceleration in the Arab-Israeli peace process and escalation of the intifada have not affected Jewish attendance, forcing a constant increase in military presence to protect pilgrims and leading in turn to renewed attacks. By the mid-1990s ceremonies at the tomb had to be heavily guarded by Israeli border police forces positioned on the roof of the tomb and houses facing the site, with concrete slabs defending the compound from car bombs and with metal detectors placed at all entrances. The tomb has become a fortified military post, but this volatile situation has only increased the number of pilgrims. At times of political volatility, prominent rabbis rally the masses for prayer at the tomb, and the Chief Rabbinate prints prayers designed for exclusive recital at this site.[8] The outbreak of the second intifada led to a further escalation of violence, including Palestinian attacks on the tomb that killed two Israeli guards, bombs thrown at the shrine, and a firefight between Israeli soldiers and Palestinian gunmen that trapped fifty Jewish worshipers inside the tomb.[9]

Israeli-Palestinian agreements about the future of the site have run into constant opposition by the religious members of the Israeli government. Although agreement to hand over the administration of Bethlehem to the Palestinian Authority was reached early on in Israeli-Palestinian negotiations, the tomb became a stumbling block with four no-confidence motions submitted by opposition parties on this issue alone. Religious members of Parliament insisted that a road bypassing Palestinian autonomy areas be constructed to link the tomb, as an Israeli enclave, with Jerusalem. Radical members of the Palestinian Authority, in turn, promised that Jews would be banned from the site should the tomb come under their control.[10]

As I recounted in chapter 5, violence escalated with yet greater ferocity at the Tomb of the Patriarchs. After the onset of common worship in 1967, the tomb became an epicenter of Jewish-Muslims violence instigated whenever Muslims tried to pray in the Jewish section of the shrine and vice versa. Individual attacks left Palestinian residents and Muslim and Jewish worshipers, as well as Israeli soldiers, dead and wounded and culminated in the massacre of twenty-nine Muslim worshipers by Israeli settler Baruch Goldstein in February 1994.

At these two West Bank sites, as well as smaller shrines across the West Bank, such as the Tomb of Joseph in Nablus, interreligious friction led to frequent and deadly violence between Jewish and Muslim worshipers. These developments stand in stark contrast with the placid state of affairs on the Temple Mount in the first two decades after the conquest of Jerusalem by Israeli forces.

Jerusalem in June 1967

By June 7, 1967, two days into the war, Israel had conquered the entire West Bank of the Jordan River, going so far as to cross the river into the Kingdom of Jordan. At this point in the war, the Old City of Jerusalem, while encircled by Israeli forces from all sides, remained formally under Jordanian control. Moshe Dayan, Israel's minister of defense, hesitated to give the order to attack within the walls, suggesting instead that Israel place a siege around the city until its residents surrendered peacefully, "waving white flags." His foremost fear, he confessed in his autobiography, was international condemnation of a violent attack that would damage the holy places in the Old City.[11] Privately, he expressed his long-term concern regarding the future of the holy sites should these fall into Israeli hands. Sharing his concern with Uzi Narkiss, chief of Central Command, he asked rhetorically: "What do we need this Vatican business for?"[12] Dayan might well have had his way, had it not been for the pressures applied by hawks in the Israeli government and religious members of the cabinet. These, led by Menachem Begin, still smarting from the loss of the Old City in 1948 and recognizing the unique opportunity of realizing a messianic vision, urged Dayan to advance into the city before the implementation of a ceasefire by the United Nations Security Council.[13]

By midday of June 7, the commander of the charging paratrooper unit, Mordechai (Mota) Gur, who had rallied his troops with a call to fulfill two thousand years of Jewish aspirations, could exclaim triumphantly, "The Temple Mount is in our hands!"[14] The conquest had taken a mere six hours. The city was attacked without the air support that had conferred swift victory upon Israeli forces throughout the war. Reportedly, Israeli forces took significant precautions to ensure the integrity of various holy sites in the city.[15] Artillery was aimed at the northwest corner of the Old City, away from the Muslim sanctuaries in the southeast, with explicit directions to avoid damaging the Church of the Holy Sepulcher at the center of the Old City. With the exception of the minaret of the al-Aqsa Mosque, in which Jordanian snipers had taken up position, none of the holy sites in the city seemed to have incurred damage. Anuar al-Hatib, the highest-ranking Jordanian official in Jerusalem, later explained to his interrogators that he had pleaded in vain with the Jordanian legionnaires to ban snipers from the minaret.[16]

Dayan displayed further sensitivity to the inviolable status of the holy places in Jerusalem in his behavior immediately following the conquest. Narkiss had ordered all soldiers to refrain from entering the mosque and dome on the Mount and placed sentries at the doors of these shrines. It is evident from soldiers' testimonies that this order was disobeyed.[17] Dignitaries arrived at the site and entered the sanctuary, and the Israeli flag was raised victoriously over the Dome of the Rock.[18] Dayan's arrival at the scene signaled the restoration of order and dignity to the Temple Mount compound. Upon spotting the flag he immediately ordered it removed.[19] Against Narkiss's urgings, he ordered all soldiers off the Mount and decreed immediate free access to the holy sites for members of all faiths. Narkiss protested once more but relented.[20] Fearing a "mass Israeli invasion" of the sanctuary, the Israeli minister of justice suggested placing Druze police units on the Mount, that is, units of Israeli police composed neither of Jews nor of Sunni Muslims. Dayan vetoed even this form of armed presence. The Israeli military withdrew from the compound and set up a single checkpoint at its southwestern entrance. This remains the only permanent Israeli presence on the Mount to this day.

In the Aftermath of the Conquest

Dayan spent the next day with Major David Farkhi, a professor of Muslim history at the Hebrew University and the military government's liaison with the Arab leadership, in order to prepare for a meeting with the Muslim dignitaries in the Haram.[21] Farkhi and Dayan discussed the status of the Noble Sanctuary in Islam and Muslim attitudes toward Israel and Judaism in general. Three days after the conquest of Jerusalem, Dayan met with the mufti of Jerusalem and the kadi of the Haram inside the al-Aqsa Mosque, all Israeli representatives having removed their shoes and disarmed at the entrance. At this meeting, Dayan reassured the representative of the Muslim Council that all administrative matters relating to the Haram would remain under their jurisdiction and requested that Muslim worship resume at their earliest convenience.

It is worth noting that these and other policies enacted by the minister of defense were implemented without consultation with the rest of the Israeli cabinet. The decision to leave the Temple Mount in Muslim hands, a decision later enshrined in successive government positions, originated exclusively with Dayan. It drew on his own religious-nationalist relationship to the site and his views on Islam, Judaism, history, and archaeology. Similar assurances regarding Christian sacred sites were granted to representatives of the Vatican and the World Council of Churches.[22]

This is not to say that Dayan respected all aspects of the status quo ante in Jerusalem. Far from it. In spite of his pro-Islamic position regarding Jewish rights to the Temple Mount, Dayan realized that a continued prohibition on Jewish access to the site was now politically unfeasible. He demanded that the Muslim authorities accept the right of Jews to access the Temple Mount. The Muslim Council responded in anger but consented, perhaps because its members had expected a far worse outcome, such as an Israeli demand to construct a synagogue on the Mount or even the destruction of the Muslim shrines.[23]

Such destruction as did take place occurred not on the plateau but adjacent to it. Israeli bulldozers demolished a residential Muslim quarter facing the Western Wall so as to create a larger area for congregation and prayer in front of the Wall. The residents of the area were forcibly evacuated, as were several members of the Muslim Council, banned from the city so as to reduce the power and influence of the council. Later that month, the Muslim Council was brought under the supervision of Israel's Ministry of Religious Affairs. On June 27, Israel officially annexed the Old City and East Jerusalem and extended its laws to these areas.[24]

By July 1967, Muslim attendance at Friday prayers in the Sanctuary had returned to the prewar level of approximately ten thousand worshipers, up from five thousand in June.[25] Religious and political actors seemed to be recovering from the shock of conquest and began reasserting their positions regarding the Mount. When the Israeli Ministry of Religious Affairs attempted to censor a quote from the Qur'an in a Friday sermon, the Muslim Council responded with a manifesto calling for an end to censorship, the repatriation of their exiled members, and independent authority over religious courts and endowments. Israel responded positively and removed the council from under the authority of the Ministry of Religious Affairs.[26] Jewish activists, meanwhile, advanced their own agenda. Several rabbis embarked on attempts to pray in sections of the Mount estimated as sufficiently distant from the former location of the Holy of Holies. These efforts were spearheaded by Rabbi Shlomo Goren, the Chief Rabbi of the Israel Defense Forces.

It seems worthwhile, at this juncture in the narrative, to add some detail to the character of this charismatic rabbi, who would become one of the chief protagonists in the struggle over a Jewish presence on the Temple Mount. Two episodes from the course of the Six Day War suffice to give some impression of Goren's impulsive character. On June 7, Goren, flouting all warnings to take cover from enemy snipers, accompanied the Israeli paratrooper units fighting their way toward the Temple Mount. He led the troops in an emotional prayer at the Wall, then ascended to the Mount and entered the Dome of the Rock to blow the shofar, a ram's horn traditionally blown as a Jewish act of celebration. It was here that a brief exchange took place between Goren and Uzi Narkiss, the contents of which Narkiss would reveal only decades later, several weeks before his death:

> I was standing alone, lost in thought, when Goren approached me. "Uzi," Rabbi Goren said to me, "this is the opportunity to place 100 kilos of explosive in the Dome of the Rock and, that's it, get rid of it once and for all." I told him: "Rabbi, stop." Goren said to me: "Uzi, this decision could get you into the history books … you don't realize the tremendous significance of this act. We must seize this opportunity now, immediately. Tomorrow it will no longer be possible." I said to him: "Rabbi, if you don't stop, I'll have you arrested." … Rabbi Goren left without saying another word.[27]

Goren's actions the next day are the stuff of much speculation and mythmaking. Convinced that Israeli forces had already occupied Hebron, Goren purportedly instructed his personal chauffeur to drive him to the Tomb of the Patriarchs in the heart of city. Goren is said to have blasted open the tomb's gates with his submachine gun, entered the shrine, sounded the shofar, and commenced praying. These actions, if true, were extraordinary not merely because Goren was the first Jew to have entered the shrine in seven hundred years but also because Goren had miscalculated the position of the Israeli military. He had, in fact, preempted the Israeli army's occupation of Hebron by hours and thus had, so to speak, "conquered" Hebron single-handedly.

Goren spent the weeks after the war organizing regular prayer services on the Temple Mount. He also elicited the cooperation of the army's corps of engineers in measuring and mapping the precise dimensions of the plateau. He concluded that Jewish prayer was permitted on a 109-yard-long section in the southern part of the Mount, based on evidence suggesting the presence of a tenth-century synagogue there and calculations as to the approximate location of the Holy of Holies.[28] Goren's activities were emulated by several groups of religious Jews who organized demonstrative prayer services on the Mount. Israel's minister of religious affairs, Rabbi Zerach Warhaftig, added his own fuel to the fire by declaring the entire Temple Mount "Jewish property," based on the biblical account of its purchase by King David.[29]

This declaration substantiated Muslim fears, rooted in Palestinian propaganda from the 1920s, about the Jewish intention of destroying the Muslim shrines on the Mount in order to rebuild their Temple. On August 22, the Muslim Council responded with a religious ruling of its own that declared its right of ownership over the Haram and warned of the far-reaching effects of changes to the status quo. The council furthermore attempted to bar entry by Israelis into the compound, to which the Israeli government responded by confiscating the keys to the southwestern entrance to the site.[30]

By August 1967, it was becoming clear that political moves to achieve accommodation between Jewish and Muslim actors had reached a dead end. The Israeli government had done everything in its power to safeguard the religious status quo ante on the Mount and allay Muslim fears about apocalyptic Jewish intentions, while at the same time satisfying Jewish demands for access. Israelis, meanwhile, began visiting the Mount in ever increasing numbers. The sudden accessibility of the holy sites released a wave of religious fervor even among those segments of the population that only weeks earlier had displayed a relative indifference to religion.[31] Three immediate consequences of Israel's conquest of Jerusalem became obvious to decision makers: Israel would extend full sovereignty over the Temple Mount, Jews would flock to the site in their hundreds, and sectarian violence would ensue.[32] As parallel events in Hebron were soon to prove, a clash between Jewish and Muslim worshipers was merely a matter of time.

All three predictions would turn out to be mistaken. For it is at this juncture that a rabbinical declaration resolved, for nearly twenty years, the problem of common prayer on the Temple Mount.[33] The declaration, published by fifty-six rabbis and eventually endorsed by three hundred additional rabbis, prohibited any Jewish entrance "male or female to any part of the Temple Mount, irrespective of the gate used for entrance." The ruling was justified in terms of the threat of desecration: "With the passage of time," explained the rabbis, "we have lost knowledge of the precise location of the Temple, so that anyone entering the Temple Mount area today might mistakenly enter the Temple and the Holy of Holies." The undersigned concluded their admonition by reminding the public of the duty to "fear and respect the Temple."[34]

This last phrase entailed an implicit warning against any attempt to circumvent the ruling by ascertaining the location of the Holy of Holies, as Goren had attempted to do. Such measurement would also constitute a sin, the undersigned authorities suggested, even if the findings were precise and even if, following such instructions, one were able to pray on the Mount without committing a desecration. This was because even the most careful of worshipers would, by risking desecration based on scientific measurement, display callous irreverence toward the sanctity of the Temple and thus transgress the duty to fear and respect the Temple. Confidently accessing the sanctuary without the fear of *potentially* committing a transgression of this magnitude was a sin in and of itself. The ruling, in other words, was watertight.

Official proclamations prohibiting Jewish access to any part of the Mount appeared in the media, on signs leading onto the Temple Mount, and on posters plastered throughout the streets of Jerusalem. A small sentry's hut was placed near the southwestern entrance of the Mount, manned by an elderly Orthodox Jew, tasked with reminding errant Jews of the sins they were bringing upon their own heads if they chose to enter the site. With impressive swiftness, Israeli courts enshrined the rabbinical ruling into civil law, preventing Jews from praying on the Temple Mount "for reasons of security." Although the Supreme Court upheld the constitutional right of Jews to pray on the Mount, it prohibited the right of worshipers to pray "provocatively."[35] The court tolerated only "the prayer of single individuals, innocently and for non-demonstrative purposes," thus charging the Israeli police with the preposterous task of divining the intentions of Jewish worshipers.[36]

In actuality, the Israeli police has prevented even individuals from praying on the plateau. The civil ruling, upheld by successive High Court judges, has effectively revoked any Israeli sovereign claim over the area. Although Israeli laws concerning construction, absentee property, or the preservation of archaeologically valuable sites are strictly enforced in other Muslim religious endowments and holy sites throughout Israel, they have never been enforced on the Temple Mount.[37] The High Court justified its decisions, stating: "The situation is unique and we doubt there is anything similar to this in the history of our country or in the entire world.... In a place such as this even the simplest question of enforcing the law, investigating a crime and all that is involved, transcend normal judicial procedure. We cannot but recognize that flexible and pragmatic considerations that are 'above and beyond the law' take precedence over the rigid letter of the law."[38]

Opinion polls from the early 1970s and 1980s demonstrated that the majority of Israelis opposed the position of the courts regarding the Temple Mount, yet chose to abide by the religious ruling.[39] In other words, civil restrictions on access to the site would have been insufficient to prevent Jews from accessing the former site of the Temple. Only when combined with the religious ruling was the civil law effective. Moreover, civil restrictions would have been unfeasible to begin with had it not been for the backing provided by the religious edict.

The violent events that did occur, or that nearly occurred, on the Mount in this period are very much the exceptions that prove the rule. Because they were committed by individuals and groups that were not part of the Jewish Orthodox mainstream, they underscore both the importance and the limits of the rabbinical ruling. In 1969, an Australian tourist, Dennis Michael Rohan, succeeded in setting fire to the al-Aqsa Mosque, destroying several of the precious historical artifacts within. In 1982, an Israeli soldier managed to smuggle a weapon into the Sanctuary and shot a Palestinian guard to death.

Moreover, by the late 1980s several plans to destroy the shrines on the Temple Mount came to light, plots that had been hatched by Jewish extremists who felt increasingly frustrated by the lack of response from their own civil legal system and who recognized the vulnerability of Arab-Israeli peace efforts to attacks on the site.[40] Yet Rohan was, to the immense relief of all involved, a born-again Christian, whereas Goodman was a paranoid schizophrenic who suffered from an extreme God complex. None of the movements plotting to blow up the Dome of the Rock found rabbis to sanction their acts. Indeed, the most significant of these groups, the "Jewish Underground," canceled a detailed plot to destroy the Muslim shrines because of repeated failures to receive rabbinical sanctions for their plan.[41]

These incidents underscored the need for a coordinated Israeli-Palestinian security policy on the Mount. The fire set by Rohan very nearly caused inter-communal rioting in Israel and was proclaimed by the Arab media as a Jewish effort to burn the al-Aqsa Mosque "in order to fulfill their ambition of building the Third Temple."[42] In focusing on Israeli disengagement from the site, Dayan had failed to detail precise arrangements for security or foreign access. Given sensitivities to the postwar status quo, the Israeli police could do little in response to these acts but increase its presence outside the confines of the Mount. To placate Muslim opinions, these police forces were placed under the command of an Arab-Israeli police officer. It was an insufficient response that would prove disastrous.

Explaining the Rabbinical Ruling

The unprecedented ruling of October 1967 occurred at a unique historical juncture, a "perfect storm" at which political and religious crises converged to align the preferences of political and religious elites. The possibility of accessing the most sacred of Jewish sites placed the government in an impossible position. It was obvious to all that Jews would throng to worship on the Mount and that the government could not justify preventing Jewish worship at the site. A political prohibition of this sort would have been physically, morally, and politically indefensible. At the same time, it was clear that common Jewish and Muslim worship at the site was a recipe for disaster.

The religious elite, on the other hand, faced a theological crisis. Two thousand years of religious-legal debates faced possible implementation now that Jews could actually access their sacred site and potentially renew ancient rites. The rabbinical ruling of October 1967 proved brilliant, not only because it offered the government a way out of its dilemma, but also because it spoke to a very particular segment of Israel's population. Those Jews who revered the site and were most likely to clash with Muslims on the Mount were also the ones who respected rabbinical authority sufficiently to abide by the ruling. Nevertheless, the events of October 1967 raise several obvious questions. First, why did the rabbis agree to prohibit all Jewish access to the Temple Mount? Second, why did the public accept this ruling? Third, what role did the Israeli government play in encouraging or orchestrating this turn of events?

At the foundation of the October 1967 ruling was an intense debate that took place at the Annual Oral Law Conference, held in Jerusalem in August 1967, at which Israel's leading rabbis met to discuss the possibility of accessing the Temple Mount. The ruling arrived at after the conclusion of the conference sought to justify the exclusion of Jews from the most sacred site in their religious landscape, a site from which they had been barred for over a millennium and to which they had sought, and fought, to return relentlessly.

To succeed, the ruling had to gloss over a long list of legal difficulties. First and foremost, traditional opinions diverged over whether the plateau had maintained its sanctity after the destruction of the Temple.[43] The rabbis argued vehemently that the prohibitions on access remained intact even two thousand years after the structure itself had been removed. Thus access to the Holy of Holies, wherever it may have been located, was still prohibited to all Jews with the exception of the High Priest, a figure of authority no longer in existence.

Second, the rabbis had to justify the incongruence between the prohibition on access to the Holy of Holies and the exclusion of Jews from the entirety of the plateau. After all, the Holy of Holies had taken up only one percent of the area of the Temple, which, in turn, had occupied less than a third of the platform. Rabbis opposing entry to the Mount argued that Jewish worshipers would be committing sacrilege even if they visited those parts of the compound to which lay access had once been permitted. They reminded those in the audience that any entry into the Temple courtyards required purification and ablution rites the precise details of which were now long lost.

Third, the prohibition had to sidestep precedents of Jewish access to the Mount. Moses Maimonides, the great medieval Jewish scholar and supreme authority in all matters pertaining to the Temple, had claimed that the impure were permitted to enter the inner courts of the Temple, even in the absence of the forgotten rites. The rabbis ruled otherwise. In his diaries, Maimonides had recorded having prayed himself on the Temple Mount. The rabbis interpreted this as a misunderstanding. They argued, instead, that Maimonides must have prayed elsewhere, perhaps in the vicinity of the Mount, surely not on it.[44]

The rabbis cited as a relevant precedent the story of the nineteenth-century Jewish philanthropist Moses Montefiore, who had bribed Ottoman authorities to gain entry into the Temple Mount and had subsequently been excommunicated by a Jerusalem rabbi.[45] They omitted the aftermath of this incident, in which the excommunicating rabbi was declared insane by the Jerusalem rabbinical courts and an official apology was tendered to Montefiore. The rabbis also failed to recount the long case history of other Jewish notables who had visited the site throughout the centuries and the possible existence of several synagogues on the Mount at various points in history.[46]

None of the speakers at the conference mentioned that the most revered rabbis present in the conference hall had themselves entered the precincts of the Temple Mount within hours of its conquest by Israel. Among them were both of the Chief Rabbis of Israel as well as the venerated Rabbi Tzvi Yehuda Kook. More embarrassingly yet, these rabbis had driven across the Temple Mount by car, not with the intention of worshiping on it but in order to gain easy access to the Western Wall below. In effect, they had used the Temple Mount as a shortcut.[47]

How then, given these obstacles, did the rabbis arrive at the ruling? Strict theological arguments aside, the rabbis offered two main arguments to back their decision to ban Jews from the site. Both are located at the nexus of political and religious decision making. The first consideration related to the sanctity of life. Several rabbis realized the obvious implications of permitting Jews and Muslims to pray at the same site. They argued that the prime Jewish directive of preserving life, *Pikuach Nefesh,* placed the safety of worshipers above the importance of prayer at that precise location. Rabbi Avigdor Navnatzel, the rabbi of the Jewish Quarter in Jerusalem, later explained, in a debate with a proponent of prayer on the Mount: "As far as Jewish law is concerned, you are correct, it is entirely permissible [to enter the Temple Mount].... But Jewish sages have always concerned themselves with preventing wars of religion.... You are asking me to risk a Jihad and the killing of Jews, and for what? For the performance of some commandment that does nothing to protect Jewish life and, on the contrary, may risk Jewish lives?"[48]

A second argument that appears in several of the statements made at the Oral Law Conference relates to physical access as a symbol of sovereign right. The rabbis who espoused this position argued that permitting Jewish access to some parts of the sanctuary and not others would signal the ceding of sovereignty over those parts to which access was barred.[49] Paradoxically, then, Muslims would receive the impression that Jews did not desire ownership of those parts of the Mount that were most holy to them. By issuing a total prohibition on access, the rabbis reserved the right to claim sovereignty over the entire Mount. Oddly, the rabbis did not reconsider their prohibition when it became all too clear that Muslims, and perhaps even the Israeli courts, were interpreting this prohibition as conceding the entire Mount.

The public had reasons of its own to accept the rabbinical ruling. First, an alternative focus of attention had been made available. The Western Wall had been used as a substitute for prayer on the Mount ever since Muslims prohibited Jewish access to the Mount. Since 1948, Jordan had prohibited Jewish prayer at the Wall as well, an act that increased the mystique of that secondary site. Now that the Wall was available for prayer once again, all attention was channeled toward it. Intense disputes between the Ministry of Religious Affairs and the Ministry of Tourism regarding arrangements for visiting and worshiping at the Wall focused much attention on that site. Israel's minister of religion went as far as to extol the virtues of the Western Wall by quoting a Mishnah passage according to which the Wall occupied the center of the world. This was a brazen act of religious revisionism, for the Mishnah, which does not mention the Western Wall at all, places the Temple Mount at the center of the universe.[50]

A second reason for the broad acceptance of the decree had to do with the overwhelming number of rabbis who endorsed it and the resolute manner in which the decree was phrased. In spite of intense disagreement among the rabbis in the period leading up to the proclamation, the rabbis left no doubt, in the language of the ruling, regarding the validity of its precedent. The rabbis reminded the readers that this precedent existed both de jure and de facto, writing: "We have been warned, since time immemorial, against entering the entire area of the Temple Mount and have indeed avoided doing so."[51] Variants of the ruling, plastered in poster form throughout the streets of Jerusalem and by the gates leading onto the Mount, warned of "death by the hand of God" to anyone transgressing the ruling. The genius of the rabbinical decree was thus not in redefining the rules that governed access to the site. It lay in convincing the public that no redefinition had taken place. To this day, a majority of Jews from across the religious spectrum accept the ruling as the natural extension of an ancient tradition that has barred Jewish access to the Mount since the destruction of the Temple, nearly two thousand years ago. In actuality, no such ancient tradition exists.

Missing from this account of the religious ruling is the seminal role played by the Israeli government in encouraging the ruling and creating conditions favorable to it. Although no direct evidence exists to show that the government influenced rabbis to arrive at a prohibition, there is ample evidence to demonstrate active government intervention in silencing those rabbis who tried to derail the ruling. Primary among these was Rabbi Shlomo Goren,

Chief Rabbi of the IDF, the chief proponent of Jewish prayer on the Temple Mount. Fortunately for the government, Goren's status as a civil servant placed him under the direct command of the chief of staff of the IDF and thus indirectly under the purview of the minister of defense, Dayan, and the government.

The government censored Goren's speech as well as his actions. When Goren tried to pray on the Mount in the weeks after the war, the government banned him from accessing the site to minimize provocations. On August 10, Goren held a four-hour lecture for a forum of military rabbis in which he explained that bans on Jewish presence on the Mount were based on "fatal mistakes" and that the decision to hand the site to Muslim authorities was the equivalent of "the destruction of a third Temple."[52] A military censor carefully rephrased reports of these statements to suggest that "a military rabbi had encouraged religious deliberations regarding Jewish access to the Mount." A week later, Goren succeeded in dodging the soldiers guarding the entrance to the Mount and commenced a prayer service but was forcibly removed by Israeli troops.[53]

The government's most blatant intervention in the rabbinical ruling had to do with Goren's crucial appearance at the Oral Law Conference. The conference program, published several days before the event, advertised that two keynote speakers would debate the topic of accessing the Temple Mount: the young Rabbi Ovadia Yoseph, who would later become Chief Rabbi of Israel, was to present arguments against Jewish access to the Mount, whereas Rabbi Goren was to present the merits of the opposite position, defending the permission (and even obligation) to access particular parts of the Temple Mount.[54] The government intervened, first, by forcing Goren to change the topic of his keynote address. He had intended to discuss the most controversial topic of all, "Constructing the Temple in Our Time," but was instructed to change the title of his address to "Accessing the Temple Mount in Our Time."[55] The government then intervened a second time, having presumably reconsidered its position. It barred Goren from attending the conference altogether.[56]

Thus, one reason why a plurality of rabbis agreed on a prohibition against Jewish access to the Temple Mount was that there was no speaker at the Oral Law Conference to defend the opposite point of view. Rabbi Yoseph presented his condemnation of Jewish access to the Mount, but no counterpoint was ever presented, leading observers to complain of "an extreme disproportion" in the balance of arguments.[57] Goren's absence from the conference caused outrage among those present, many of whom had attended the conference primarily out of a "fascination with the issues regarding entry to the Temple Mount in general and the sacrificing of animals in particular."[58] The specific topic of access had been added to the program at the last minute in response to strong public demand. "The fact that Rabbi Goren was barred from speaking at this learned forum is unacceptable," raged the conference organizer, Yitzhak Raphael, to the sound of cheers from the crowd: "Our purpose here is not to deal in politics. This conference has no implications beyond the theoretical. And yet, only those who disagreed with Rabbi Goren's opinions appeared here, whereas his own opinion was never presented. Some even disagreed with opinions he never voiced and does not adhere to. We look forward to hearing what he has to say and expect him to publish a pamphlet in which he will elaborate his opinions on these issues."[59]

Goren did elaborate his opinions in writing, but they remained unpublished for twenty-four years. *The Temple Mount Book,* a detailed tome that includes sets of maps documenting those areas of the Mount accessible to Jews, appeared only in 1991. It is an inflammatory text, in both content and style. It recounts in dramatic detail the debates and physical confrontations between Goren's followers and the Israeli government in the weeks following the war, as the former attempted time and again to establish a permanent Jewish prayer site on the Mount. The eventual publication of the volume would bolster and accelerate the provocative actions taken by an extremist Jewish movement that advocated a Jewish presence at the site.

The lay public, however, knew little of Goren's opinions between 1967 and 1991. The vast majority of observant Jews accepted the prohibition on entering the site, if only because of the overwhelming number of rabbis who signed onto the ruling and had backed it with reasonable theological arguments. Moreover, the public was under the impression that the ruling had resulted from an extensive and open debate. In actuality, the debate over accessing the Temple Mount had involved as much political intrigue as religious discussion. Contrary to the public perception, the Oral Law Conference did not end in unanimous agreement on a ban against Jewish access to the Mount. In spite of protest by supporters of the ban, most speakers at the conference concluded that it was too early to issue a ruling about entry into the Mount, because not all the facts were available and had been examined.[60] Their hesitation may, in part, explain why proclamations of the ban appeared only in mid-October, six weeks after the conference ended.[61]

There is little to no information about the process by which the rabbis arrived at a common resolution banning Jewish access to the Mount in the intervening weeks. Evidence from the religious press, at least, indicates that disagreement over this issue remained intense until the very end, with various camps lambasting one another with accusations, evidence, and emotional appeals.[62] In the interim, the government maintained constant pressure on

Goren to stay out of the debate. The chief rabbis, presumably encouraged by the government's attitude toward Goren, refused to even meet the maverick rabbi. A conciliatory meeting, arranged by the minister for religious affairs, at which Goren was to present his opinions to the Chief Rabbis, was canceled at the last minute. Both Chief Rabbis justified their refusal to meet with Goren by expressing dismay at Goren's provocative actions on the Temple Mount, castigated as an attempted to present them with a fait accompli.[63] Goren's meetings with Dayan, on the other hand, resulted in shouting matches.[64]

On August 17, while the Oral Law Conference was still in full swing, a ministerial committee, convened to discuss the Temple Mount, announced to the press that Goren would cancel future plans to pray on the site.[65] Goren, banned from both the conference and the Mount and barred from access to both the political and the religious elites, ceased promoting his cause. Weeks later, in response to the publication of the rabbinical ruling, Jewish presence on the Temple Mount slowed to a trickle and then stopped altogether.

Turmoil Resumes

Why, given the success of the ruling of October 1967, did the Temple Mount become embroiled in interreligious conflict nearly twenty years later? The answer, once again, lies at the juncture of religious and political decision making. A religious counterruling in 1986 opened the floodgates for Jewish worship on the Mount, driven by right-wing despair over the Israeli withdrawal from the Sinai. At the same time, the policy of disengagement from the Temple Mount, initiated by Dayan, was proving increasingly incapable of allaying the tensions between Israeli and Palestinian nationalist groups at the site.

In August 1986, fifty rabbis met in Jerusalem, under the guidance of Rabbi Goren, to issue a proclamation permitting Jewish prayer on the Mount. In their counterruling, the rabbis stressed that praying on the Mount was a religious duty and sacred obligation.[66] This announcement gave impetus to a variety of Jewish groups, up to forty members in size, that began to arrange demonstrative prayer services on the Mount. Jewish protesters in their tens of thousands marched toward the plateau demanding access to the Sanctuary.[67] Prime among these groups was a radical movement, led by the secular nationalist Gershon Salomon, called the "Temple Mount Faithful," which began planning in earnest for the construction of the Temple on the Mount and the demolition of the Muslim structures. Its members began raising funds for purchasing the materials required for constructing the Temple and the implements required for priestly worship. The group's propaganda posters showed the Jerusalem skyline, digitally retouched so as to replace the Dome of the Rock with an artist's impression of the future Temple.[68]

The first sectarian conflict on the Temple Mount since its occupation in 1967 followed in October 1990. It was prompted by a message from the Lubavitcher rabbi, Meir Schneerson, leader of the largest Jewish Orthodox movement in America. From his seat in Crown Heights, Brooklyn, Rabbi Schneerson called on the faithful to pray on the Temple Mount to commemorate the Jewish festival of Succoth (Tabernacles), a traditional date of Jewish pilgrimage to the Temple in Jerusalem.[69] Motivated by this message, the Temple Mount Faithful marched toward the Mount on October 8, 1990. A scuffle between Salomon's followers and Muslim worshipers devolved into violence. The Muslim Council called on the faithful, via loudspeakers on the minarets, to rush to the site. Two thousand Muslims on the Mount pelted the thirty thousand Jews praying at the Western Wall plaza below with stones. A three-hour battle against armed Israeli policemen ended with the death of seventeen Muslim worshipers by Israeli fire. One hundred fifty others were wounded. A week of riots ensued, followed by the general strike of half a million businesses across the Palestinian territories.[70] From this point on the violence on the Mount would mirror, and eventually surpass, the levels of violence that had prevailed throughout the smaller shrines in the West Bank since the Israeli conquest in 1967.

Muslim authorities did not remain passive in light of this escalation. Now that Israeli rule over Jerusalem could no longer be dismissed as a temporary state of affairs, the autonomy granted by Dayan to the Muslim Council was recast as a humiliating Muslim concession, coerced by Israeli force.[71] In the ensuing intifada, the Haram was to play a seminal role, not only as a religious-nationalist symbol of Jerusalem, the future Palestinian capital, but also as a secure location for voicing criticism against Israel in public sermons and secret gatherings of Islamic terror cells.[72]

Over the course of two intifadas, the Palestinian Authority has employed the controversy over the site in order to mobilize the Palestinian public, most dramatically during the "tunnel riots" of September 1996. These incidents demonstrated how much had changed since 1967. The need for executive approval to open an additional entrance to a tourist attraction, the unanimous vote against the move by the Israeli cabinet, and its shocking aftermath, a week of gunfighting between Palestinians and Israelis resulting in seventy-five dead, all indicated that Israel had lost any ability to control the politics of the Temple Mount.[73] One Israeli member of Parliament lamented: "The Temple Mount, of which Mota Gur said 'it is in our hands!' is in our hands no more."[74] Michael Dumper summarized the situation as follows: "Despite full military control and the assertion of total Israeli sovereignty over the whole of Jerusalem and the surrounding area, the Israeli government found that it was obliged to accept restrictions and ambiguities with regard to the full application of its law and administration.... Parts of the Old City, such as the Haram al-Sharif compound, were virtually autonomous areas, beyond Israeli civil jurisdiction.... perceived by both Palestinians and Israelis as an enclave separate from Israeli political control."[75]

Faced with increasing troubles from Jewish radicals and Muslims alike, Israel tried to involve Jordan in managing the Temple Mount.[76] The 1993 Israeli-Jordanian peace agreement confirmed Jordan's position as custodian of the holy sites, promised Jordan "special priority" in the event of final negotiations over Jerusalem, and placed the management of the affairs of the Haram in the hands of the Jordanian Ministry of Religion. Arab leaders, in turn, began vying with Jordan over patronage of the Sanctuary.[77]

Currently, Israel's police force, acting on Israeli Supreme Court rulings, continues to bar access to the site to Jews, with occasional exceptions for Jewish tourists in secular attire. Access to all non-Muslims is prohibited on Fridays. Any attempts to access the site by Israeli members of Parliament, police, or the army have provoked violent Muslim reactions.[78] Israeli courts have elected not to enforce Israeli law on the Mount and have barred archaeologists from digging at or near the compound. The Supreme Court has also rebuffed attempts by Jewish activists to prevent the construction of a 4,500-square-meter mosque under the Haram platform. The mosque opened its doors to worshipers in December 1996. Because the construction project was not supervised by professional archaeologists or architects, it caused irreparable damage to the Temple Mount's architectural integrity.[79]

The Israeli government has gone from ecstatic celebration over the conquest of the site most holy to Judaism to desperate attempts at passing responsibility for the Mount back to Jordan. The army has gone from gaudy victor to incompetent bystander. The Israeli public, once overjoyed to return to the Temple Mount, has become wary of approaching the site. Religious parties have made the prohibition on Jewish access to the Mount a condition for joining ruling coalitions.[80] Few Israelis have ever been to the Temple Mount— even fewer would care to visit it today. Radical elements within the Jewish camp have gone from grief over the destruction of the Temple to incarceration for plotting to blow up the Dome of the Rock. Muslim officials no longer depend on Dayan's charitable gestures: they are now the ones setting the rules on the Temple Mount.

For Jewish extremists the Mount has become the primary locus of nationalist identity, a position that has only become entrenched after failures in

Israeli courts. For Muslims the Haram has become a source of unity and strength under Israeli occupation. Their successes in the face of Israeli power and the activities of the Jewish religious right have galvanized this posture. For Palestinian nationalists, the Haram has become the prime symbol of Palestinian sovereignty. Religious and political ideas about the Temple Mount have gradually affected the value of that site to political and religious actors alike, just as religious and political realities have affected ideas in turn.

Several aspects of the ruling of October 1967 must, however, remain shrouded in mystery. Why did the rabbis not reverse the ruling once its increasingly detrimental effect on Jewish claims to the Temple Mount became obvious? Moreover, if the ruling was based on the risk of desecration by impure Jewish worshipers, why did the rabbis make no attempt to bar non-Jewish worshipers from the site? Finally, if the ruling was driven by a regard for the sanctity of life, why did the rabbis not apply similar rulings to other contested sites, such as the Tomb of the Patriarchs in Hebron or Rachel's Tomb in Bethlehem? Although the problems of impurity and desecration that exist on the Temple Mount would not have applied to these sites, other reasons to prohibit access would certainly have presented themselves. The rabbis could, for example, have extended the Jewish prohibition on praying in Christian churches to the tombs in Hebron and Bethlehem, which functioned as mosques when they were occupied in 1967.[81] Why did the rabbis fail to prevent conflict at these sites, yet apply their extreme prohibition to the single most sacred site in Judaism?

Any answer to these questions must rest on speculation. One provocative guess draws on institutional theory to explain the rabbis' behavior. Since the destruction of the Temple in 70 CE, Judaism has revolved around rabbis as figures of authority and has focused on synagogues as primary sites of congregation. Yochanan ben Zakkai and the rabbis who followed in his footsteps designed these institutions, and the complex sets of rites, rules, and practices surrounding them, to replace and displace pre-Diaspora Judaism, which had centered on worship at the Jerusalem Temple under the guidance of the priestly class. A renewal of Jewish worship on the Temple Mount after the victory of 1967 would have constituted a complete upheaval in the structure and logic of Judaism, second only to the cataclysm of 70 CE. If such worship were to include the potential resumption of ancient practices, from long-lost rites of ablution to animal sacrifices and even an aspiration to rebuild the Temple, it would throw the institution of rabbinical Judaism into utter disarray. In issuing their ruling, the rabbis may have sought to protect not only Jewish life and the sanctity of the Temple Mount but also the foundations of modern Judaism. To put it more bluntly, they may well have worried about their job security.

This institutional explanation, while speculative, might go a long way toward explaining why Rabbi Goren suppressed *The Temple Mount Book* for a quarter of a century. In 1964, three years before the war, Goren had lost the elections for the position of Israel's Chief Ashkenazi Rabbi to Rabbi Issar Y. Unterman by only three votes.[82] In 1967, Unterman, in his capacity as Chief Rabbi, led the opposition to Goren's camp, pushing successfully for a prohibition on Jewish access to the Mount. In 1972, however, Goren defeated the incumbent Unterman to finally become Israel's Chief Ashkenazi Rabbi. Ironically, the man elected to become his counterpart, the Chief Sephardic Rabbi, was none other than Ovadia Yoseph, who had defended the prohibition on entering the Mount in August 1967.

It is reasonable to assume that Goren's provocative text was suppressed in part owing to government pressure on the now Chief Rabbi. It is equally reasonable to suppose that Goren himself stifled the publication of the volume in order to mend relations with Rabbi Yoseph and thus strengthen the institution of the chief rabbinate. Finally, Goren may have realized that his transformation from rebellious rabbi to chief representative of the rabbinical council carried with it not only significant influence but also considerable moral responsibility. In his capacity as Chief Rabbi he continued to advocate for a Jewish presence on the Mount and even tried, unsuccessfully, to organize a rabbinical consensus around a ruling that would remove the ban on Jewish access. Yet he ridiculed calls for the construction of a Temple and denied having ever called for the destruction of the Muslim shrines.[83]

In 1983, Goren retired from his position as Chief Ashkenazi Rabbi of Israel. That same year, he published the first volume of a four-part series on religion, the state, and the practice of war, *Meshiv Milchama* (loosely, "Fighting Back"). The fourth and final volume in this series was *The Temple Mount Book*. When it finally appeared in print in 1991, only three years before Goren's death, it became the theological manifesto of the extremist Temple Mount movements.

In May 2007, in commemoration of the fortieth anniversary of the liberation of Jerusalem by Israeli forces, three leading Israeli rabbis published a newspaper ad calling on Jews to "in purity, ascend at this time to the places permitted for Jews to enter" on the Temple Mount.[84] In so doing, these rabbis joined a growing number of rabbis, estimated in the dozens, who now encourage their followers to pray on the Temple Mount. The extraordinary ruling of October 1967 is now in the process of being overturned.

11. Interior of the Grand Mosque in Mecca: pilgrims circumambulating the Ka'ba. Thousands of worshipers were held hostage inside the mosque during the 1979 insurgency. Photo copyright Kazuyoshi Nomachi/Corbis.

Chapter Eight

SUCCESSFUL CONFLICT MANAGEMENT

Mecca, 1979

In November 1979, the Saudi government was forced to confront an impossible dilemma. Insurgents had taken thousands of hostages inside the Grand Mosque in Mecca, the holiest site in Islam. The hostile takeover of this inviolable shrine was designed as a blow to the prestige of the House of Saud, custodian of the Holy Mosque, which based its legitimacy on political and religious control over this site. Yet the Saudi regime could find no effective means of dealing with the insurgents because the use of force in the mosque was prohibited by Muslim law. Seventy-two hours later the crisis was resolved by means of an auspicious ruling by the ulema, the religious elite, that offered an interpretation of Muslim law permitting the use of force in the Grand Mosque. There followed several days of intense fighting in the mosque, ending with the death and execution of the insurgents.

What are the conditions for a reconfiguration of sacred space in the manner performed by the ulema? In the following pages I argue that the unique relationship between the House of Saud and the Saudi ulema, drawing on the historical bond between Ibn Saud and the descendants of Abd al-Wahab, as well as the characteristics of the Hanbali school of Islam practiced in Saudi Arabia, permitted the ulema and the Saudi regime to collude in an unprecedented reconfiguration of the parameters of the Grand Mosque in Mecca, with significant implications for the future of this most sacred of Muslim sites.

The Grand Mosque in Mecca

The Grand Mosque in Mecca is the center of the Muslim universe, the place toward which all prayers are directed and the focus of the world's largest annual pilgrimage, the *hajj*.[1] It is the *axis mundi* of Islam, by Muslim belief the first shrine created by man for God, tightly intertwined with the pre-Islamic origins of Arabia, the lives of the Muslim patriarchs Abraham and Ishmael, the life of the Prophet Muhammad and history of the early Muslim community. Millions of Muslims perform pilgrimage to Mecca every year in the sacred pilgrimage month to fulfill the obligation of the hajj, one of the five pillars of Islam. This commandment is set forth in Sura 22:26–27: "Clean my house for those who will circumambulate it, stand (in reverence) and bow in homage; Announce the Pilgrimage to the people. They will come to you on foot and riding along distant roads."[2]

Upon arriving from destinations near and far, the pilgrims enter a state of ritual purity and don consecrated robes. They then perform a series of rituals within the mosque compound and at nearby Mina, Muzdalifah, and Arafat, as commanded in Sura 2:158 and 198. The Grand Mosque contains several additional shrines, of which the most prominent are the place of Abraham, the well of Zamzam, and the hillocks of Safa and Marwa. The highlight of every pilgrimage and the goal of a "lesser pilgrimage" is the counterclockwise circumambulation (*tawaf*) of the Ka'ba. This is the large cuboid structure at the center of the Grand Mosque, 12 × 10 × 16 meters in size, which holds a black meteorite.

In performing the rites of the hajj at Mecca, the pilgrims imitate the acts of Abraham, Ishmael, and Muhammad at the religious and spiritual center of Islam, seeking proximity to the one God. The Ka'ba links the believer both to the origins of Islam and to the heavens; it is an earthly reflection of the celestial temple surrounding the throne of God. The Ka'ba is revered not on its own accord, for it is empty, having been cleansed of idols by the Prophet himself, but on account of its symbolic force. In design it reflects geometric perfection; in orientation it signifies the four pillars of the traditional cosmos; and by containing a meteorite it implies the cosmos beyond the earth.

The huge area within the mosque (three times the size of Yankee Stadium) is a *haram:* a sanctuary within which the truce of God reigns and neither man nor animal may be harmed. Its 209,000 square meters can hold more than seven hundred thousand people at one time, with an additional hundred fifty thousand on the roof and surrounding areas. Fighting, killing, even swatting flies or cutting trees is prohibited in this courtyard. The taboo on violence of any sort within this precinct is unequivocal, as are prohibitions on the cutting of nails and hair, committing acts of rudeness, wickedness, and indecency, wearing shoes, or covering the head.

The relevant passages in the Qur'an define the boundaries of the sanctuary and circumscribe behavior within it. Sura 2:125 defines the Ka'ba as "a place of congregation and safe retreat." Sura 3:97 tells of the foundation of Mecca by Abraham and promises that "anyone who enters it will find security." The Hadith (oral traditions relating to the sayings and deeds of the Prophet Muhammad) report a declaration by the Prophet defining the mosque as "a sanctuary," specifying not only that the shedding of blood was prohibited but also that "its thorny bushes should not be cut, its game should not be chased, and its fallen things should not be picked up."[3]

Entry to within the fifteen-mile radius of the city is restricted to members of the Muslim faith, who must undergo ablutions and don a shroud, the *ihram,* several miles before entering the city.[4] Signs on the roads leading to the city warn non-Muslims to keep their distance; special circuit roads, known as the "non-Muslim roads," lead travelers from Jeddah to Ta'if on a detour that makes a wide arc around Mecca. Few Western travelers who have risked their lives to see Mecca have lived to tell the tale. Sura 9:18 reminds the faithful that "only those who believe in God and the Last Day, who fulfill their devotional obligations, pay the zakat, and fear no one but God, can visit the mosques of God," and later in the same Sura: "O believers, the idolaters are unclean. So they should not approach the Holy Mosque" (9:28).

Like the taboo on violence, the restrictions on access to Mecca are codified in the Hadith as well as the Qur'an. Both sources report the attempt by the Ethiopian prince Abraha to destroy the Meccan shrine near the year of Muhammad's birth, 570 CE, an attempt foiled by miraculous forces of nature.[5] The Qur'an also offers detailed reports of the wars between the Prophet and the Quraysh tribe of Mecca, between the years 622 and 630 CE. During this brutal period of war between the followers of the Prophet and the Meccan idol worshipers, Muhammad refused to use force in taking the city, and truce reigned within the sanctuary. The Prophet and his men entered the city unarmed in 629, as agreed in the treaty of al-Hudaybiyah, and worshiped at the site, despite a long history of deceit and mistrust between the parties.[6] Muslim sources repeatedly stress that Muhammad conquered the city "without striking a single blow," a symbolic victory (*fat'h*) that vindicated his prophetic claim and led to the conversion of his most committed enemies.[7]

The historical record lists only two noteworthy cases in which the sanctity of the mosque was violated.[8] In 692 CE, Abd Allah ibn al-Zubayr, a claimant to the caliphate, sought refuge in the mosque and the Ummayad caliphs placed

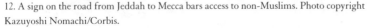

12. A sign on the road from Jeddah to Mecca bars access to non-Muslims. Photo copyright Kazuyoshi Nomachi/Corbis.

an eight-month siege against Mecca. In 930 CE the Qarmatians, members of an Ismaili sect, desecrated the mosque and temporarily removed the meteorite from the Ka'ba.[9] The infrequency of attacks on the mosque is noteworthy, given the regularity with which the city was conquered and reconquered by successive Muslim dynasties. These conquerors took great pains to eschew the use of force, even though the city was unfortified and of immeasurable political value. Some were prohibited from doing so by their religious advisors; others encountered apparitions of the Prophet in their dreams, warning them not to use force in their conquest of Mecca.[10]

Since 1979, however, there has been a spate of violent incidents in Mecca against the background of Iranian-Saudi tensions.[11] The Saudi response, given the precedent of the 1979 ulema ruling, has been brutal in all cases. In 1986 Iranian Revolutionary Guards posing as pilgrims tried to smuggle weapons and explosives into the mosque. In 1987 more than four hundred fifty pilgrims were shot in the mosque and surrounding streets by the Saudi National Guard, after a demonstration by Iranian pilgrims. In 1988, sixteen Kuwaiti pilgrims were beheaded for their alleged involvement in the detonation of two bombs in the vicinity of the mosque that killed one pilgrim and wounded sixteen others.

In a sense, the Meccan ruling is the counterpoint to the 1967 Temple Mount ruling: In Jerusalem the religious ruling created an unprecedented period of stability in a volatile context. The 1979 ruling by the ulema opened the floodgates for violence in a space where the use of force had been unprecedented. Although this ruling did not resolve a longstanding dispute over sacred space or mitigate its indivisibility, it did fundamentally affect the restrictions regulating access to and behavior within a sacred space, with both short-term and long-term implications for that space. How can we explain the decision by the ulema to issue this decisive fatwa? How can we explain its acceptance?

The Ulema and the House of Saud: Historical Background

The ulema are theological and legal experts who have gained the respect and recognition of the community and the political authorities.[12] In Saudi Arabia, the ulema are a loosely defined group of religious experts and office holders in religious courts with close ties to the Saudi regime. Since the founding of the modern state of Saudi Arabia in 1932, the ulema have come to occupy a prominent position in the state's leadership, unparalleled in any modern Sunni state. Their extraordinary status derives from the historical ties between the House of Saud and the House of al-Shaykh; the particular form of Islam practiced in Saudi Arabia, namely the Hanbali legal tradition within Sunni Islam; the prominent position of Islam in the laws and institutions of the Saudi state; and the influential offices held by members of the ulema in the public sphere.

Modern Saudi Arabi is the product of an alliance struck between the Islamic revivalist Shaykh Muhammad ibn Abd al-Wahhab and a Bedouin chief, Muhammad ibn Saud of Diriyah.[13] In 1744, these two swore an oath of mutual allegiance, ushering in the first Wahhabi kingdom, which would eventually become, after the demise of the second Wahhabi kingdom, modern Saudi Arabia. The pact between Abd al-Wahhab and ibn Saud created a powerful political movement that united the tribes of Arabia and, by 1802, succeeded in ruling over Mecca and Medina. Ibn Saud committed himself to using his military prowess to realize the rigorous religious reform advocated by Abd al-Wahhab and consistently consulted with the shaykh before leading believers into battle. Abd al-Wahhab and his descendants, the al-Shaykh clan, in turn justified the policies of ibn Saud by authoring pamphlets and texts that identified his rule with Wahhabism.

The two leaders came to depend on one another for their survival and the success of their complementary objectives: Abd al-Wahhab gained a political arm for his teachings whereas ibn Saud gained a body of converts capable of extending his political control over the Arabian peninsula. Wahhabi ideology became a basis for the consolidation of Saudi rule, with obedience defined as a religious duty and rebellion as sin. The union of these twin forces of Islam was symbolized in the Saudi flag, combining the confession of faith with the swords of ibn Saud and Abd al-Wahhab. Descendants of Abd al-Wahhab, the al-Shaykh clan, form the core of the Saudi ulema to this day.

Having been defeated and exiled by the Ottomans in 1818, descendants of the House of Saud returned to rule the Arabian peninsula at the turn of the twentieth century, under Abd al-Aziz ibn Abd al-Rahman al-Saud. In 1902 Abd al-Aziz married a member of the al-Shaykh clan, the first in a long line of marriages between the Houses of Saud and Abd al-Wahhab. Appealing once more to Islam as a tool for reuniting the tribes of the peninsula, and deploying analogies to the union of Muslim warriors under Muhammad, Abd al-Aziz managed to recruit a Bedouin army and recapture the Najd region in 1906 and the Hijaz region in 1925, imposing a central government on the tribes of Arabia in 1932. His Bedouin army was organized into the Brotherhood of Believers, the Ikhwan, numbering some thirty thousand warriors by 1930, committed to spreading Wahhabi doctrine in Arabia. The Ikhwan were indoctrinated into Wahhabi ideology by Shaykh Abd Allah al-Shaykh to suit Abd al-Aziz's political objectives and became the kingdom's elite military force. Mobilized with the message "Islam is a seditious religion" they became an ideological force that would soon prove difficult to control.[14]

Throughout the history of the third Saudi kingdom, the ulema have proved a reliable source of support for the king, not only offering convenient interpretations of the law but also counseling on a wide range of issues ranging from domestic affairs to war. The consultative relations between the ulema and the House of Saud are anchored not only in the historical ties between these elites but also in the Hanbali legal tradition and in traditional Sunni political theory, especially the teachings of ibn Taymiyya and al-Ghazali.[15] Both thinkers argued for tight interdependence between the coercive power of the state and the moral power of the Shari'a (Islamic law), suggesting that the ideal Muslim state required close cooperation between the religious and political elites. They conceived of religion and state as tightly linked: the purpose of government was to enforce the dictates of the Shari'a, thus becoming the ultimate source of divine intervention.

Hanbali law is the strictest and most rigid of Islamic law schools. It attributes legal and moral weight to any ruling issued by a member of the religious elite and leaves no doubt about the importance of obedience. But the Hanbali tradition is also unique among Muslim legal schools in permitting change, adaptation, and even modernization in those issues on which the law is silent. Moreover, unlike other Sunni law schools, the Hanbali legal tradition has kept the doors of reinterpretation (*ijtihad*) relatively open, permitting the Saudi government to introduce modern regulations in areas not explicitly covered by traditional law.

The utility of the ulema was demonstrated at several critical historical junctures. In 1918 the ulema issued a ruling that consolidated the king's rule over the Ikhwan and settled religious tensions between the Bedouin and townspeople of the Arabian peninsula. In 1923, when the king considered advancing against Mecca, the ulema ruled that liberating the city from foreign occupation was mandatory. Upon successful conquest they issued an additional fatwa urging all Muslims to obey the new and legitimate ruler of the holy places.

When the Ikhwan revolted, in 1929, the king was once again able to rely on the ulema to quell the uprising. The Ikhwan had denounced the king's slackening of religious faith, criticized the regime's conciliatory policies toward the European powers, and protested the introduction of symbols of modernity such as the automobile and telegraph. The ulema responded with a fatwa supporting the king and justifying the cessation of the brotherhood's jihadist activities. Islam, they now proclaimed in a complete reversal of the 1930s ruling, was not a seditious force but a "religion of the middle road."[16] By compelling the Ikhwan to swear allegiance to the king, the ulema may well have saved Abd al-Aziz's throne.[17] Rebellious Ikhwan were defeated at the battle of Sibila in 1929; the rest were incorporated into the National Guard.

The first permanent forum created to officially serve the king's need for religious authorization and approval was the Council of the Grand Ulema (Majlis Hay'at Kibar al-Ulema), founded in 1971 and headed by the late Shaykh Abd al-Aziz ibn Abd Allah ibn Baz. It was designed to issue religio-legal opinions and adapt the Shari'a to present-day requirements. The council deals with a variety of topics, but its power derives from fatwas on political questions.[18] Both Abd al-Aziz and his heir, King Faysal, were able to rely on the ulema in withstanding religious opposition to modernization. The ulema cited prophetic history and traditions to justify the employment of non-Muslim oil technicians, the use of the telephone, automobiles, and even women's education.[19] In the case of radio and television a compromise was struck: the media were to be used for news and recitation of the Qur'an only. On other issues the king succeeded in overruling the ulema: Abd al-Aziz refused to modify his military's modern uniforms and continued to support the Allies during World War II, even though his religious advisors saw no reason to become embroiled in a "quarrel between unbelievers."[20] When King Faysal authorized the construction of television stations across the kingdom, however, the ulema arranged a popular revolt, leading to violent confrontations with the police.[21] At the same time, the ulema proved of utility in confronting the threat of pan-Arab socialism, in condemning the revolutionary regime in Iran, and in mobilizing Saudi volunteers to fight the Soviets in Afghanistan.[22] During Operation Desert Storm, the Saudi ulema declared the war against Saddam Hussein to be the highest form of jihad.[23]

In conclusion, while not accommodating the regime across the board, the Saudi ulema have consistently supported the House of Saud at critical historical junctures, a collaboration that has contributed to the elite's privileged status. This accommodation is relatively flexible. Where king and ulema have disagreed, persuasion rather than imposition was the common mode of conduct.[24] The ulema adhere to the original Wahhabi ideology, which ostensibly resists all foreign or modern influence in Saudi Arabia, but they never openly criticize the Saudi regime for promoting such influence. Despite the regime's shortcomings, the ulema see the Saudis as the best defense available for Islamic values.[25] This accommodation has led, inevitably, to a decline in the credibility of the ulema as an independent political force and has prompted criticism from religious radicals, including the insurgents that occupied the Grand Mosque in 1979.

The Ulema in Contemporary Saudi Arabia

The conjunction of religion and politics in Saudi Arabia extends beyond the consultative relationship between the ulema and the Saudi regime. The regime has enhanced its legitimacy by rationalizing its policies in religious terms. Saudi Arabia and Iran are the only Muslim regimes relying on religion as the exclusive basis for legitimacy. The Basic Law for the kingdom defines the Qur'an as the constitution. It provides that the king be limited by the Shari'a and that all legislation be in accordance with the Sunna (the practices of the Prophet Muhammad). Indeed, the king is the nominal head of the ulema. Unfettered by legislature, constitution, or political parties, the monarch's absolute power is limited only by the advice of the ulema and Consultative Council.

By virtue of their influence and their historical allegiance to the royal household, the ulema form one of three power centers of the kingdom, alongside the members of the royal court and the heads of the major tribes. The descendants of Muhammad ibn Abd al-Wahhab are the most prominent among the ulema class and hold the most important positions at the great mosques, universities, the Council of the Grand Ulema, and the World Islamic League. There is also a high degree of intermarriage between the al-Shaykh and al-Saud families. Although the most important government offices are held by members of the royal family, the Ministries of Justice, Higher Education, Hajj (pilgrimage), and Awqaf (religious endowments) are held by ulema. Several ulema are members of the Consultative Council, hold responsible positions in the civil service, and carry out important diplomatic functions. In the public sphere the ulema exercise a monopoly over religious and social morals through their membership in and leadership of the "religious police" (formally, Councils for Exhortation to Good and Interdiction of Evil). These committees ensure public observance of the commandments of the Shari'a, enforced by police powers.

Unlike their counterparts in Egypt or Iran, the ulema have established a convenient relationship with the Saudi royal dynasty by balancing religious and political interests. In Egypt, leaders have traditionally subordinated the ulema to the regime by depriving them of an independent economic base.[26] Iran's leaders ignored the religious elite altogether before 1979.[27] Consequently, unlike the ulema in Egypt or Iran, the Saudi ulema have refrained from mobilizing the population as a means of influencing policies. Instead, the ulema voice their disagreements in private consultations with the king. The king, on the other hand, involves the ulema in the state apparatus, provides them with an independent source of revenue, accords them due respect and protocol, and consults frequently with them on matters of state.

The ulema became an important stabilizing factor in the kingdom, mediating between the regime and various social strata, guaranteeing obedience to the regime and legitimizing moderately reformist policies. Having learned from the mistakes of the Iranian monarchy, the royal household was careful to integrate the ulema into the ruling elite and treated them with due respect and protocol, avoiding all open confrontation and seeking their support through persuasion. Because the ulema enjoyed the benefits of this arrangement, they came to identify the good of the state with the good of the regime and remained committed to the status quo.

This collusion came at a heavy price for the religious elites. In the years leading up to the 1979 Meccan crisis the power of the ulema gradually waned. The suppression of the Ikhwan and the modernization of the army had weakened the ability of the ulema to tip the scales between the royal household and alternative power centers. Increased urbanization and literacy, the influx of migrant workers, the establishment of modern education centers, the rise in the number of Saudis traveling abroad, all threatened the traditional values of Saudi society. Saudi ties with other Muslim countries led to an increase in the popularity of Islamic doctrines that competed with the traditional Hanbali school of thought that had dominated Saudi Arabian schools and courts in earlier decades. With increased openness to Western culture, the strength and influence of the religious police declined and the influence of the ulema in the sphere of education eroded.

The increased wealth of the Saudi regime and the development of an oil economy enhanced government activity at the expense of the ulema's jurisdiction. After the 1960s, the ulema came to depend on the state for revenue, its leaders were appointed by the king, and its activities came to be regulated by state laws.[28] After the death of the last Grand Mufti of Saudi Arabia in 1969, the legal functions of the mufti were assumed by the minister of justice. The king and government passed administrative regulations and laws in spheres such as commerce, labor, and international relations that did not strictly conform to the Shar'ia, thus confining the role of the ulema to civil and criminal law.

All this was to change in the aftermath of the Meccan crisis, an incident that further tightened the link between the regime and the religious elite in Saudi Arabia, forging a new accommodation in which the government granted the ulema enhanced freedoms and powers in return for unconditional political support.

The Events of November 1979

On November 20, 1979, hundreds of armed insurgents locked the gates of the Grand Mosque in Mecca, trapping thousands of pilgrims inside.[29] Their leader, Juhayman al-Utaybi, was a religious scholar and a former member of the National Guard. To the amazement of those present, he proclaimed his brother-in-law, Muhammad ibn Abd Allah al-Qahtani, to be the Mahdi, the messianic redeemer, and demanded allegiance from all those present.[30] Utaybi denounced the corrupt rule of the Saudi royal family, condemned the ulema for their collaboration with the regime, and called for the establishment of a traditional Muslim society on the Saudi peninsula.

Utaybi and several leaders of the insurgency were members of a radical Islamist movement that had been launched by Shaykh ibn Baz, the chairman of the Council of the Grand Ulema, during his tenure as dean of Medina's Islamic University.[31] Ibn Baz had sanctioned this missionary movement, a revival of the very same Ikhwan movement founded and later quelled by ibn Saud, to reinvigorate Wahhabi devotion. It quickly spread throughout the country and slipped out of the immediate control of the cleric.[32] Many members of the ulema, increasingly concerned over the modernizing direction the regime was assuming, encouraged or at least tolerated the brotherhood's militant activities. Indeed, ibn Baz had been instrumental in the release from custody of members of Utaybi's network who had been apprehended a mere year before they struck in Mecca.[33] This link in origin and purpose between the ulema and Utaybi's network explains why the ulema would condemn the insurgents' violation of the shrine but refused to denounce the insurgents as heretics.[34]

Nonetheless, the differences between Utaybi and his teacher were at the core of the brotherhood's resentment of the regime. Ibn Baz and the rest of the ulema, who were on the government's payroll and had intertwined their fates with the fortunes of the House of Saud, were willing to forgive the regime its shortcomings.[35] The purist Utaybi was unwilling to make concessions on Islamic values and despised the ulema for their accommodating stance toward the regime. Utaybi wrote of his teacher ibn Baz: "[He is] in the pay of the al-Sauds, little better than a tool for the family's manipulation of the people.... Ibn Baz may know his Sunna well enough, but he uses it to bolster corrupt rulers."[36]

Utaybi's movement had adopted millenarian ideas, not shared by the ulema, that confirmed the justness of their cause and the need for rebellion against the corrupt state.[37] Utaybi had chosen Muhammad al-Qahtani as redeemer because his name, lineage, and tribal origin as well as his physical features (high forehead, hooked nose, a red scar on the cheek) matched those associated with the Mahdi in prophecies attributed to the Prophet Muhammad. The date for the attack was chosen in light of a Hadith that predicted that the Mahdi would present himself, at the northern corner of the Ka'ba, right after the pilgrimage season and at the turn of the Islamic century.[38] The movement thus envisioned the occupation of the shrine to be the ideal means for accelerating history and bringing the al-Saud regime to its end.[39]

If Saudi authorities knew about this prophecy, they may have ignored the most advanced early warning in the history of armed conflict: a description of the time, location, and identity of an insurgency, given fourteen hundred years before the event. In actuality, the authorities needed three hours to respond to the takeover and arrive at the scene. Saudi troops soon surrounded the large mosque with soldiers and armored vehicles, placed a curfew on Mecca, and rolled in tanks and trucks, yet ordered no attack.[40]

Because of the ban on foreign presence in Mecca, information about the Saudi response to the crisis is spotty and often contradictory. It seems that the Saudi National Guard refused to attack the mosque without the written approval of the ulema and even rejected outright a proposal by the minister of defense, Prince Sultan, that several local sheikhs approve the attack. Some soldiers refused to even point their weapons at the mosque unless ibn Baz himself instructed them to do so, despite threats, later realized, to imprison or execute disobedient soldiers.[41] The military's oath to the king explicitly stipulated that obedience could not contradict Islamic principles.[42] Since the strict letter of Islamic law called for dismemberment of anyone desecrating the holy shrine, soldiers were torn between the belief that expelling the insurgents from the sacred site would guarantee them a place in paradise and the fear that desecrating the mosque would secure them the torments of hell.[43]

Even if the Saudi regime had succeeded in motivating its troops to fight in Mecca, it would still have had to manage the popular outrage, in the Arabian peninsula and throughout the Muslim world, in response to an unauthorized desecration of the shrine. This became all too clear early on in the standoff as Muslims around the world instigated riots against U.S., British, and Christian targets in response to rumors of Western involvement in the Meccan crisis. In Pakistan a mob attacked the U.S. embassy in Islamabad and nearly burned all 137 personnel inside alive. Five Pakistanis and two Americans died in the attack.[44] Assaults on businesses and missions linked to the United States soon followed in Rawalpindi, Lahore, Karachi, and Islamabad, all in response to rumors about an American occupation of Mecca. Protesters in Izmir, Turkey, attacked the residence of the U.S. consul. In Dhaka, Bangladesh, mobs tried to burn down the American embassy. In Calcutta, protesters pelting the U.S. consulate with stones had to be dispersed with tear gas and proceeded to wreak havoc in the city. In Hyderabad, Muslim radicals turned their anger on Hindus, leading to days of communal violence.[45]

The urgency of the need for a decisive clerical sanction for a military operation in the mosque was now beyond doubt. Utaybi and his followers were challenging the authority of the House of Saud at the very sacred sites in which this authority was anchored.[46] Desperate to reaffirm its legitimacy, the Saudi monarch turned to the ulema to confer about his right to send armed troops into the mosque.

The Fatwa and Its Aftermath

Because there is no single legislative authority or hierarchical clergy structure in Sunni Islam, leaders are compelled to look to the ulema for religious sanction of each and every decree. Saudi leaders, including the current monarch, King Abdullah bin Abdul Aziz al-Saud, continue to consult with the ulema on a weekly basis and often grace its members with visits at their private residences. The legal opinions, or fatwas, of the ulema maintain a crucial importance, a point demonstrated succinctly during the 1979 crisis. Unlike judgments of religious courts, fatwas are not binding and are intended as elucidating informational opinions, issued at the request of the enquirer. Important fatwas, however, are considered to have broader applicability, greater importance, and higher impact on legal precedent than court judgments.[47]

King Khalid's consultation with the ulema at the height of the Mecca crisis led to a period of deliberation as the clerics, led by ibn Baz, weighed the theological implications of the monarch's request. To effectively justify the use of force in the Grand Mosque, the ulema had to overcome several obstacles. For one, the clerics had to persuasively argue that the insurgents lacked religious legitimacy. Moreover, the only Qur'anic passage that delineates conditions for using force in a mosque, Sura 2:191, had never before been used to justify the use of force in Mecca, let alone violence against fellow Muslims. The verse reads: "Do not fight them by the Holy Mosque unless they fight you there. If they do, then slay them: Such is the requital for unbelievers." Relying on this passage to justify military force in Mecca posed a formidable challenge, given the verse's emphasis on "unbelievers." The insurgents were Muslim, after all. The ulema thus had to show, contrary to the claims of the insurgents inside the mosque, that the regime had not fired the first shot and that Sura 2:191 applied not only to infidels but to Muslims who are "unbelievers" as well.

By one account, the initial ruling issued by the ulema permitted combat in the mosque on the condition that no live fire be employed. This ruling is said to have resulted in the immediate death of one hundred Saudi paratroopers, dropped into the mosque unarmed. Cut down by the rebels' automatic weapons, not one of the paratroopers reached the ground alive.[48] The ulema may have hesitated with issuing a fatwa, or may have permitted the use of force only in a second fatwa issued on November 24, in order to use the crisis as a means of placing pressure on the royal house.[49] In either case, prior to the publication of the fatwa that permitted the unlimited use of force in the mosque, Saudi troops fought under exceedingly constrained conditions in order to avoid damaging the mosque. For example, the artillery employed to cover the initial attacks fired flash-bang shells, designed to stun the insurgents by means of noise and light, but not explosive shells that would produce lethal fragments.[50] Absent appropriate artillery coverage, these initial assaults culminated in the veritable massacre of the military units involved.

The fatwa ultimately issued by the ulema eliminated all tactical constraints. In an unprecedented ruling, it sanctioned the full use of force in the shrine. The fatwa reads, in part:

> We gave him [King Khalid] our opinion, namely that it was necessary to call on them to surrender and lay down their arms. If they did so that would be accepted and they should be imprisoned then until their case was considered according to the Shari'ah. If they refused, every measure should be taken to seize them even if it led to fighting them and killing those who are not arrested or who had surrendered, in accordance to what the Almighty says: "But fight them not in the Holy Mosque unless they fight you there. But if they fight you, slay them. Such is the reward of those who suppress faith." ... Therefore fighting in the Haram has been permitted unanimously by the Ulema, in accordance with what the Prophet said.[51]

To overcome the theological challenges posed by the insurgency, the ulema first proposed, in a communiqué attached to the fatwa, that various conditions for the arrival of the Mahdi as spelled out in prophecies had not yet been fulfilled.[52] The signatories of the fatwa reminded their readers that the Mahdi was said to appear in opposition to a corrupt ruler. Since the current government enforced the Shari'a, argued the clerics, the insurgents in the mosque had to be impostors and their rebellion thus constituted treason deserving of death.[53] Second, the elders conceded that Sura 2:191 "concerns the infidel," yet also insisted that this verse applied to the insurgents all the same because they "wanted to divide the Muslims and go against their Imam,"[54] that is, the Saudi king. In English translations of the fatwa, the term "unbelievers" from Sura 2:191 was rendered "those who suppress the faith," thus mitigating some of the difficulty in applying these conditions to Muslim insurgents. Yaroslav Trofimov captures the significance of this fatwa: "The gloves were now off. Up until then, the government's paramount concern was not to damage the Grand Mosque ... now the Saudi state no longer had to worry about theological cover. It could finally unleash on Juhayman's rebels the full might of the latest American and European weaponry."[55]

With a green light from the ulema the Saudi National Guard began pounding extremist positions in the mosque with howitzers and machine guns, finally entering the courtyard with armored personnel carriers four days after the takeover.[56] Antitank missiles were fired at the mosque's minarets, annihilating the sniper positions at their tops. Entire walls of the mosque were reduced to rubble, most windows, gates, and doors were blown out, and remaining surfaces were riddled with bullets and shell fragments. Burnt-out military vehicles blocked hallways, artillery shells caused stairways to collapse, and the ensuing blaze melted and twisted metal fixtures and decorations on the ceilings and walls.[57]

Saudi troops soon managed to clear the mosque courtyard and main structures of insurgents, but they could not dislodge the insurgents from the tunnels and caverns under the mosque. Underground fighting continued for two weeks, culminating in the deployment of tear gas to flush out the insurgents. By some accounts, chemical weapons were also used for this purpose. The toll of these operations in pilgrim, insurgent, and counterinsurgent lives remains uncertain, with estimates ranging from dozens (according to the Saudi government) to many thousands (according to foreign media and some scholars).[58]

Given the absolute and unequivocal ban on the presence of non-Muslims anywhere near the city of Mecca, not to mention the interior of the most sacred of mosques, and given the public outcry in the Muslim world in response to rumors of non-Muslim involvement in the insurgency, it is surprising to encounter persistent reports of foreign involvement in the Saudi operation. Several sources claim that American special forces were called in to end the crisis after a series of failed Saudi attempts.[59] Other sources report that members of the French Foreign Legion or members of the Groupe d'Intervention de la Gendarmerie Nationale participated in training Saudi troops before the close combat under the mosque as well as supplying the chemical weapons required to complete the operation.[60] These foreign advisors are alleged to have undergone perfunctory conversions to Islam upon their arrival in Saudi Arabia.[61] Saudi Arabia has categorically denied such reports. If these accounts are true, then the ulema's fatwa seems to have inspired unparalleled boldness in the Saudi regime.

Several factors made possible the dramatic shift in the rules governing the Grand Mosque in Mecca in November 1979. First and foremost was the traditional support by Sunni ulema across the Muslim world of political institutions in power, based on dominant philosophical traditions within the Sunni orthodoxy. In Saudi Arabia, this support was bolstered by the historical ties between the ulema and the House of Saud, dating back to the eighteenth century, and the successful incorporation and bureaucratization of the ulema into the Saudi political apparatus. These factors outweighed the strict prohibitions on violence surrounding the Grand Mosque, permitted the king to approach the ulema with a request for help, and granted the ruling issued by the ulema the weight necessary for acceptance by the Muslim community, within and without Saudi Arabia.

The ulema's support for the Saudi monarchy did not end with the fatwa issued at the height of the Meccan insurgency. In sermons and televised interviews after the resolution of the crisis, clerics stressed the sinful nature of the insurgents, the piety of the Saudi regime, the prohibition on rebelling against just rulers, and the inherently moderate nature of Islam.[62] Two months after the insurgency, the ulema convened again at the monarch's request to issue death verdicts against thirty-six insurgents that had been captured alive. The executions, by steel sword, were staged simultaneously in eight cities across Saudi Arabia.[63]

The tighter relations between the religious and political elite in Saudi Arabia in the aftermath of the Mecca crisis resulted in regime concessions to the ulema on the religious front and a Wahhabi revival in Saudi Arabia. The government appointed a member of the al-Shaykh clan as director of public security, closed down video stores of dubious repute, raised the salaries of the ulema, and allocated additional funds to the building of mosques and propagation of Islam. In the immediate aftermath of the Mecca insurgency, 241 mosques were built with these funds, and an additional 37 mosques underwent renovation.[64] The government also expanded the powers of the religious police, which in turn moved to close down women's hairdressing salons and clubs as well as cultural centers and movie theaters. Female announcers were dismissed from television stations, songs were banned from television, and women were prohibited from studying abroad.[65]

By embracing Wahhabi fundamentalism and aiding the ulema in their dissemination of this extremist doctrine, the Saudi regime indirectly fostered a generation indoctrinated by Salafism, the most radical variant of Wahhabi Islam. The regime then encouraged young members of this radicalized cohort to join the anti-Soviet insurgency in Afghanistan, an effort aided once again by the Saudi ulema, who declared this struggle a legitimate jihad. It was in Afghanistan that many young Saudi radicals received their combat training and began transforming the Salafi ideology that had motivated Utaybi into the ideology of a transnational terror movement.[66]

One of these radical youths was Osama bin Laden, twenty-two years old at the time of the Mecca insurgency. He had witnessed the events of November 1979 at close hand. His father, Muhammad bin Laden, had been the Saudi government's chief contractor, responsible for the sixfold expansion and embellishment of the Grand Mosque structure in the 1950s, 1960s, and 1970s. Osama bin Laden's half-brother, Salem bin Laden, was the Saudi government's sole source for blueprints of the mosque and its subterranean passageways during the crisis.[67] Bin Laden had stark memories of how the regime had "defiled the sanctity of the Grand Mosque" and recalled seeing the imprint of tracked military vehicles on the tiles of the mosque and the smoke rising from the minarets. The insurgents had been "true Muslims," he opined, "innocent of any crime," yet they were "killed ruthlessly."[68]

The collusion between the political and religious elite in Saudi Arabia thus had a paradoxical effect on bin Laden and many of his followers. By supporting the ulema, the Saudi regime had helped spread and fund the very doctrine that motivated and radicalized Salafi extremists. By bolstering the regime time and again, the ulema discredited themselves as an impartial source for religious rulings in matters political. The clerics' decision to compromise religious principles for political expedience led to a loss of legitimacy for the ulema; one angry elder characterized Saudi Arabia as "the graveyard of the ulema."[69] The events of 1979 were thus formative in leading extremist Wahhabis to denounce the ulema for their subservience to the regime and to oppose the House of Saud and its American backers.

13. A mosque in Pec, Kosovo, destroyed by Serbian militia during the Yugoslavian civil war. Photo copyright Antoine Gyori/Corbis Sygma.

Chapter Nine

LESSONS FROM CONFLICTS
OVER SACRED PLACES

This volume offered an investigation into the causes, properties, and potential means of managing conflicts over sacred sites. Sacred sites are prone to
conflict because they provide valuable resources for both religious and political actors. To believers, sacred sites offer the possibility of communicating with
the gods, receiving divine favors, and achieving insight into the deeper meanings of their faith. These characteristics lead to competition between religious
groups who wish to control a sacred space both in order to exclude rivals from
practicing potentially conflicting rituals in the sacred space and in order to
assert the legitimacy of their particular sect. Sacred sites then become attractive targets for political actors who hope to control believers and their religious movements. These conflicts are particularly difficult to resolve because
sacred sites pose an indivisibility problem: they cannot be shared because the
religious prerequisites for safeguarding them from desecration require believers to have complete and exclusive control over access to and conduct within
them.

The second half of this volume focused on the mitigation of conflicts over
sacred places. Managing these disputes requires recognizing that the religious
elements of these conflicts are inextricably intertwined with their political
components. Cooperation between political leaders who are interested in
promoting conflict resolution and religious leaders who are capable of shaping and reshaping the meaning, value, and parameters of sacred places can

ameliorate or even resolve disputes over sacred space, as exemplified in the case studies I presented in chapters 7 and 8.

In this final chapter I review the implications of my argument for the management of conflicts over sacred places and expand my findings beyond the study of sacred space to the analysis of territorial disputes and the broader topic of religiously motivated violence. Territorial disputes can enhance the salience of conflicted sacred sites as tensions from one type of conflict spills over into the other. The indivisibility of sacred places can also shed light on the manner in which territorial disputes become increasingly resistant to resolution. Religious actors can even imbue contested secular territory with religious characteristics so as to mobilize believers in defense of a territory. If participants begin conceiving of the space as civil-religious sacred space over time, disputed territory can take on quasi-sacred qualities. Influential leaders can undo this process and resolve the most entrenched territorial disputes by persuading their domestic audiences to rethink their perceptions of the disputed territory.

Finally, I discuss the implications of my argument for the future of research on religion and international relations. To mitigate worrisome trends in contemporary analyses, I propose an approach that both traces the pathways by which the origins of the content and meaning of religion impact international affairs and offers generalizable findings at the international level of analysis. This *thick religion* methodology requires a sensitivity to theology, religious organizations, iconography, ceremony, and belief as well as a willingness to abstract from particular religious movements, regions, or instances in order to arrive at broader conclusions about international affairs.

Explaining, Understanding, and Shaping Disputes over Sacred Places

Throughout this volume I have employed three approaches for analyzing conflicts over sacred places: materialism, interpretivism, and constructivism. These methodologies offer contrasting but not contradictory accounts of the causes and consequences of these disputes. To truly understand these conflicts, we have to combine insights from all three methodologies. The materialist account emphasizes the political ramifications of bargaining over an indivisible good such as sacred space. The interpretivist account focuses on the significance of sacred places to believers. The constructivist account highlights the role of leaders in creating and reshaping these places. By drawing on all three, we may arrive at an understanding that is as sensitive to the weight of religious ideas as to the processes through which such ideas are constructed and redefined, as well as their material underpinnings and their political ramifications.

In this section, I explore the implications of each of these accounts for the management of conflicts over sacred places. The materialist component of my argument suggests that political actors should seek advice from experts in religion before attempting to intervene in conflicts over sacred sites. Such consultations are rare, even though religious experts possess important information about the parameters that govern the indivisibility of sacred places. The interpretivist viewpoint goes a step further to recommend that religious leaders, and not merely religious experts, be included in consultations about these conflicts. Whereas experts can offer explanations for conflicts by providing empirical data about the components, boundaries, and value of these sites, religious leaders can convey an understanding of these conflicts, providing insight into the meaning and significance of sacred sites to believers. Finally, the constructivist aspect of the foregoing analysis implies that certain religious leaders may be able to assist in the management of conflict over sacred places by modifying the parameters that control access to these sites and behaviors within them.

Explaining Conflicts over Sacred Places

Because conflicts over sacred places mesh political and religious interests, addressing these disputes requires both political and religious intelligence. The former is easier to come by than the latter: governments have set agencies in place for collecting, analyzing, and disseminating information about the material interests and capabilities of political actors. Indeed, governmental institutions are adept at processing economic, geographic, legal, demographic, and other data that might influence decision making and conflict resolution. No parallel mechanisms for gathering or interpreting data about religion exist in American executive agencies. Writing about the salience of religion as a factor in international politics during her tenure at the State Department, Madeleine Albright reported: "When I was secretary of state, I had an entire bureau of economic experts I could turn to, and a cadre of experts on nonproliferation and arms control, whose mastery of technical jargon earned them a nickname, 'the priesthood.' With the notable exception of Ambassador [Robert] Seiple, I did not have similar expertise available for integrating religious principles into our efforts at diplomacy. Given the nature of today's world, knowledge of this type is essential."[1]

The failure to integrate religious intelligence into the American diplomatic apparatus is a legacy of the doctrine of the separation of church and state. Although governmental ignorance of the variables that drive religiously motivated violence comes at a heavy cost, decision makers remain distrustful of religious influence on matters of state and hesitant to incorporate religious expertise into their calculations. Yet experts in religion can provide decision makers with crucial information about the three indivisibility parameters discussed in chapter 3: cohesion, boundaries, and uniqueness. An expert on sacred sites can thus provide answers to three important questions: What are the components of the site and how do they hang together? What are the boundaries of the site? Why do believers value this site?

Indian authorities learned this lesson in their disastrous confrontation with a Sikh insurgency in the Golden Temple complex in Amritsar, alluded to in the second chapter of this book. In 1980, an extremist preacher and leader of a radical Sikh separatist movement, Sant Jarnail Bhindranwale, sought refuge from the Indian police in this most sacred Sikh temple.[2] Over the course of four years, Bhindranwale's forces turned the temple into a fortified stronghold, replete with fortified machine gun nests and ammunition depots. In 1984, Indian special forces began planning a complex operation focused on eliminating the insurgents. Their attack, code-named Operation Blue Star, led to the surrender of the insurgents, but it also destroyed many of the ancient structures in the temple complex and burned invaluable manuscripts housed inside.

The public outrage that followed Operation Blue Star was driven not only by the destruction of the temple and the sacrilegious behavior of soldiers within the complex but also by the Indian government's insensitivity to Sikh religious sensibilities as demonstrated by the date chosen for the operation. The Indian army chose to attack the temple on the date commemorating the martyrdom of the Sikh guru and founder of the temple, Guru Anjun. Guru Anjun had undergone religious persecution and was ultimately executed, an act marking the evolution of the Sikh movement from one of pacifist reform to one of ritual militancy. When the attack occurred, Amritsar was crowded with visitors who were there to commemorate the occasion. The attack also coincided with the fifth day of a lunar month, a particularly auspicious day for bathing in the temple's lake. Indian authorities did not consult with Sikh experts and seemed blissfully unaware of the significance of the date chosen for the attack and its tactical implications. Consequently, about one thousand pilgrims lost their lives during Operation Blue Star. Six months after the event, Indian prime minister Indira Gandhi was assassinated by her Sikh bodyguards, unleashing months of sectarian riots across India.

A similar refusal to consult with religious experts characterized all three parties to the Camp David negotiations in 2001, analyzed in chapter 5. Political scientist Menahem Klein summarized the Israeli delegation's attitude toward consultation with religious experts:

> The lack of a religious discourse within the Israeli establishment that prepared for the summit and the failure to initiate a religious dialogue between the Israeli and Palestinian representatives were critical once the question of the Temple Mount was raised in the way it was raised. The religious issue seems to have deterred the Israeli decision makers. They were afraid to deal with it because they themselves were not religious and lacked familiarity with the philosophical and legal world of Judaism.[3]

Understanding Conflicts over Sacred Places

Yet Israeli, Palestinian, and American representatives to Camp David committed an even greater blunder in their refusal to integrate religious leaders into the negotiation process. All agreements reached by the negotiators were criticized and eventually scuttled by religious leaders excluded from the negotiations. These saw their religious rights and values threatened by the negotiators and refused, on principle, to extend their support to bargains after the fact.

Similarly, when reporters asked Sikh religious leaders why they had not issued an edict to oust the insurgents from the Golden Temple before Operation Blue Star, one Sikh high priest replied, "No one complained to me about this matter."[4] There is no indication that the Indian government ever discussed the crisis with the high priests. Had government officials done so, they would have learned at the very least that the hostel at which Bhindranwale had resided in the months leading up to the operation, although near the temple, was not considered by Sikhs to be part of the sacred temple complex. The military had been reluctant to apprehend him there because Indian commanders were ignorant of the temple's precise boundaries and uncertain as to the response that an incursion into the hostel would provoke. The government's refusal to consult with Sikh leaders to ascertain the parameters of the Amritsar shrine would ultimately result in the deaths of thousands.

Moreover, serious consultation with religious leaders can supply religious intelligence that experts are ill equipped to provide. As outsiders, analysts and academics can accumulate empirical data about sacred sites, such as details about their layout, the rules governing access and behavior within, or the history of the conflict. These specialists cannot, however, accurately convey the believers' intuition about the significance of these sites.

The difference between the expert's point of view and the religious practitioner's vantage point is best captured in the distinction between "explaining" and "understanding" that lies at the basis of the difference between materialist and interpretivist analyses.[5] Explaining entails offering causal accounts, rooted in a positivist and empiricist conception of human behavior that applies natural science tools to decipher social action. Analysts engaged in explaining use measurements and testing to arrive at general laws that explicate reasons for social behavior. Understanding, on the other hand, focuses on meaning and beliefs. To arrive at the meaning of sacred places for believers, for example, requires locating beliefs about the sacred in the wider context of religious meanings and historically contingent particulars. Religious leaders are uniquely suited for both understanding and interpreting these meaning and beliefs. Involving religious leaders in the process of managing disputes over sacred places not only increases their goodwill toward the political process but also informs the decision makers' intuition regarding the processes and motivations driving the dispute, a prerequisite for addressing these disputes.

Shaping Conflicts over Sacred Places

Religious leaders can add one final arrow to the decision makers' quiver: the possibility of reshaping the meaning of sacred space to believers in a manner that will promote conflict management or even resolution. As I argued in chapter 6, religious leaders are uniquely suited for reconfiguring sacred space because they enjoy significant social influence as well as a proficiency in the traditions, rituals, and religious-legal precedents of a religious movement. Religious leaders transform sacred places on a routine basis, but their ability to do so in a manner conducive to conflict amelioration depends on the importance of the sacred site involved, the nature and timing of the proposed change, the position of the leader in the religious hierarchy, and the ability of secular leaders to induce the cooperation of religious leaders. Only rarely do all these variables line up correctly. Although the reconfiguration of sacred space is the most remarkable skill that religious leaders can bring to the table, aspiring to change the status of a sacred site offers the least practical means for addressing a dispute.

I examined two salient cases in which political and religious circumstances did align to enable such a reconfiguration. The rabbinical ruling of October 1967, examined in chapter 7, prevented sectarian conflict on the Temple Mount for decades by restricting Jewish access to that sacred site. Despite the significant centrality and vulnerability of the disputed site, the rabbis succeeded in convincing their followers to abstain from entering their most sacred space, while the government blocked opponents of the ruling from exerting their influence. Although this reconfiguration did not resolve the dispute over the Temple Mount, it succeeded in managing the conflict in the medium to long term. The 1979 ruling by the Saudi ulema, on the other hand, was designed not to mitigate conflict but rather to enable the deployment of military force where religious principles would have prohibited its use. By temporarily lifting the ban on violence in the Grand Mosque in Mecca, the ulema helped the Saudi government confront an insurgency at a site of prime religious significance.

At the same time, the aftermath of the Mecca insurgency entails a warning about the costs of involving religious actors in the management of disputes over sacred space. The cooperation between the Saudi regime and the ulema came at a significant cost for both parties. In return for their cooperation, the government was forced to offer the religious elite political and financial concession that enhanced the power of the ulema at the expense of the regime. At the same time, the ulema's decision to compromise religious principles in order to gain the regime's favor led to its discrediting, a common trend across Muslim states in which regimes have co-opted religious elites.[6]

Religious leaders wary of "blowback" effects will prove reluctant to cooperate in managing disputes over sacred places, particularly when such cooperation entails reshaping sacred sites counter to existing religious traditions and sensibilities. Because participants in these disputes know that their legitimacy can be undermined by religious leaders, they may even threaten these leaders into compliance. Faced with intimidation, leaders may choose to ignore the costs of continued conflict at sacred sites or even direct responsibility for conflict onto the government. Decision makers can encourage cooperative behavior by treating religious leaders as sensitive assets that require protection.

At the same time, religious leaders should be willing to provide information that can help minimize damage to their shrine, keep their followers out of harm's way, and reduce the risk of sacrilege and desecration. They may be able to predict, interpret, and even influence public perceptions regarding the dispute or act as go-betweens at times of crisis. Some religious actors may exact a higher price for their cooperation, a concession decision makers should be wary of extending. Thus, far from offering a panacea for the resolution of these disputes, the possibility of reconfiguring sacred sites requires religious and political leaders to engage in a delicate bargain that will affect their respective fortunes as well as the fate of the disputed sacred space.

Sacred Places and Disputed Territories

The causes and consequences of conflicts over sacred places also bear implications for the resolution of "secular" territorial disputes. Territorial disputes are disagreements between states over the ownership of land or the location of boundaries. At their most basic level of interaction, territorial disputes enhance the salience of conflicted sacred sites. Sacred sites can come to represent the larger territorial disputes within which they are embedded, and violence from one type of conflict can spill over into the parallel dispute.

Second, although secular territorial disputes lack the inherent characteristics that produce indivisibility in sacred spaces, rivals increasingly come to perceive territorial disputes as indivisible as time passes. As these disputes become entrenched, the disputed territories undergo changes in cohesion, boundaries, and uniqueness that match the three aspects that render sacred space indivisible. The indivisibility of sacred places can thus shed light on the manner in which territorial disputes become increasingly resistant to resolution. Moreover, under restricted circumstances, religious actors can imbue contested secular territory with religious characteristics so as to mobilize believers in defense of a territory.

Third, even where religious actors have not intervened to consecrate disputed secular space, such space can take on quasi-sacred qualities over time if participants begin conceiving of the space as civil-religious sacred space. By occupying the middle ground between secular and sacred territory, these spaces provide the nation with the ability to experience, celebrate, and commemorate its past, present. and future. This provides rivals with the incentive to produce civil-religious sacred space in contested territory, linking the territory with the ethos and destiny of the nation and thus enhancing its value.

The antithesis of this process of civil consecration, namely, a process of reevaluation leading to the devaluation of disputed territory, is required to resolve entrenched territorial disputes. This is the fourth and final lesson for secular territorial disputes that can be drawn from disputes over sacred space. Just as religious elites can play a crucial role in mitigating disputes over sacred places by redefining their cohesion, boundaries, or value, so can influential leaders resolve the most entrenched territorial disputes by engaging in a process of persuasion with their domestic audiences that shapes public perceptions of the disputed territory.

The Relationship between Secular and Sacred Territorial Disputes

When territorial disputes fall along sectarian lines, as in the Israeli-Palestinian dispute over the West Bank, for example, they elevate the salience of the sacred sites within the disputed territories, thus increasing the likelihood of conflict at disputed shrines. These holy sites then become symbols of the larger territories within which they are embedded. Disputes over these shrines can come to represent the greater territorial disagreements between the two communities. As the parallel disputes, the sacred and the secular, become enmeshed, violence can spill over from one setting into the other. Furthermore, setbacks in the resolution of one type of dispute can impede progress in the other.

The prolonged dispute between India and Pakistan over the Himalayan region of Jammu and Kashmir (Kashmir for short) exemplifies this feedback process well. Kashmir harbored religious significance to participants long before the outbreak of the interstate dispute between India and Pakistan. Kashmiris have often referred to the region as Jannat-ud-Duniya (Paradise on Earth) and Bagh-i-Jannat (the Garden of Paradise). Nonetheless, the onset of the Indo-Pakistani dispute in 1947 further enhanced the salience of existing sacred sites, led to the production of new sacred sites, and fostered conflict at salient shrines.

One measure of the religious significance of Kashmir lies in the number and importance of sacred shrines and pilgrimage sites in the region. Every year, thousands of Hindu pilgrims make the five-day trek to the Sri Amarnath cave, at six thousand meters altitude, to celebrate the festival of Rakshabandan. The cave, near Srinagar, contains sacred idols of Shiva, Parvati, and Ganesh, as well as a miraculous ice lingam. Pilgrims also flock to the Vaishno Devi cave near Jammu to worship the three mother goddesses of Hinduism.[7] The Raghunath Temple in Jammu, one of the largest temple complexes in India, was designed to establish Jammu as a great religious center, rivaling the sacred city of Varanasi in India.[8] Hindus have also identified the spot at which Vishnu, pursued by Bhasmasure, rested his foot as Kawnsarang Lake in Kashmir, for "if ever an immortal placed his foot anywhere on earth, this must surely be the place."[9]

Muslims revere the mosque of Charar Sharif for its association with the Sufi patron saint of the Vale of Kashmir, Sheikh Noor-ud-Din Noorani, whose tomb is nearby.[10] The most sacred site to Muslims in Kashmir is the Hazratbal Mosque in Srinagar where a hair of the Prophet Muhammad is kept in a glass phial.[11] The Rauzabal Mosque in Srinagar contains the tomb of Yus Asaf, revered as the founder of the Quadiani sect of Islam. Some Muslims identify him as Jesus who, having survived the crucifixion, returned to Kashmir where he had spent his youth and died a natural death.[12] In Murree, believers may worship the tomb of Mary and the rod of Jesus.[13]

With the entrenchment of the Kashmir dispute, these sacred sites have risen in salience, drawing growing numbers of visitors from both religious communities who seek to assert their dominance over the disputed region. The sacred sites in Kashmir have come to represent these rival communities and thus pose tempting targets for assault by opponents. These attacks, in turn, often lead to retaliatory assaults and have adverse effects on the larger interstate dispute. The Hazratbal Mosque, by virtue of its status as the most important Muslim shrine in Kashmir, has repeatedly suffered the brunt of attacks and has served as a rallying symbol in a conflict that has increasingly assumed communalist dimensions.

In 1963, the sacred relic was stolen from the Hazratbal Mosque. Although it was soon located by Indian intelligence operatives, authenticated by Muslim clerics, and returned to its place, the incident sparked the retaliatory theft of sacred images from a temple in Jammu. This in turn led to Muslim protests in Srinagar, Hindu protests in Jammu, anti-Indian sentiments throughout Kashmir, and violent communal rioting in Calcutta. Pakistan interpreted these protests as a cry for liberation on the part of Kashmir's Muslims, ready to revolt against India, and initiated a military incursion into Kashmir a year later.[14]

In 1992, following the Ayodhya affair (described in chapter 5) and widespread communal violence in India, similar strife broke out in Jammu and Kashmir. The chief minister of Jammu and Kashmir had permitted Muslim state employees to pray near an old Hindu temple, located in the states office in Jammu. Hindus perceived this as the construction of a mosque near the temple; their protests led to clashes and in turn to curfews on towns throughout Kashmir. In spite of increased intervention by the Indian army and paramilitary forces, the violence forced a first wave of a hundred thousand fearful Hindu refugees to leave the valley.[15]

In 1993, the Hazratbal Mosque became once again the focus of communal violence. Having learned their lesson from the disastrous attack on the Sikh shrine in Amritsar in 1984, the army chose not to invade the shrine and the militants surrendered after one month of negotiations.[16] Two years later, Indian forces failed to resolve a similar crisis in the mosque at Charar Sharif. A group of sixty to one hundred insurgents, led by a former Afghan Mujahid, barricaded themselves in the mosque and fortified the shrine with explosives. A fire that broke out ten weeks into the siege consumed the shrine and much of the town, as well as the 650-year-old mausoleum of Sheikh Noor-ud-Din Noorani.[17] Widespread protests took place in both countries, and communal violence erupted throughout Kashmir. In 1996, attention turned once again to the Hazratbal Mosque in Kashmir, where members of the Jammu and Kashmir Liberation Front had ensconced themselves. This time the Border Security Force was instructed to charge the shrine rather than negotiate, and thirty insurgents were killed.[18]

Attacks on sacred sites in Kashmir continue unabated. In July 2002, an attack by gunmen disguised as Hindu holy men on a temple in Jammu left more than twelve dead and over twenty injured.[19] In August that year, gunmen attacked pilgrims on their way to the annual worship at the Sri Amarnath cave near Srinagar, leaving nine dead.[20] A month later, gunmen attacked a Hindu temple in Gandhinagar, killing twenty-nine before Indian commandos stormed the temple to flush out the attackers.[21] As long as the Indo-Pakistani dispute over Kashmir remains unresolved, sacred sites in the region will continue to bear the brunt of sectarian violence.

This interaction between disputes over sacred space and conflicts over profane space is not confined to the Indo-Pakistani or the Arab-Israeli dispute. In disputes that fall along religious divides, such as the Greek-Albanian dispute over northern Epirus, the Turkish-Greek dispute over Cyprus, the civil war in the former Yugoslavia, or the dispute between Armenia and Azerbaijan over Nagorno Karabakh, parties have invested significant efforts in constructing and embellishing shrines while accusing their opponents of marginalizing, desecrating, or even destroying religious sites on the other side of the border. Each dispute type amplifies the other, creating a dangerous feedback effect to the detriment of both conflicts.

The Entrenchment of Territorial Disputes

Territorial disputes are among the most common and costliest interstate disputes, directly affecting the frequency, severity, and duration of international crises and wars.[22] These disputes are also particularly resistant to resolution. Only half of the two-hundred-odd territorial disputes in the twentieth century were resolved in less than twenty years, and a full third required more than forty years to resolve, if they were resolved at all. These troubling empirical data on territorial disputes are accompanied by an even more worrying statistical trend: territorial disputes, unlike wars, have no innate tendency to subside over time. Instead, these disputes behave like institutions: the more they persist, the more entrenched and embedded they become.[23] Entrenchment is the process by which disputes become increasingly resistant to resolution over time, marked by an enhanced reluctance to offer, accept, or implement compromises or even negotiate over territory. This entrenchment is often accompanied by an escalation of hostile rhetoric regarding the territory and even armed clashes. Why is that the case?

Although territorial disputes are qualitatively different from conflicts over sacred sites, these sites can shed some light on the processes of entrenchment that territorial disputes undergo as they mature. All territorial disputes move toward indivisibility over time, as a result not only of top-down manipulations by wily or shortsighted leaders but also of gradual shifts in the meaning, content, and definition of issues as perceived by society. These shifts involve three characteristics that match the three indivisibility aspects of sacred space:

cohesion, boundaries, and uniqueness. Territorial disputes become more difficult to resolve over time because the disputed territory grows increasingly cohesive over time, its boundaries rigidify, and its subjective value rises, adding layers of emotional, nationalist, and religious value to what may well have started off as a dispute over strategically or materially valuable land.

Each of these three processes is driven by distinct and observable mechanisms. Changes in territorial cohesion are driven by population growth and infrastructure improvement and construction as well as by the extension of legal and administrative frameworks, for example. These link disparate parts of the territory both to one another and to the homeland, leading these parts to become increasingly interdependent and difficult to separate from one another. Boundaries become increasingly rigid as a result of mapping, the public statement of negotiation positions, and declarations about the disputed land. Changes in the fungibility of territory are driven by loss of life in defense of the disputed land but also by the emotional attachment to homes, landscapes, and symbolic sites, such as memorials or religious shrines.

These processes serve to entrench territorial disputes over time. Over time, territory tends to become more, rather than less, developed; more, and not fewer, soldiers will die defending a patch of disputed land; more maps of the disputed territory are produced, never fewer. Moreover, some of these mechanisms are self-enforcing. For example, the higher the value assigned to the land, the more effort goes into defending it, the more likely are future sacrifices. Similarly, the more developed land is, the more settlers will want to move there, the more likely it is to undergo further development. These feedback loops help shape territorial disputes into enduring and self-sustaining institutions, often lasting into the fifth or sixth decade since inception.

Many of these mechanisms can be driven by policy, like construction and settlement tactics designed to appropriate contested territory. But construction and settlement need not be the outcome of conscious policy, whereas other mechanisms cannot be the outcome of purposive policy, such as the personal investment of locals in the territory. In other words, disputed territories move toward indivisibility irrespective of whether leaders involved in the dispute wish them to do so.

Sacred places, by virtue of being perfectly indivisible, define the end point of the path down which territorial disputes move as they mature. Territories involved in exceedingly protracted disputes can gradually take on the characteristics of civil-religious sacred space, a phenomenon I discuss in the next section, but they cannot become sacred space in the absence of acts of consecration by charismatic religious leaders. Where such leaders have become involved in territorial disputes, however, their consecration of secular space has often thwarted peaceful attempts at conflict resolution.

The failure to take into account the influence of religious leaders on secular territorial disputes led to an unexpected crisis during Israel's evacuation of Sinai settlements. In 1982, Israel began evacuating its settlements in the Sinai in a move toward returning the Sinai to Egypt, as agreed in the 1978 Camp David accords. The Israeli populace indicated no resistance to the evacuation of these settlements, and any protest by settlers was quickly overcome by "adjusting" the compensation payments offered.[24] Religious reasons for holding onto the Sinai were never discussed, even though then prime minister Menachem Begin was an observant Jew with deep religious convictions. According to biblical and legal definitions of the boundaries of the Land of Israel, the Sinai was not part of the Promised Land but just beyond its southern boundary.[25]

To Begin's dismay, however, an influential group of rabbis, the leaders of Jewish settlement in the West Bank and Gaza, issued religious rulings to the contrary.[26] They sponsored a movement to resist the evacuation, long after most permanent residents had left, by convincing four hundred families to move from the West Bank to the Sinai town of Yamit in the months before its evacuation. Once there, the settlers organized the city for a siege, storing food and erecting barricades, accompanied by an intensification of ceremonies, prayers, and millenarian sermons. "The entire Yamit territory was named a 'holy land' and the settlers, a 'holy public.' Everything there became in fact holy: 'holy struggle,' 'holy purpose' and 'holy movement.'"[27] Nine-year-old Yamit was added to the canonical list of sacred cities of Israel, its name substituted for Jerusalem in the Passover rituals of 1982.[28] The rabbis had overturned any ambiguity that might have surrounded the biblical borders of Israel, the significance of these borders, and the practical implications of that significance.

When the time came to evacuate the settlement of Yamit, violence erupted. Settlers hurled stones and bottles at soldiers armed with hoses and tear gas while an extremist group in an air raid bunker threatened mass suicide. The images of soldiers dragging women and children off the roofs by means of cages, beating students coming out of shelters, and bulldozing through barricades constituted the first round in a continuing struggle between the government of Israel and settlers over "Greater Israel." Similar scenarios repeated themselves during the evacuation of Israeli settlements in the Gaza Strip in September 2005, with leading rabbis calling on soldiers to refuse orders to participate in the evacuation because of the sanctity of the land that was about to be abandoned.[29] This evacuation was complicated by the presence of thirty synagogues in the Gaza Strip that had to be destroyed by Israeli forces, prompting a local rabbi to compare the evacuation to "the destruction of the Holy Temple," albeit at the hand of Jews.[30]

Muslim Palestinian leaders have taken similar actions to raise the perceived value of occupied Palestine. Muslim notables led by the Grand Mufti of

Jerusalem, Sheikh Ekrima Sabri, have expanded the boundaries of "al-Aksa," a term that previously referred only to the mosque in the Noble Sanctuary in Jerusalem, to encompass not only the entire sanctuary platform but the city of Jerusalem and surrounding Palestine as well. The territories disputed in the Israeli-Palestinian conflict have thus been transformed into a *waqf,* an Islamic endowment, the transfer of which to non-Muslims is strictly prohibited by Muslim law.[31]

Similar attempts at expanding the boundaries of sacred space so as to subsume the entirety of a disputed territory are apparent in proclamations by Buddhist nationalists, protesting Sinhalese efforts at autonomy, that declare the whole island of Sri Lanka to be indivisible because it was destined by the Buddha himself to be a pure source for Buddhist teaching and practice.[32] Noteworthy is also the fatwa issued in 1996 by Osama bin Laden, subtitled "Expel the Infidels from the Arab Peninsula," in which bin Laden pronounced the presence of U.S. troops in Saudi Arabia a desecration of the sacred cities of Mecca and Medina.[33] Although U.S. troops were not based in or near these cities, bin Laden's declaration successfully mobilized Muslims worldwide by extending the boundaries of Mecca and Medina to include all of Saudi Arabia. This call for a jihad against the U.S.-led West, first implemented through a 1996 attack against U.S. forces in Dhahran, Saudi Arabia, culminated in the attacks of September 11, 2001.

Rulings such as these demonstrate the ability of religious actors to complicate the resolution of territorial disputes by transforming secular space into disputed sacred space through declaratory acts and corresponding rituals. As in the resolution of disputes over sacred space, eliciting the cooperation of religious actors to support the resolution of territorial disputes can prove a daunting task. Yet the damage caused by religious actors who are left out of the resolution process can be prohibitive.

Civil-Religious Sacred Space

Most territorial disputes do not undergo consecration by religious actors. The connection between sacred space and entrenched territorial disputes may nevertheless run deep if participants to a territorial dispute come to conceptualize the disputed land as a civil-religious sacred space. Civil-religious sacred spaces are secular spaces, such as memorials, cemeteries, or museums, that serve emotive and ritualistic functions for a nation that parallel the functions sacred space serves for a religious movement.[34] Instead of offering access to the divine, civil-religious sacred space provides the community with the means for visualizing, celebrating, and memorializing the nation, both past and present. The layout and design of civil-religious sacred space commemorate the nation's revered history by displaying key actors and events, permitting visitors to reenact and relive these venerated occasions. Patriotic discourse links these spaces to the nation's ethos, history, and destiny.

Civil-religious sacred space can play a particularly important role in solidifying a state's hold on disputed land. In encouraging citizens to conceive of the disputed territory as civil-religious sacred space, elites can highlight its irreplaceable value, integrate the space into the nation's narratives, and link its future to that of the homeland. Leaders may do so by adopting a quasi-religious discourse that associates the disputed territory with the identity of the state, its history, and the nation's sacrifices at times of war.

Yet another means of enhancing the civil-religious value of disputed territory is to mark its landscape with civil-religious shrines such as war memorials, military cemeteries, monuments, museums, and national parks.[35] At these sites citizens can experience the otherwise ineffable nature of the nation more effectively. Tourists can explore the link between the territory and their nation's history, schoolchildren can learn about their fatherland, and soldiers can honor lost comrades. These sites also serve as the public setting for commemorative rituals, celebrations, and rites of passage that link the territory to the national calendar. Although these ceremonies focus on particular sites, they enhance the nationalist value of the surrounding disputed territory as a whole until it becomes increasingly prized for aspects other than its inherent economic or strategic value. The result is a territory that is an intermediary between sacred and secular space: disputed territory of such high civil-religious value as to be exceedingly difficult to divide.

The territorial dispute between Peru and Ecuador illustrates this link between disputed territory, sacred space, and the resulting synthesis, civil-religious sacred space. The dispute over El Oriente concerned a hundred-thousand- square-mile region in the heart of the Amazon. Described as the most difficult territorial dispute in the Western Hemisphere, it lasted for 170 years and "caused more trouble than any other in America...baff[ling] repeated attempts at settlement by direct negotiation and repeated efforts at mediation on the part of other friendly nations."[36] General Paco Moncayo, Ecuador's leading military intellectual, captured the significance of the disputed territory to his countrymen:

> I believe that I, just like all Ecuadorians, have lived anguished by the territorial problem....It is because no one who loves his country can truly live without anguishing about the destiny of his country. The territorial problem...is the very basis of our historical projection and the very survival of our nation. The

anguish is a vital anguish of the Ecuadorian people. We are born with this anguish the way Christians are born with original sin.[37]

As the parties neared resolution of the dispute in 1998, the main point
of contention became a single military outpost, Tiwintza, which Ecuador
had managed to defend against a Peruvian assault at the cost of twelve
casualties.[38] This 250-acre plot of land, consisting of a collection of huts
and trenches, lost in the inaccessible mountain ranges and hidden under a
triple-canopy jungle, came to symbolize the entire disputed territory and the
very essence of the Peruvian-Ecuadorian rivalry. Three-quarters of Ecuadorians polled during the 1995 war between Peru and Ecuador stated that
they would support a renewed offensive against Peru, should Tiwintza ultimately fall into enemy hands.[39] U.S. ambassador Luigi Einaudi, who acted
as intermediary in the ensuing peace talks, reported: "Typically, the parties
could agree neither on its precise location nor even on the spelling of its
name. For Ecuadorians, "Tiwintza" symbolized national dignity. For Peru-
vians, "Tiwinsa" symbolized Ecuadorian aggression. Ecuador claimed it
had successfully defended Tiwintza against Peruvian attacks. Peru claimed
it had recaptured Tiwintza, preserving Peru's sovereign rights. Both sides
had watered its soil with the blood of their soldiers. Neither could conceive
of yielding it to the other."[40]

These examples of civil-religious discourse provide evidence of attempts by
elites to raise the value of disputed territory by imbuing it with civil-religious
"sanctity." They parallel efforts by religious actors to encumber the resolution of disputes over sacred sites by expanding the boundaries, increasing the
cohesion, or enhancing the value of these sites. By the same token, political
leaders should be able to mitigate territorial disputes by reducing the emotive
value that disputed territories have accumulated over time, thus reversing the
entrenchment effects that have driven these disputes toward indivisibility.

Resolving Territorial Disputes

States have resolved their territorial disputes by dividing the disputed territory, redefining its boundaries in a manner that permits both claimants to
achieve their objectives, compensating one claimant for territorial gains, or some
combination of these approaches.[41] Territorial disputes become harder to resolve
over time because partition, redefinition, and compensation become more difficult to implement as disputes mature and move toward indivisibility.

My argument regarding territorial dispute entrenchment suggests that advanced territorial conflicts, like conflicts over sacred places, are self-sustaining

institutions that cannot be dismantled by means of common conflict resolution approaches. Indeed, strategies that espouse reciprocal trust-building measures have to contend with the adverse effects of time on these disputes. Instead, by analogy with the mitigation of conflicts over sacred space, the resolution of territorial disputes must involve idea entrepreneurs capable of redefining social perceptions of dispute indivisibility in a manner that permits partition, redefinition, or compensation. The idea entrepreneur might suggest, for example, that some symbols of integration are more significant than others or that the territory does, in fact, lend itself to subdivision quite naturally in one way or another. She might succeed in contracting, expanding, or otherwise shifting the perceived boundaries of the territory. Finally, he could contest the symbolic value of the territory, by suggesting that some other good or issue has a value higher than previously believed. The idea entrepreneur could propose, for example, that value can be derived from the territory even in the absence of full sovereignty or that utility previously attributed to the entire disputed space can be derived from a small part of the territory.

The challenge facing these idea entrepreneurs stems, in part, from the fact that the political authority required to define and shape ideas about disputed territories is far more diffuse than the religious authority required to shape ideas about sacred space. By virtue of their monopoly over knowledge and their charisma, religious leaders are uniquely capable of shaping their followers' perceptions of sacred space. The ability to reconfigure perceptions of secular territory, on the other hand, lies as much in the hands of the media, scholars, educators, and the public itself as it does in leaders. Nonetheless, particularly influential leaders have succeeded in reshaping social perceptions in a manner conducive to conflict resolution, as exemplified by Presidents Alberto Fujimori of Peru and Jamil Mahuad of Ecuador in resolving the protracted dispute over the Oriente region.

Both presidents had placed the resolution of the dispute at the top of their political agenda, realizing the costs of conflict and the opportunities of peace.[42] As the peace process between Peru and Ecuador threatened to collapse in late 1998 over the issue of Tiwintza, both men forged a close personal relationship and engaged in direct presidential diplomacy, meeting one-on-one seven times in various Latin American capitals.

Mahuad succeeded in redefining his state's position by inducing two simultaneous changes. First, he stressed the Ecuadorian victory over Peru in the war of 1995, as opposed to the humiliating defeat at the hands of Peru in 1941. Having evened the score with their traditional enemies, he argued, the people of Ecuador could now negotiate territorial concessions without diminishing the nation's honor.[43] Second, he changed the focus of the dispute from those territories lost in 1941 to those territories successfully defended in 1995, replacing old with new aspirations.

Carlos Espinosa described the dramatic changes in Ecuador's position during the 1998 negotiations: "Ecuador's leaders had to address emotional needs in laborious ways in order to arrive at a lasting peace. Ecuador's treatment of its territorial aspirations underwent a remarkable evolution in the course of the 1995–1998 negotiations… Ecuador's perception of the territorial issue had partially shifted away from the problem of Amazonian sovereignty to the retention of the sites Ecuador had held in the 1995 war. That displacement made possible Ecuador's downscaling of the sovereign access aspiration."[44]

The last hurdle to be overcome was the status of Tiwintza, the aforementioned 250-acre plot of land that Ecuadorian soldiers had defended against a Peruvian assault at the cost of their lives. Ecuadorians reacted furiously to the suggestion that all territory gained in the 1995 conflict, including Tiwintza, be returned to Peru because this seemed to render Ecuador's sacrifices and victory futile.[45] The status of Tiwintza was equally emotional for Peru: the Peruvian military had been less than forthcoming regarding its poor showing in the conflict and claimed to have dislodged Ecuador from all its bases. Turning over the military sites would have forced the Peruvian military to reveal the truth about its defeat in 1995.

It was at this point that both leaders displayed their most dramatic personal diplomacy, starting with a four-hour meeting in Brasilia, without aides or intermediaries. Two weeks later, with the support of third-party arbitrators (Chile, Argentina, Brazil, and the United States), the two leaders arrived at a solution: the disputed territories would remain in Peruvian hands, but Tiwintza would be granted to Ecuador as private property.[46] Mahuad bolstered this solution by publicly declaring ownership over Tiwintza sufficient to ensure that Ecuador's honor was intact.[47] The Act of Brasilia, concluding the longest territorial dispute in the history of the Americas, was signed three days later in an emotional ceremony at which the leaders exchanged military mementos from the 1942 war, "taming" the memories of the past.[48]

Support for this agreement in Ecuador was, in part, the outcome of a successful public relations campaign waged by Mahuad to prepare the public for territorial concessions.[49] He recognized that a final agreement would depend on convincing Ecuadorians that peace would benefit the country even if it did not fulfill entrenched historical aspirations and claims attached to national identity.[50] As resolution approached, Ecuador's top-ranking diplomats began making occasional statements that signaled the diminished odds that Ecuador's historic position would prevail.

Starting in January 1998, for example, the phrase "sovereign" was dropped from the slogan "sovereign access to the Amazon" in all official statements.[51] Later that year, the Foreign Ministry began rewriting Ecuador's history, in a process that came to be known as the "truth bath" (*baño de verdad*). In meetings with the press and sectors of civil society, the Foreign Ministry explained that Ecuador had never in its history exerted sovereignty over the Amazon. The Foreign Ministry encouraged the view that "national honor lay in social justice or 'governance' and not in the retention of territories defended in war" and hinted that Ecuador lacked juridical rights to the disputed region.[52] The new agreement, the regime argued, would bring Ecuador closer than it had ever been to the Amazon since colonial times. When the final agreement was revealed, it was received as the product of a national debate that had created a consensus for peace, although it did lead to acrimonious debate over whether and how Ecuador should rewrite its own history and the way that history was to be taught in its schools.[53]

The resolution of the Peru-Ecuador dispute, Carlos Espinosa writes, "offers important lessons on how to deal with emotionally charged issues in the context of conflict management. It points to both the force and the malleability of emotional constraints to a mutually beneficial peace."[54] Ending this territorial dispute required influential leaders to engage in a process of persuasion by proposing new conceptions of the dispute that better conformed to reality. Mahuad appealed to the heroism of 1995 and the symbolic significance of a single military base that had been valiantly defended, to supplant deeply rooted historical aspirations for expansive territory. Similar reconfiguration efforts are apparent in the resolution of other protracted disputes, resolved when leaders succeeded in convincing their constituents to rethink the meaning and value of the disputed territory by employing symbolic maneuvers, persuasive arguments, and public campaigns.

Ongoing Disputes over Sacred Places

Since the inception of this volume, conflicts at sacred sites have continued to dominate national and international headlines. In Israel alone, conflicts since the start of the new millennium have involved a gamut of religious groups pitted against one another in various combinations as they competed to control sacred sites. In 2005, for example, Israel's secret service raised its estimate of the probability of an extremist Jewish attack on the Muslim shrines in the Noble Sanctuary in Jerusalem to "level 8," exceeding its estimate of a threat to the life of the prime minister (at level 6).[55] This assessment emerged from a series of meetings with extremist rabbis at which members of the secret service learned about the conditions under which these rabbis would sanction such attacks. These meetings also afforded the Israeli government an opportunity to warn the rabbis about the disastrous repercussions of an attack on the Muslim shrines.[56]

On the Temple Mount itself, work to repair a crumbling pedestrian ramp that leads onto the Haram platform led to violent protests in February 2007. Palestinian protestors claimed that the construction was part of a plot to undermine the foundations of the Muslim shrines in the Noble Sanctuary. After hundreds of Palestinian protesters clashed with Israeli soldiers, work on the ramp resumed under Turkish inspection, with webcams by the Israeli Antiquities Authority permitting viewers to survey progress on the excavations online.[57]

In December 2007, Greek Orthodox and Armenian priests attacked one another with brooms and stones inside the Church of the Nativity in Bethlehem, revered as the site of Jesus' birth. The fight erupted because of a disagreement about the rights to clean parts of the church claimed by members of both movements. The scuffle, involving fifty Orthodox priests and thirty Armenians, was broken up by Palestinian policemen who had to form a human cordon to separate the two camps.[58] One expert on Christian disputes in the Holy Land estimates that "hardly a Christmas or Easter went by without an incident in the Bethlehem basilica."[59]

Meanwhile in Nazareth, a city linked in Christian belief to Jesus' childhood, a dispute between Christians and Muslims over the construction of a giant mosque in front of the Basilica of the Annunciation ended on July 2, 2003. Under the cover of darkness, an Interior Ministry demolition crew, accompanied by five hundred policemen and special forces units, demolished the unlicensed mosque's foundations. It had been designed to mark the tomb of Shehab al-Din, nephew of famed crusade vanquisher Saladin, and would have dwarfed the large Christian shrine in the center of Nazareth.[60] Its intended construction had caused strains in the relations between Israel, the Vatican, the Palestinian Authority, Saudi Arabia, and local Arabs of both Muslim and Christian persuasion.[61]

Outside the Middle East, several disputes involved not conflicts between religious groups but conflicts between religious actors and secular actors. In Mexico City, archaeologists had to cease excavations on an eighteen-yard-tall Teotihuacan pyramid from the sixth century, discovered under the site of a nineteenth-century crucifixion reenactment. The archaeologists filled in the excavation pits and reburied the pyramid for fear that the million or so spectators who attend the traditional Easter ritual would damage the invaluable find.[62] In Hong Kong, the monks of the Po Lin Monastery clashed with the government over tourist access to a giant Buddha statue, after the government proposed the construction of a cable car and tourist market near the statue. "Horrified by the thought of tourists trying to carry Big Macs and chicken legs past holy relics," the monks declared the plans a threat to their religious freedom.[63]

In Sand Springs, Oklahoma, "a battle between God almighty and the almighty dollar" raged over the future of a small church, destined to be demolished to make way for a new shopping mall. "The Lord didn't send me here to build a mini mall," exclaimed the church's pastor, who was said to be praying over a more lucrative counteroffer from city officials. Despite citizen protest, the city has threatened to seize the land and demolish the church under eminent domain.[64] Meanwhile, in northern California, protests have erupted over plans by the energy company Calpine to construct a geothermal plant at Medicine Lake near Mount Shasta, land sacred to the Pit River tribe. The tribe is concerned over the environmental impact of the proposed plant as well as the effect that the extraction of geothermal energy will have on the healing powers of the lake.[65]

Sacred places also served as the arena or pretext for international hostilities. In Cambodia, an angry mob attacked the Thai Embassy, ambassador's residence, and Thai businesses in January 2003, killing at least one Thai citizen and causing $50 million in damages. These riots occurred in response to comments, attributed to a Thai actress, alleging that Cambodia had stolen Angkor Wat from Thailand. Thai-Cambodian tensions over the temple can be traced to the Siamese sacking of Angkor Wat in 1431.[66] Hundreds of Thai citizens were evacuated from Cambodia aboard military transport aircraft, as the two states suspended diplomatic and economic ties.[67] The incident caused protracted anti-Thai resentment in Cambodia, unleashed counterriots in Bangkok, and severely strained relations between the two states.[68]

In Iraq, Afghanistan, and Pakistan, attacks on mosques continue to fuel sectarian conflict between Shi'a and Sunni Muslims, mobilized by the U.S. invasion of Iraq. In the Balkans, March 2004 saw Albanian mobs destroying scores of Orthodox churches and monasteries as violence in Kosovo reached levels unprecedented since 1999.[69] The fighting, which left nineteen people dead and wounded hundreds, also demolished the scriptures, icons, records, and structures of one hundred fifty churches in what amounted to an all-out attack on the Serb cultural heritage. Vengeful Serbs in the town of Nis set fire to the local mosque and then stretched out on the ground in front of the burning building to prevent fire engines from reaching it.[70]

Disputes over sacred places exemplify conflicts over territory at their most difficult. The problems associated with negotiating over increasingly indivisible territory reach their zenith in this category of disputes. At the same time, the resolution of these disputes, when it occurs, exemplifies the reconfiguration of indivisibility perceptions at its clearest because specific actors control the meaning and significance of these places in the eyes of believers.

Thick Religion

The in-depth study of a clearly delimited research topic such as conflicts over sacred sites affords an opportunity for interdisciplinary progress by encouraging a focused theoretical exchange between international relations (IR) scholars and sociologists of religion. A mutually beneficial dialogue of this sort is more necessary now than ever before. The convergence of religion and violence has posed increasing challenges to regional and international peace and stability in the post-cold-war world. Yet the study of religion and conflict lags far behind these challenges. Social scientists have yet to offer incisive explanations for the causes and characteristics of contemporary religious violence. American academia has grappled with the problematic interaction between religion and international conflict for several decades, an intellectual struggle revived in response to the Iranian revolution in 1979 and most recently accelerated by the events of September 11, 2001. But the results, so far, have been less than promising.

At the core of the challenge facing those who wish to study the confluence of religion and violence stands a series of ontological and epistemological problems that have yet to be resolved. We do not have a working definition of religion; an ability to differentiate its effects as a set of beliefs from its effects as a set of identities, practices, or symbols; or a clear understanding of the levels of analysis or methodologies best suited for studying religious conflict across cases. It is because of these challenges that analyses of religion and international relations have experienced a bifurcation, diverging into a *broad* route and a *deep* route. In the former case, authors focus their attention on the international arena at the cost of examining religion in depth. Their analyses tend to essentialize religion and reduce it to its social, economic, or political implications. Authors espousing the *deep* route place their emphasis on an intimate familiarity with a particular religious movement or a particular geographical region, without offering generalizations for the international sphere.

This state of affairs, in which authors choose between generalizability and interdisciplinary rigor, is the exception to the norm in international relations, the very epitome of an interdisciplinary field. International relations scholars habitually borrow insights, themes, and even methods from disciplines as far afield as geography, psychology, sociology, and anthropology. Yet they do not simply assert that regional or state geography, for example, has immediate implications for global politics, nor are they content to conclude their analyses with findings at the subglobal level. Rather they have taken great care to expand and link these accounts to the international outcome they are trying to explain. Similarly, scholars who seek insight into international affairs from psychology or anthropology have eschewed treating these fields of inquiry as mere metaphors for international affairs. Instead, they have linked findings at the individual level of analysis (for psychology) or the societal level of analysis (for social psychology and anthropology) to the international level of analysis by means of carefully traced causal chains.

Few IR scholars have extended this courtesy to religion. The most-cited text on religion and international affairs, Samuel Huntington's *Clash of Civilizations and the Remaking of World Order,* for example, offers one of the clearest examples of the *broad* approach.[71] Although Huntington's argument is ostensibly about clashes between civilizations, it is, in essence, an argument about conflicts between large religious blocks.[72] Nonetheless, *The Clash of Civilizations* offers no insight into civilizational identity, not to mention religious identity. Relying explicitly on distinctiveness theory, Huntington presents a billiard-ball theory of religious conflict in which all cultural disagreements are zero-sum, all religious blocks in contact are also at war, and all clashes are uniform in kind and degree irrespective of what the particular religions involved happen to be.[73] Religions clash not because of what they are but because of what they are not: a religious identity serves merely as a tag to differentiate one side of a conflict from the other. There is little about Islam or Christianity, for example, that explains conflict between these two civilizations other than the fact that Islam is not Christianity. The mechanisms driving Huntington's global clash of religions are primarily demographic, economic, technological, and political, not religious. The disconnect between the explanatory outcome, at the international level of analysis, and the underlying religious cause does not invalidate Huntington's claim or detract from the value of his analysis, but it does suggests that although Huntington is writing *on* religion, he is not writing *about* religion.

In contrast, Martin Marty and Scott Appleby's "Fundamentalism Project" exemplifies the *deep* approach to religion and international affairs.[74] In over one hundred case studies spread over five volumes, some of the foremost scholars of comparative religion, experts on extremist movements, and country specialists examine the problem of fundamentalism, using either the religious movement or the geographical region as their unit of analysis. The analysis, throughout, is sensitive to religious practices and beliefs, the content of scripture, exegesis, and interpretation, rituals and symbols, religious hierarchies, and leadership structures. Together, these volumes offer the most meticulous and comprehensive survey of fundamentalism available.

The multiple contributions in the Fundamentalism Project do not, however, amount to an international theory of fundamentalism. The disparate chapters remain distinct case studies, and their findings are not generalized beyond the particular region or religion each discusses, despite introductory chapters that emphasize similarities and differences across cases. Because the project offers no generalized system-level explanation, it remains a text in comparative politics, not a contribution to international relations theory, no matter how thorough its coverage of the globe.[75]

The two approaches exemplified by Huntington, on the one hand, and Marty and Appleby, on the other, as well as the vast majority of texts on religion and IR currently available, can be located in a two-dimensional space that represents the relationship between an argument's level of analysis and its methodology. In this two-dimensional space, one axis forms a continuum ranging from the domestic to the international. This represents the level of analysis on which research into religious behavior focuses. The other axis captures the degree to which research engages religion in a materialist or reflectivist manner. A materialist approach rationalizes religion by measuring its empirical effects in some parallel sphere, be it demography, ethnic identity, trade, and so forth, whereas a reflectivist approach attempts to understand religious behavior by describing religious beliefs and practices.

Research in the *broad religion* category falls toward the international end of the level of analysis continuum because it tends to emphasize the effects of religious behavior on the international sphere. At the same time, this research has, so far, tended to restrict its methodology to materialism. These authors are interested in the effects of religion on international conflict and cooperation, diplomacy or globalization, but they have been hesitant to trace these effects to their origins in religion itself.

Research in the *deep religion* category, on the other hand, has adopted a reflectivist stance on religion and politics by using a religious context to understand religious behavior. At the same time, this research has, so far, restricted itself to operating at or below the domestic level of analysis. These authors study a single religious movement or region in depth, often revealing insights regarding ritual practice, the meaning of symbols and language, the implications of theology and exegesis, and the role of beliefs in local political practices, but they seldom if ever extend these conclusions to the international sphere.

What is lacking is an approach that combines an international relations focus with an interpretivist methodology. This is the approach that I call *thick religion*. The term is an obvious nod toward Clifford Geertz's seminal text on the study of culture[76] as well as a useful mnemonic for those aspects of religion in which studies of religion and international relations should be grounded: theology, religious organization (hierarchy), symbol (iconography), ceremony, and belief (or knowledge—hence "t-h-i-c-k"). A *thick religion* analysis should thus be anchored in answers to one or more of the following questions: What are the tenets of this religious movement, and what do its most important texts and scholars propose (theology)? How is the religious movement organized socially and politically, who rules and makes decisions, and how are these individuals chosen and ranked (hierarchy)? How does this religious movement use symbols, myths, images, words, or sounds to convey its ideas, and how do believers treat these icons (iconography)? How do believers act out the theology, hierarchy, and iconography of this religious movement, and what are their rituals, practices, feasts, and commemorations (ceremony)? And finally, what do members of this religious community believe in, and what are the foundations of their faith (belief)? We need to know at least some of this before we can proceed to critically examine the role religion plays in current affairs.

This approach offers not a critique of or substitute for its alternatives but a complementary method that ties a deep understanding of religion to broad-ranging effects at the international level. The challenge facing this approach is thus twofold: it must bridge the levels of analysis separating religion from international relations, and it must adapt a reflectivist methodology, useful for gaining insight into religious beliefs and practices, to a discipline with a materialist orientation.

Given this formidable methodological challenge, the decision by most international relations scholars to opt for a *broad* or a *deep* approach is understandable. Linking an explanation from outside the political realm to an outcome in IR necessitates shifts in both levels of analysis and epistemology. Whereas international relations works its immediate effects at the very top of the level-of-analysis ladder, religion affects the individual and group levels most directly. Scholars can approach either discipline with any of a variety of available epistemologies. Yet if they choose to employ a different epistemology for religion, on the one hand, and IR, on the other, then connecting the various levels of analysis that separate the individual or group level from the international level will also require "translating" one epistemology to the other, possibly using an intermediary epistemology to bridge the two. Connecting religion and IR thus requires ascending the level-of-analysis ladder while presenting arguments with the appropriate methodology for each rung.

Thick religion implies an issue-area approach that focuses the analysis on a particular topic of concern in which religion and international affairs interact. Instead of identifying mere correlations, this method traces a comprehensive logical chain, from the content of specific religious ideas to particular outcomes in international politics, and thus identifies causal or even constitutive relationships between religious ideas and political behavior. *Thick religion* starts its investigation with the religious microfoundations of a political phenomenon and then constructs successive layers of explanation, each more removed from the religious and closer to the political, until it reaches the outcome to be explained.

This approach rests on the assumption that the study of religion and international politics is necessarily an interdisciplinary exercise. Merely viewing religion through a political lens will not do. In addition to politics, we ought also to study religion directly, be it through the sociology of religion, comparative religious analysis, or theology.

Throughout this book, I have tried to exemplify an alternative approach to the study of religion and international relations that is both *deep,* in that it traces the pathways by which sacred space influences international affairs to their origins in the content and meaning of the sacred, and *broad,* in that it offers generalizable implications across states and regions. A *thick religion* approach to the study of religion and international politics requires an understanding of religious detail but also a willingness to generalize from particular religious movements, regions, or instances to arrive at broader conclusions.

I began by examining the religious underpinnings of sacred space, using an interpretivist epistemology to get at the meaning of this space to individuals and groups of believers. I examined the rituals and symbols that accompany and establish these meanings and the religious customs and laws that regulate access to and behavior within these spaces. I then moved to a level of analysis appropriate for the study of a religious movement in its entirety. I relied on an argument from the sociology of religion, Max Weber's account of the institutionalization of charismatic authority, in order to rank sacred places by significance within and across religious traditions.

I then shifted to the political level of analysis, employing a materialist methodology to explain why these beliefs and rules produce an indivisibility problem. By drawing on examples from comparative politics, I showcased the range of contingent conditions under which sacred places become contested, for reasons ranging from military doctrine to real estate. These empirical findings, combined with the indivisibility argument, provide an explanation for the frequency of disputes over sacred space and their resistance to resolution efforts. The institutionalization argument contributes the added ability to predict which sacred places are most likely to experience conflict. I repeated this process in the second half of the book to examine strategies for ameliorating or resolving these disputes.

By cutting a thin slice out of the religion and violence sphere, I have striven to employ a methodology that is equally accessible to students of religion and to students of politics. If successful, this methodology can provide the impetus for investigations into other issue areas at the confluence of religion and international affairs, such as work on religious authority, the link between religious education and conflict, or the study of rituals and war. In the present volume my goal was more modest: an endeavor to investigate the causes and characteristics of conflict over a good valued for its religious attributes, namely, sacred space.

Acknowledgments

Many colleagues and friends helped nurture this project along the path to publication. I am grateful to Lynn Eden, Arnold Eisen, Stephen Krasner, and Scott D. Sagan for their mentoring, wisdom, counsel, and leadership. The faculty, fellows, and graduate students at the Charles and Louise Travers Department of Political Science of the University of California, Berkeley; the Stanford Department of Political Science; and the John M. Olin Institute for Strategic Studies at Harvard University provided support, constructive criticism, and encouragement throughout. I could not have conceived of this project, let alone completed it, without the selfless support of my colleagues at these institutions. My work at Stanford and Harvard was generously funded by the John D. and Catherine T. MacArthur Foundation and the John M. Olin Foundation, respectively.

I had the privilege of completing this manuscript at Stanford's Center for International Security and Cooperation (CISAC), an exceptionally nurturing academic environment that, under the guidance of Scott Sagan and Lynn Eden, has grown to become the greatest research center at which a young security scholar could aspire to work.

My thanks go out to all those who read and commented on my work throughout the years. They include Vinod Aggarwal, Carol Atkinson, Benjamin Beit-Hallahmi, Nora Bensahel, Hamutal Bernstein, Mia Bloom, Risa Brooks, Daniel Byman, David Collier, Ruth Collier, Keith Darden, Laura

Donohue, Alex Downes, Monica Duffy Toft, Brent Durbin, David Edelstein, C. Christine Fair, Tanisha Fazal, James Fearon, Steven Fish, Page Fortna, Taylor Fravel, Roger Friedland, Sumit Ganguly, George Gavrilis, Stacie Goddard, Hein Goemans, Gary Goertz, Arman Gregorian, John Hall, Richard Hecht, Paul Hensel, Ann Hironaka, Jacques Hymans, Michael Innes, Patrick Johnston, Paul Kapur, Michael Kenney, Helen Kinsella, Menachem Klein, Ronald Krebs, Gail Lapidus, Jennifer Lind, Charles Lipson, Paul MacDonald, Dinshaw Mistry, Alex Montgomery, Kevin Narizny, Daniel Nexon, Barry O'Neill, Robert Pape, Seohyun Park, David Patel, Daniel Philpott, Daryl Press, Amnon Ramon, Yitzhak Reiter, Holger Schmidt, Jacob Shapiro, Frank Smith, Lisa Stampnitzky, Scott Thomas, Benjamin Valentino, Leslie Vinjamuri, Steven Weber, Jessica Weeks, and Marie-Joelle Zahar. Since I cannot hope to list all those who contributed to the development of this manuscript in its various reincarnations, I beg forgiveness from those friends whose names I have omitted.

Two anonymous reviewers provided valuable comments on an earlier draft of this manuscript. Andrius Galisanka provided excellent research assistance. Roger Haydon, Susan Barnett, Susan Specter, and Susan Tarcov at Cornell gently shepherded the manuscript through the publication process. Special credit goes to Tonya Putnam for suggesting the book's title.

Finally, I wish to thank my family for their confidence, patience, and love.

Notes

Prologue: "A Terrifying and Fascinating Mystery"

1. Raymond D'Aguilers, *The History of the Franks Who Captured Jerusalem,* trans. John Hugh Hall and Laurita L. Hill (Philadelphia: American Philosophical Society, 1968), 128.

2. Ibid., 127–28. The name "Raymond" in D'Aguilers's account refers to Raymond IV of Toulouse, one of the leaders of the first crusade.

3. F. E. Peters, *Jerusalem: The Holy City in the Eyes of Chroniclers, Visitors, Pilgrims, and Prophets from the Days of Abraham to the Beginnings of Modern Time* (Princeton: Princeton University Press, 1985), 171, citing F. Conybeare, "Antiochus Strategos' Account of the Sack of Jerusalem in A.D. 614," *English Historical Review* 25 (1910): 502–16.

4. Peters, *Jerusalem,* 116, and Eric H. Cline, *Jerusalem Besieged: From Ancient Canaan to Modern Israel* (Ann Arbor: University of Michigan Press, 2004), 126, both citing Josephus Flavius, *The Jewish War* 6.4.6.

5. Exodus 3:2. Here and throughout I use Robert Alter's remarkable new translation of the Torah, which displays a refreshing awareness of the rhyme and rhythm of the Hebrew original. Robert Alter, *The Five Books of Moses: A Translation with Commentary* (New York: W. W. Norton, 2004). The Muslim variant of this exchange appears in verses 20:12 and 79:16 of the Qur'an.

6. Exodus 3:3–5.

7. Daniel Libeskind, master architect for the design of the new World Trade Center, noted that the Temple Mount in Jerusalem offered a precedent for his plan to rebuild Ground Zero in Manhattan because the Mount is "one of the most positive

sites of all, yet a site of total destruction." Jörg Häntzschel, "Ein Zeichen der Hoffnung: Daniel Libeskind über seinen Entwurf für Ground Zero," *Sueddeutsche Zeitung,* February 28, 2003, http://www.gf-kuehn.de/feature/wdrnyczero1.htm (accessed September 5, 2008), my translation.

8. Rudolph Otto, *The Idea of the Holy,* trans. John W. Harvey (Oxford: Oxford University Press, 1923). Mircea Eliade traces the dual meaning of the term to its earliest origins in *Patterns in Comparative Religion,* trans. Rosemary Sheed (New York: New American Library, 1974), 15. For Freud's discussion of the term "taboo" and its twin meanings, both "sacred" and "forbidden," see Sigmund Freud, *Totem and Taboo* (New York: Routledge and Kegan Paul, 1950), 18–25. Freud, in turn, is drawing on Wilhelm Wundt's analysis of the primitive taboo as denoting a demonic being or place, uniting both awe and aversion. See Franz Steiner, *Taboo* (London: Cohen & West, 1956), 128–33.

9. For the term *deinon* and its significance in Sophocles' *Antigone,* see Martin Heidegger, *Introduction to Metaphysics,* trans. Ralph Manheim (New York: Yale University Press, 1959), 144–65. The Arabic *haram* shares its etymology with the Hebrew *herem,* meaning that which is banned to humans and dedicated to God. See John J. Collins, "The Zeal of Phinehas: The Bible and the Legitimation of Violence," *Journal of Biblical Literature* 122, no. 1 (2003): 3–21.

10. Genesis 28:16–17.

1. On Sacred Grounds

1. In the absence of a comprehensive worldwide catalog of conflicts over sacred places it is difficult to estimate precisely what percentage of these sites has undergone conflict. Single-country compilations suggest that this number is quite high: Roger Eaton, for example, has counted 80 incidents of Hindu temple desecration in India by Muslims between 1193 and 1729. The index to the most comprehensive legal history of conflicts over sacred places in Israel and the Palestinian Territories, Shmuel Berkovits's *The Battle for the Holy Places,* lists some 450 sites, including 21 disputed churches, 11 monasteries, 7 mosques, 7 sacred caves, and 33 sacred tombs. The Sacred Lands Film Project lists, as a sample of ongoing disputes over Native American sacred space in the United States, 21 conflicts. This list, which does not claim to be exhaustive, excludes conflicts among Native American tribes over sacred space, for example. See Richard M. Eaton, "Temple Desecration in Pre-modern India," *Frontline* 17, nos. 25 and 26, (December 22, 2000, and January 5, 2000); Shmuel Berkovits, *The Battle for the Holy Places: The Struggle over Jerusalem and the Holy Sites in Israel, Judea, Samaria, and the Gaza District* (OrYehuda, Israel: Hed Arzi, 2000); Sacred Land Film Project, http://www.sacredland.org/endangered.html.

2. For fictitious accounts of the Temple Mount dispute in Jerusalem, for example, see Robert Stone, *Damascus Gate* (Boston: Houghton Mifflin, 1998); Tom Clancy, *Sum of All Fears* (New York: Putnam, 1991); and the award-winning Israeli film *Ha-Hesder* (Time of Favor), Joseph Cedar, 2000. For recent histories of the Jerusalem dispute, see, for example, Karen Armstrong, *Jerusalem: One City, Three Faiths* (New York: Knopf, 1996); Bernard Wasserstein, *Divided Jerusalem: The Struggle for the Holy City*

(London: Profile Books, 2001); Gershom Gorenberg, *The End of Days: Fundamentalism and the Struggle for the Temple Mount* (New York: Free Press, 2000); Nadav Shragai, *Har Ha-merivah: Hama'avak al Har Ha-Bayit: Yehudim u-Muslemim, Dat u-Politikah Meaz 1967* [The Temple Mount Conflict, in Hebrew] (Jerusalem: Keter, 1995); Roger Friedland and Richard Hecht, *To Rule Jerusalem* (Berkeley: University of California Press, 2000).

3. Only a handful of texts on conflicts over sacred space go beyond studies of a single event or repeated disputes over one sacred site. See Eaton, "Temple Desecration"; Roger W. Stump, *Boundaries of Faith: A Geographical Perspective on Religious Fundamentalism* (Lanham, MD: Rowman and Littlefield, 2000); Ifrah Zilberman, *Yerushalayim Ve-Ayodyah: Deyokana Shel Haktsanah Datit-Politit* (Jerusalem: Mekhon Yerushalayim Leheker Yisrael, 1997); and Roger Friedland and Richard Hecht, "The Bodies of Nations: A Comparative Study of Religious Violence in Jerusalem and Ayodhya," *History of Religions* 38, no. 2 (November 1998): 101–49. Eric H. Cline, *Jerusalem Besieged: From Ancient Canaan to Modern Israel* (Ann Arbor: University of Michigan Press, 2004), draws on archaeological and scriptural sources to offer a compelling history of conflict over Jerusalem across history, with a particular focus on the Temple Mount. The classicist F. E. Peter contrasts the urban development of Mecca and Jerusalem without focusing on conflicts over sacred sites in *Jerusalem and Mecca: A Typology of the Holy City in the Near East* (New York: New York University Press, 1986).

4. On indivisibility, see James D. Fearon, "Rationalist Explanations for War," *International Organization* 49, no. 3 (Summer 1995): 379–414; Barbara F. Walter, "The Critical Barrier to Civil War Settlement," *International Organization* 51, no. 3 (Summer 1997): 335–64; Stacie E. Goddard, "Uncommon Ground: Indivisible Territory and the Politics of Legitimacy," *International Organization* 60, no. 1 (Winter 2006): 35–68; Monica Duffy-Toft, "Issue Indivisibility and Time Horizons as Rationalist Explanations for War," *Security Studies* 15, no. 1 (January–March 2006): 34–69; Monica Duffy-Toft, *The Geography of Ethnic Violence: Identity, Interests, and the Indivisibility of Territory* (Princeton: Princeton University Press, 2003); Robert Powell, "War as a Commitment Problem," *International Organization* 60, no. 1 (Winter 2006): 169–203.

5. A cohort of young scholars publishing on religion and international affairs is now striving to overturn this trend. See Daniel Philpott, *Revolutions in Sovereignty: How Ideas Shaped Modern International Relations* (Princeton: Princeton University Press, 2001); Fabio Petito and Pavlos Hatzopoulos, eds., *Religion in International Relations: The Return from Exile* (New York: Palgrave Macmillan, 2003); Jonathan Fox and Shmuel Sandler, *Bringing Religion into International Relations* (New York: Palgrave Macmillan, 2004); Pippa Norris and Ronald Inglehart, *Sacred and Secular: Religion and Politics Worldwide* (Cambridge: Cambridge University Press, 2004); Scott M. Thomas, *The Global Resurgence of Religion and the Transformation of International Relations: The Struggle for the Soul of the Twenty-first Century* (New York: Palgrave Macmillan, 2005); Elizabeth Shakman Hurd, *The Politics of Secularism in International Relations* (Princeton: Princeton University Press, 2007); Daniel Philpott, "Explaining the Political Ambivalence of Religion," *American Political Science Review* 101, no. 3 (August 2007): 505–525; Monica Duffy-Toft, "Getting Religion? The Puzzling Case of Islam and Civil War," *International Security* 31, no. 4 (Spring 2007): 97–131. An evaluation of the state of the art on religion and politics appears in Kenneth D. Wald

and Clyde Wilcox, "Getting Religion: Has Political Science Rediscovered the Faith Factor?" *American Political Science Review* 100, no. 4 (November 2006): 523.

6. For the origins of the constructivist agenda in sociology see Peter L. Berger and Thomas Luckmann, *The Social Construction of Reality: A Treatise in the Sociology of Knowledge* (Garden City, NY: Anchor Books, 1966); Pierre Bourdieu, *Outline of a Theory of Practice* (London: Cambridge University Press, 1977); Anthony Giddens, *The Constitution of Society: Outline of a Theory of Structuration* (Berkeley: University of California Press, 1984); W. F. Sewell, "A Theory of Structure: Duality, Agency, and Transformation," *American Journal of Sociology* 98, no. 1 (July 1992): 1–29; John Meyer, J. Boli, G. Thomas, and F. Ramirez, "World Society and the Nation State," *American Journal of Sociology* 103, no. 1 (1997): 144–81. For the development of this program by the English school of international relations and its American successors, see Hedley Bull, *The Anarchical Society: A Study of Order in World Politics* (London: Macmillan, 1977); Roy E. Jones, "The English School of International Relations: A Case for Closure," *Review of International Studies* 7 (1981): 1–13; Barry Buzan, "From International System to International Society: Structural Realism and Regime Theory Meet the English School," *International Organization* 47, no. 3 (1983): 327–52; Friedrich Kratochwil and John G. Ruggie, "International Organizations: A State of the Art on the Art of the State," *International Organization* 40, no. 4 (1986): 753–75; Alexander Wendt, "The Agent-Structure Problem in International Relations Theory," *International Organization* 41, no. 3 (1987): 335–70; David Dessler, "What's at Stake in the Agent-Structure Debate?" *International Organization* 13, no. 3 (Summer 1989): 441–74.

7. This is elucidated and illustrated in, for example, Theodore F. Abel, "The Operation Called *Verstehen,*" *American Journal of Sociology* 54, no. 1 (November 1948): 211–18; Hedley Bull, "International Theory: The Case for a Classical Approach," *World Politics* 18, no. 3 (April 1966): 361–77; Clifford Geertz, "Thick Description: Toward an Interpretive Theory of Culture," in *The Interpretation of Cultures* (New York: Basic Books, 1973), 3–30; Martin Hollis and Steve Smith, *Explaining and Understanding International Relations* (Oxford: Oxford University Press, 1991); Alex Wendt, "Constructing International Politics," *International Security* 20, no. 1 (Summer 1995): 71–81.

8. Giddens, *Constitution of Society.* For structuration theory in international relations, see Alexander Wendt, "Anarchy Is What States Make of It," *International Organization* 46, no. 2 (Spring 1992): 391–425; and Alexander Wendt, *Social Theory of International Politics* (Cambridge: Cambridge University Press, 1999).

9. See, for example, Martha Finnemore and Kathryn Sikkink, "International Norm Dynamics and Political Change," *International Organization* 52, no. 4 (Autumn 1998): 887–917; Thomas Risse, "'Let's Argue!': Communicative Action in World Politics," *International Organization* 54, no. 1 (2000): 1–39; Jeffrey Checkel, "Ideas, Institutions, and the Gorbachev Foreign Policy Revolution," *World Politics* 45, no. 2 (January 1993): 271–300; Kathryn Sikkink, "The Power of Principled Ideas: Human Rights Policies in the United States and Western Europe," in *Ideas and Foreign Policy: Beliefs, Institutions, and Political Change,* ed. Judith Goldstein and Robert O. Keohane (Ithaca, NY: Cornell University Press, 1993), 139–172; Amy Gurowitz, "Mobilizing International Norms: Domestic Actors, Immigrants, and the Japanese State," *World Politics* 51, no. 3 (1999): 413–45; John S. Duffield, "Political Culture and State Behavior:

Why Germany Confounds Neorealism," *International Organization* 53, no. 4 (1999): 765–803; Ted Hopf, *Social Construction of International Relations: Identities and Foreign Policies, Moscow 1955 and 1999* (Ithaca, NY: Cornell University Press, 2002); Audie Klotz, *Norms in International Relations: The Struggle against Apartheid* (Ithaca, NY: Cornell University Press, 1995).

10. See, for example, Jeffrey T. Checkel, "International Norms and Domestic Politics: Bridging the Rationalist-Constructivist Divide," *European Journal of International Relations* 3, no. 4 (1997): 473–95; Richard K. Herrmann and Vaughn P. Shannon, "Defending International Norms: The Role of Obligation, Material Interest, and Perception in Decision Making," *International Organization* 55, no. 3 (Summer 2001): 621–54; Jeffrey W. Legro, "Whence American Internationalism," *International Organization* 54, no. 2 (Spring 2000): 253–289; Michael Barnett and Raymond Duvall, "Power in International Relations," *International Organization* 59, no. 1 (Winter 2005): 39–75; Peter Katzenstein, ed., *The Culture of National Security* (New York: Columbia University Press, 1996), 153–85.

11. Variants of this argument are debated in Emanuel Adler, "Seizing the Middle Ground: Constructivism in World Politics," *European Journal of International Relations* 3, no. 3 (1997): 319–63; John Gerard Ruggie, "What Makes the World Hang Together? Neo-utilitarianism and the Social Constructivist Challenge," *International Organization* 52, no. 4 (Autumn 1998): 855–85; James Fearon and Alex Wendt, "Rationalism v. Constructivism: A Skeptical View," in *Handbook of International Relations,* ed. Walter Carlsnaes, Thomas Risse, and Beth Simmons (London: Sage, 2002), 52–72; Jeffrey T. Checkel, "The Constructivist Turn in International Relations Theory," *World Politics* 50, no. 2 (1998): 324–48; Ted Hopf, "The Promise of Constructivism in International Relations Theory," *International Security* 23, no. 1 (Summer 1998): 171–200.

12. For critical assessments of the constructivist agenda by international relations scholars, see Michael Desch, "Culture Clash: Assessing the Importance of Ideas in Security Studies," *International Security* 23, no. 1 (Summer 1998): 141–70; John S. Duffield, Richard Price, and Theo Farrell, "Correspondence—Isms and Schisms: Culturalism versus Realism in Security Studies," *International Security* 24, no. 1 (Summer 1999): 156–80; Paul Kowert and Jeffrey Legro, "Norms, Identity, and Their Limits: A Theoretical Reprise," in Katzenstein, *Culture of National Security,* 451–97; Robert Keohane et al., "Forum on Alexander Wendt's *Social Theory of International Politics,*" in *Review of International Studies* 26, no. 1 (January 2000): 123–180.

13. For a critique of the interpretivist approach as overly essentialist and apolitical, see Richard D. Hecht, "The Construction and Management of Sacred Time and Space: *Sabta Nur* in the Church of the Holy Sepulcher," in *NowHere: Space, Time and Modernity,* ed. Roger Friedland and Deirdre Boden (Berkeley: University of California Press, 1994), 221–23; and Friedland and Hecht, "Bodies of Nations," 108–9.

14. Friedland and Hecht, "Bodies of Nations"; and Friedland and Hecht, *To Rule Jerusalem.*

15. See, for example, Douglas Johnston and Cynthia Sampson, eds., *Religion: The Missing Dimension of Statecraft* (New York: Oxford University Press, 1995); Douglas Johnston, ed., *Faith-Based Diplomacy: Trumping Realpolitik* (New York: Oxford University Press, 2003); R. Scott Appleby, *The Ambivalence of the Sacred: Religion, Violence, and Reconciliation* (New York: Rowman & Littlefield, 1999); Marc Gopin, *Holy War, Holy Peace: How Religion Can Bring Peace to the Middle East* (New York:

Oxford University Press, 2002); Marc Gopin, *Between Eden and Armageddon: The Future of World Religions, Violence, and Peacemaking* (New York: Oxford University Press, 2002); David R. Smock, *Interfaith Dialogue and Peacebuilding* (Washington, DC: USIP, 2002); and Mohammad Abu-Nimer, "Conflict Resolution, Culture, and Religion: Toward a Training Model of Interreligious Peacebuilding," *Journal of Peace Research*, 38, no. 6 (November 2001): 685–704.

16. Gerardus Van der Leeuw, *Religion in Essence and Manifestation*, trans. J. E. Turner (Princeton: Princeton University Press, 1986), 393–407.

17. David Chidester and Edward T. Linenthal, eds., *American Sacred Space* (Bloomington: Indiana University Press, 1995), 6 and 18.

18. Jonathan Z. Smith, *Map Is Not Territory* (Chicago: University of Chicago Press, 1978), 291.

19. Chidester and Linenthal, *American Sacred Space*, 17.

20. Friedland and Hecht, "Bodies of Nations," 110–11.

21. Chidester and Linenthal, *American Sacred Space*, 14, my italics.

22. Ibid., 7.

2. What is Sacred Space?

1. For alternative definitions and typologies of sacred sites, see, for example, Yi-Fu Tuan, *Space and Place: The Perspective of Experience* (Minneapolis: University of Minnesota Press, 1977); Seth Kunnin, "Judaism," in *Sacred Place*, ed. Jean Holm and John Bowker (London: Pinter, 1994); and Richard H. Jackson and Roger Henrie, "Perception of Sacred Space," *Journal of Cultural Geography* 3 (1983): 94–107.

2. Emile Durkheim, *The Elementary Forms of the Religious Life*, trans. Joseph Ward Swain (New York: Free Press, 1915).

3. Kenneth Bolle, "Speaking of a Place," in *Myths and Symbols: Studies in Honor of Mircea Eliade*, ed. Joseph M. Kitagawa and Charles Long (Chicago: University of Chicago Press, 1969).

4. Mircea Eliade, *Patterns in Comparative Religion* (New York: New American Library, 1974), 367.

5. For historical and architectural details about these and other sacred sites mentioned in this chapter, I consulted Norbert C. Brockman, *Encyclopedia of Sacred Places* (New York: Oxford University Press, 1997); James Harpur, *The Atlas of Sacred Places* (New York: Henry Holt, 1994); Colin Wilson, *The Atlas of Holy Places and Sacred Sites* (Toronto: Penguin Studio, 1996); John Esposito et al., *Geography of Religion: Where God Lives, Where Pilgrims Walk* (Washington, DC: National Geographic, 2004); Brad Olsen, *Sacred Places, North America: 108 Destinations* (Santa Cruz, CA: CCC Books, 2003); and Martin Gray's *Places of Peace and Power* website at http://www.sacredsites.com/.

6. Nicole Price, "Tourism and the Bighorn Medicine Wheel: How Multiple Use Does Not Work for Sacred Land Sites," in *Sacred Sites, Sacred Places*, ed. David L. Charmichael, Jane Hubert, Brian Reeves, and Audhild Schanche (London: Routledge, 1994).

7. Eliade, *Patterns in Comparative Religion*, 367. See also Alan Morinis, ed., *Sacred Journeys: The Anthropology of Pilgrimage* (New York: Greenwood Press, 1992).

8. Joel P. Brereton, "Sacred Space," in *The Encyclopedia of Religion,* ed. Mircea Eliade (New York: Macmillan, 1987), 12:526–35.

9. Eliade, *Patterns in Comparative Religion,* 231–33, 366–85.

10. Peters emphasizes parallel processes, employing terms like "enshrinement" and "personification." See F. E. Peters, *Jerusalem and Mecca: The Typology of the Holy City in the Near East* (New York: New York University Press, 1986), 5–26.

11. Max Weber, "Bureaucracy and Charisma: A Philosophy of History," "Politics as a Vocation," "The Sociology of Charismatic Authority," and "The Social Psychology of World Religion," in *From Max Weber, Essays in Sociology,* ed. H. H. Gerth and C. Wright Mills (New York: Oxford University Press, 1958).

12. On the relationship between holy places and their urban environments, see Peters, *Jerusalem and Mecca.*

13. Victor Turner and Edith Turner, *Image and Pilgrimage in Christian Culture: Anthropological Perspectives* (New York: Columbia University Press, 1978), 239; Ian Reader, "Japanese Religions," in Holm and Bowker, *Sacred Place,* 187–202.

14. Chris. C. Park, *Sacred Worlds: An Introduction to Geography and Religion* (London: Routledge, 1994), 258–85.

15. Anurandha Roma Choudhury, "Hinduism," in Holm and Bowker, *Sacred Place,* 70.

16. Roger Friedland and Richard Hecht, "The Bodies of Nations: A Comparative Study of Religious Violence in Jerusalem and Ayodhya," *History of Religions* 38, no. 2 (November 1998): 106–7. The authors suggest that narratives linking Ayodhya to creation and to Manu, the first man, are the product of recent political events that enhanced the salience of the city for Muslims and Hindus.

17. Park, *Sacred Worlds,* 283, citing T. G. Jordan and L. Rowntree, *The Human Mosaic: A Thematic Introduction to Cultural Geography* (New York: Harper and Row, 1990).

18. Mishnah, Tractate Kelim, 1:6–9.

19. Abu Hamid Muhammad al-Ghazali, *Ihya 'Ulum al-Din* (The Revival of the Religious Sciences), 1.7.1: "The Excellence of Medina the Noble over Other Lands."

20. Douglas Davies, "Christianity," in Holm and Bowker, *Sacred Place,* 45.

21. On Muslim rites of purity, see A. Kevin Reinhart, "Impurity/No Danger," *History of Religions* 30, no. 1 (August 1990): 1–24.

22. Arthur Charles James, *Taboo among the Ancient Hebrews: A Study of Certain Phases of Early Hebrew Legislation* (Philadelphia: University of Pennsylvania Press, 1925), 41.

23. Friedland and Hecht, "Bodies of Nations."

24. Ibid., 112.

3. The Indivisibility Problem

1. Steven J. Brams and Alan D. Taylor, *From Cake Cutting to Dispute Resolution* (Cambridge: Cambridge University Press, 2002).

2. James D. Fearon, "Rationalist Explanations for War," *International Organization* 49, no. 3 (Summer 1995): 379–414.

3. Ibid., 381–82 and 408.

4. Barbara F. Walter, "The Critical Barrier to Civil War Settlement," *International Organization* 51, no. 3 (Summer 1997): 335–64; Barbara F. Walter, "Explaining the Intractability of Territorial Conflict," *International Studies* Review 5, no. 4 (December 2003): 137–53; Monica Duffy-Toft, *The Geography of Ethnic Violence: Identity, Interests, and the Indivisibility of Territory* (Princeton: Princeton University Press, 2003); Monica Duffy-Toft, "Issue Indivisibility and Time Horizons as Rationalist Explanations for War," *Security Studies* 15, no. 1 (January–March 2006): 34–69.

5. Stacie E. Goddard, "Uncommon Ground: Indivisible Territory and the Politics of Legitimacy," *International Organization* 60, no. 1 (Winter 2006): 35–68.

6. The expression "ideas all the way down" is Alex Wendt's, paraphrasing an expression in Clifford Geertz, "Thick Description: Toward an Interpretive Theory of Culture," in *The Interpretation of Cultures* (New York: Basic Books, 1973). Wendt uses it to distinguish the constructivist research program in international relations, in which ideas are layered over material reality, from postmodern approaches in which ideas are layered on other ideas "all the way down." Alexander Wendt, *Social Theory of International Politics* (Cambridge: Cambridge University Press, 1999).

7. On social facts and the social construction of reality, see Pierre Bourdieu, *Outline of a Theory of Practice* (London: Cambridge University Press, 1977); Peter L. Berger and Thomas Luckmann, *The Social Construction of Reality: A Treatise in the Sociology of Knowledge* (Garden City, NY: Anchor Books, 1966); John Searle, *The Construction of Social Reality* (New York: Free Press, 1995); and Ian Hacking, *The Social Construction of What?* (Cambridge: Harvard University Press, 2000).

8. Barry O'Neill, "Risk Aversion in International Relations Theory," *International Studies Quarterly* 45, no. 4 (2001): 617–40.

9. Thomas L. Brewer, "Issue and Context Variations in Foreign Policy: Effects on American Elite Behavior," *Journal of Conflict Resolution* 17, no. 1 (March 1973): 89–114; Richard W. Mansbach and John A. Vasquez, *In Search of Theory* (New York: Columbia University Press, 1981); Richard W. Mansbach and John A. Vasquez, "The Effect of Actor and Issue Classifications on the Analysis of Global Conflict-Cooperation," *Journal of Politics* 43, no. 3 (August 1981): 861–74; James N. Rosenau, "Pre-theories and Theories of Foreign Policy," in *Approaches to Comparative and International Politics,* ed. Barry R. Farrell (Evanston, IL: Northwestern University Press, 1966); James N. Rosenau, "Foreign Policy as an Issue-Area," in *Domestic Sources of Foreign Policy,* ed. James N. Rosenau (New York: Free Press, 1967); John A. Vasquez, "The Tangibility of Issues and Global Conflict: A Test of Rosenau's Issue Area Typology," *Journal of Peace Research* 20, no. 2 (1983): 179–92.

10. John A. Vasquez and Richard W. Mansbach, "The Role of Issues in Global Cooperation and Conflict," *British Journal of Political Science* 14 (September 1984): 411–33; John A. Vasquez, *The War Puzzle* (Cambridge: Cambridge University Press, 1993).

11. Roy Licklider, "How Civil Wars End: Questions and Methods," in *Stop the Killing: How Civil Wars End,* ed. Roy Licklider (New York: New York University Press, 1993).

12. Fred Ikle, *Every War Must End* (New York: Columbia University Press, 1971), 95.

13. Paul R. Pillar, *Negotiating Peace: War Termination as a Bargaining Process* (Princeton: Princeton University Press, 1983), 24.

14. Cecilia Albin, "Negotiating Indivisible Goods: The Case of Jerusalem," *Jerusalem Journal of International Relations* 13, no. 1 (1991): 45–76; Ian Lustick, "Reinventing Jerusalem," *Foreign Policy* 93 (Winter 1993–94): 41–59.

15. Brams and Taylor, *From Cake Cutting,* 51. See ibid., note 1, for an exhaustive list of references within the game theory literature.

16. For a discussion of indivisible cultural resources and religious conflict that equates indivisibility with uniqueness, see Fred Kniss, "Ideas and Symbols as Resources in Intrareligious Conflict: The Case of American Mennonites," *Sociology of Religion* 57, no. 1 (Spring 1996): 8–9. The prohibition on measuring commitments to sacred values along instrumental lines is analyzed in Jeremy Ginges, Scott Atran, Douglas Medin, and Khalil Shikaki, "Sacred Bounds on Rational Resolution of Violent Political Conflict," *Proceedings of the National Academy of Sciences of the United States* 104, no. 18 (May 2007): 7357–60. Alan Page Fiske and Phillip E. Tetlock refer to unique relationships that cannot be exchanged contingently or proportionately as "communal sharing relationships," without reference to indivisibility. "Taboo Trade-Offs: Reactions to Transactions That Transgress Spheres of Justice," *Political Psychology* 18, no. 2 (June 1997): 258 and 267.

17. King James Bible, 1 Kings 3:26.

18. For background information, I have relied on the resources listed in chapter 2, note 5, above, as well as Percy Brown, *Indian Architecture: Buddhist and Hindu Periods* (Bombay: D. B. Taraporevala Sons, 1942); George Michell, *The Hindu Temple: An Introduction to Its Meaning and Forms* (London: Elek Books, 1977); Titus Burckhardt, *Art of Islam: Meaning and Message* (London: World of Islam Festival, 1976); Seyyed Hossein Nasr, *Traditional Islam in the Modern World* (London: KPI, 1987). Jean Holm and John Bowker, eds., *Sacred Place* (London: Pinter, 1994), offer an excellent resource on sacred sites across religious traditions.

19. Anurandha Roma Choudhury, "Hinduism," in Holm and Bowker, *Sacred Place,* 78–80; Chris C. Park, *Sacred Worlds: An Introduction to Geography and Religion* (London: Routledge, 1994), 204–5.

20. Not coincidentally, the same term, *Meru,* is used in Hinduism to describe the earth's axis of rotation, the vertical axis of a temple, and the mythical mountain at the center of the universe. Choudhury, "Hinduism," 79 and 86.

21. Emile Durkheim, *The Elementary Forms of the Religious Life,* trans. Joseph Ward Swain (New York: Free Press, 1915), 55.

22. Choudhury, "Hinduism," 68; and Park, *Sacred Worlds,* 246, citing E. Issac, "Mythical Geography," *Geographical Review* 57 (1967): 123–25, and R. Christinger, "Notions préliminaires d'une géographie mythique," *Le Globe* 105 (1965).

23. William Robertson Smith, *Religion of the Semites,* ed. J. S. Black (London: Adam & Charles Black, 1894), 145.

24. In Numbers 16, for example, three Israelites and their families are swallowed up by the earth for attempting to perform the priestly functions in the sanctuary. Two hundred fifty of their followers are consumed by a divine fire. In 2 Maccabees 3, Heliodorus, a gentile, is nearly trampled to death by a divine apparition of a horseman, while attempting to enter and loot the Temple treasury. In Acts 21: 17–29, Paul is accused of having violated the sanctity of the Temple by entering it in the company of a gentile.

25. Leviticus 10:9. Similar warnings appear in Exodus 28:43, Exodus 30:17–21 and elsewhere.

26. Benjamin Mazar, *The Mountain of the Lord* (Garden City, NY: Doubleday, 1975), 113–14.

27. Martin Boord, "Buddhism," in Holm and Bowker, *Sacred Place,* 10.

28. *Gopurams* (cow gates) provide a similar function in Hindu temples.

29. Both the waterfall and the mountain example appear in Ian Reader, "Japanese Religions," in Holm and Bowker, *Sacred Place,* 190–91.

30. Joel P. Brereton, "Sacred Space," in *The Encyclopedia of Religion,* ed. Mircea Eliade (New York: Macmillan, 1987), 12:526.

31. Douglas Davies, "Christianity," in Holm and Bowker, *Sacred Place,* 59.

32. Mary Curtius, "Holy Site Paramount among Obstacles to Mideast Peace," *Los Angeles Times,* September 5, 2000.

4. Conflict over Sacred Places

1. Nathan Jeffay, "Lag b'Omer Unity Shattered by Battle for Grave of Kabbalah Rabbi Bar Yohai," *Ha'aretz,* May 18, 2008.

2. Richard N. Ostling and Joan K. Ostling, *Mormon America* (New York: Harper-Collins, 2000), xviii and 334–35.

3. James Walker, *Watchman Expositor* 7, no. 2 (1990).

4. For syncretism, see Charles Stewart and Rosalind Shaw, eds., *Syncretism/Anti-Syncretism* (London: Routledge, 1994); Jerald D. Gort, Hendrik M. Vroom, Rein Fernhout, and Anton Wessels, eds., *Dialogue and Syncretism: An Interdisciplinary Approach* (Grand Rapids, MI: William B. Eerdmans, 1989).

5. Annabel Jane Wharton uses the term to describe the al-Aqsa Mosque in Jerusalem in *Selling Jerusalem: Relics, Replicas, Theme Parks* (Chicago: University of Chicago Press, 2006), 56. Bernard Wasserstein characterizes the entire Temple Mount as "a kind of religious palimpsest." *Divided Jerusalem: The Struggle for the Holy City* (London: Profile Books, 2001), 317.

6. Both claims are made by Eric H. Cline, *Jerusalem Besieged: From Ancient Canaan to Modern Israel* (Ann Arbor: University of Michigan Press, 2004), 32 and 2, respectively. For a listing of these conflicts, see ibid., 8–10.

7. Martin Lev, *The Traveler's Key to Jerusalem: A Guide to the Sacred Places of Jerusalem* (New York: Knopf, 1989); F. E. Peters, *Jerusalem: The Holy City in the Eyes of Chroniclers, Visitors, Pilgrims, and Prophets from the Days of Abraham to the Beginnings of Modern Time* (Princeton: Princeton University Press, 1985), 5–26; Karen Armstrong, *Jerusalem: One City, Three Faiths* (New York: Knopf, 1996).

8. Richard M. Eaton, "Temple Desecration in Pre-modern India," *Frontline* 17, nos. 25 and 26 (December 22, 2000, and January 5, 2000); "VHP Body Threatens Stir over Prayer Ban at Mosque," *Hindustan Times,* December 14, 2000; "Ominous Rumblings," *Hindu,* November 17, 2000; and "VHP Bid for Puja in Delhi Mosque," *Statesman,* November 14, 2000.

9. S. Guhan, "Dark Forebodings," in *Ayodhya and the Future of India,* ed. Jitendra Bajaj (Madras, India: Center for Policy Studies, 1993), 78–79; K. N. Panikkar, "A Historical Overview," in *Anatomy of a Confrontation: The Rise of Communal Politics in India,* ed. Sarvepalli Gopal (London: Zed Books, 1991).

10. For the case of Sun Dance lodges in Wyoming, see Ake Hultkrantz, "Pagan and Christian Elements in the Religious Syncretism among the Shoshoni Indians of Wyoming," in *Syncretism,* ed. Sven S. Hartman (Stockholm: Almquist & Wiksel, 1969). For Shi'ite-Zoroastrian shrines, see Michael J. Fischer, "Sacred Circles: Iranian (Zoroastrian and Shi'ite Muslim) Feasting and Pilgrimage Circuits," in *Sacred Places and Profane Space,* ed. Jamie Scott and Paul Simpson-Housley (New York: Greenwood Press, 1991). Other cases are listed in Chris C. Park, *Sacred Worlds: An Introduction to Geography and Religion* (London: Routledge, 1994), 252, and L. Grinsell, "The Christianization of Prehistoric and Other Pagan Sites," *Landscape History* 8 (1986): 27–37.

11. Cline, *Jerusalem Besieged,* 163, citing Meir Ben-Dov, *In the Shadow of the Temple: The Discovery of Ancient Jerusalem* (New York: Harper and Row, 1982), 241.

12. Eaton, "Temple Desecration."

13. Robert Franklin and Pamela Bunte, "When Sacred Land Is Sacred to Three Tribes: San Juan Paiute Sacred Sites and the Hopi-Navajo-Paiute Suit to Partition the Arizona Navajo Reservation," in *Sacred Sites, Sacred Places,* ed. David Carmichael, Jane Hulbert, Brian Reeves, and Audhikd Schanche (London: Routledge, 1994), 253.

14. Ibid., citing A. Frigout, "Hopi Ceremonial Organization," in *Southwest,* ed. A. Ortiz, in general *Handbook of North American Indians,* vol.9, ed. W. G. Sturtevant (Washington, DC: Smithsonian Institution, 1979), 564–76. See also Anthony Ramirez, "Die like an Eagle: Indian Rights versus a National Sanctuary," *New York Times,* November 19, 2000; Ted Williams, "Eagles for the Gods," *Audubon,* March 2001, 32–39.

15. "Police Fire Tear Gas at Ultra-Orthodox Jewish Protesters," *Toronto Star,* January 4, 1993; Dina Shiloh, "Bones of Contention," *Jerusalem Post,* July 25, 1997; Rebecca Trounson, "Science, Religion Clash in Debate over Graves," *Los Angeles Times,* July 11, 1998; Laura King, "Jerusalem Tomb Dig Divides Israel; Excavations Seen as Affront to Jewish Dead," *Toronto Star,* August 9, 1998.

16. Matti Friedman, "Jerusalem Tolerance Museum Sparks Fight," Associated Press, September 23, 2008.

17. "Hawaiians Protect Sacred Sites," *Maui News,* January 1, 1996.

18. Carmichael, Hulbert, Reeves, and Schanche, *Sacred Sites.*

19. Brian Reeves and Margaret Kennedy, eds., *Kunaitupii: Coming Together on Native Sacred Sites* (Calgary, Alberta, Canada: Archaeological Society of Alberta, 1993); Ron E. Hassner, "Native American Sacred Grounds," in *Encyclopedia of American Religion and Politics,* ed. Paul A. Djupe and Laura R. Olson (New York: Facts on File, 2003), 399–400.

20. "Uluru's Unlucky Spell on Tourists," *CNN World News,* March 7, 2003.

21. Russell Means, *Where White Men Fear to Tread: The Autobiography of Russell Means* (New York: St. Martin's Press, 1996), 182–86.

22. Yitzhak Nakash, *The Shi'ites of Iraq* (Princeton: Princeton University Press, 1994), 279.

23. Ibid. Also Douglas Jehl, "From Southern Iraq, Hints of a New Wave of Sectarian Unrest," *New York Times,* October 3, 1999; Liz Thurgood, "Saddam Drive on Shiite Holy Cities," *Guardian,* July 23, 1991; Ed Vulliamy, "Blood and Hatred Stain Shrines at Iraq's Holy Places," *Guardian,* May 1, 1991.

24. John F. Burns, "U.S. Seeks Arrest of Shiite Cleric," *New York Times,* April 6, 2004, A1; Alex Berenson and John F. Burns, "Eight-Day Battle for Najaf: From Attack to Stalemate," *New York Times,* August 18, 2004, A1; Sabrina Tavernise, "Cleric Keeps

Grip on Najaf Shrine, Even While Saying He'll Yield It," *New York Times,* August 22, 2004, A4.

25. Dexter Filkins and Robert F. Worth, "U.S. Troops Set for Final Attack on Fal-luja Force," *New York Times,* November 13, 2004, A1; Thom Shanker and Eric Schmitt, "Falluja Data Said to Pressure Guerrillas," *New York Times,* December 3, 2004, A12. For the report, see http://www.defenselink.mil/news/Dec2004/d20041203entire.ppt; Robert F. Worth, "Marines Find Vast Arms Cache in Falluja Leader's Mosque," *New York Times,* November 25, 2004, A22.

26. Ron E. Hassner, "Fighting the Insurgency on Sacred Ground," *Washington Quarterly* 29, no. 2 (Spring 2006): 149–66.

27. These cases are analyzed in depth in C. Christine Fair and Sumit Ganguly, eds., *Treading on Hallowed Ground: Counterinsurgency Operations in Sacred Spaces* (New York: Oxford University Press, 2008). For the Kashmiri, Palestinian and Punjabi cases, see Wajahat Habibullah, "Siege: Hazratbal, Kashmir, 1993," *India Review* 1, no. 3 (July 2002): 73–98; Victoria Schofield, *Kashmir in the Crossfire* (London: I. B. Tauris, 1996), 258–59; Sumit Ganguly, *The Crisis in Kashmir: Portents of War, Hopes of Peace* (Princeton: Woodrow Wilson Center Press, 1997), 119–20; Joshua Hammer, *A Season in Bethlehem: Unholy War in a Sacred Place* (New York: Free Press, 2003); Mark Tully and Satish Jacob, *Amritsar: Mrs. Gandhi's Last Battle* (London: Jonathan Cape, 1985).

28. Eaton, "Temple Desecration."

29. John Swain, "Saddam Stamps on Embers of Southern Revolt," *Sunday Times,* November 29, 1998; Doug Struck, "Tourists in Iraq See Ample Signs of Carnage, Portraits of Hussein," *Phoenix Gazette,* February 17, 1995; John Lancaster, "Iraq Turns Shiite South into Tourist Showcase; Islamic Shrines in Once Rebellious Area Have Been Polished Up as Signs of Saddam's Success," *Washington Post,* February 16, 1995; Joyce N. Wiley, *The Islamic Movement of Iraqi Shi'as* (Boulder, CO: Lynne Rienner, 1992); Daniel Williams, "Cleric's Killing Arouses Shiites; Iraqi Officials Nervous about Turmoil in South," *Washington Post,* March 16, 1999; John Daniszewski, "Iraqis Said to Riot after Cleric's Slaying," *Los Angeles Times,* February 21, 1999; Anthony Shadid, "Fear and Loathing in Southern Iraq," *Ottawa Citizen,* December 11, 1998.

30. "Violence Flares in Bosnia Ceremony," *CNN International,* June 18, 2001, at www.cnn.com/WORLD/.

31. Shimon Samuels, ed., "Worldwide Antisemitic Hate Crimes and Major Hate Incidents" (Los Angeles: Simon Wiesenthal Center, November 3, 2000); David Usborne, "Attacks on Jews Worldwide 'Worst Since Nazi Germany,'" *Independent,* October 28, 2000, 16; Chani Cohen, "UN Must Condemn Wave of Antisemitic Violence," *Jerusalem Post,* October 20, 2000, 5A; Yair Sheleg, "A Rise in the Extent of Anti-Semitism in 2001," *Ha'aretz,* April 9, 2002, 1.

32. Martin Boord, "Buddhism," in *Sacred Place,* ed. Jean Holm and John Bowker (London: Pinter, 1994), 15.

33. John F. Burns, "A Region Inflamed: Violence; At Least 143 Die in Attacks at Two Sacred Sites in Iraq," *New York Times,* March 3, 2004, A1; Dexter Filkins and Eric Schmitt, "A Region Inflamed: Security; Other Attacks Averted in Iraq, a General Says," *New York Times,* March 4, 2004, A1; Vali Nasr, "Iraq's Real Holy War," *New York Times,* March 6, 2004, A15.

34. "Iraq on the Brink," *New York Times,* March 1, 2006, A18; Volkhard Windfuhr and Bernhard Zand, "Religious Strife Is Pushing Iraq toward Civil War," *New York*

Times, March 6, 2006, citing *Der Spiegel,* trans. Christopher Sultan; Jeffrey Gettleman, "Eighty-five Bodies Found in Baghdad in Sectarian Strife," *New York Times,* March 15, 2006, A1; "Excerpts from the President's News Conference on the Iraq War and Iran," *New York Times,* March 22, 2006, A10.

35. Leonard Hammer, Yitzchak Reiter, and Marshall Breger, eds., *Holy Places in the Israeli-Palestinian Conflict: Confrontation and Co-Existence* (London: Routledge, 2009).

36. Anne Bigelow, "Practicing Pluralism in Malerkotla, Punjab," *Items & Issues* 3, nos. 1–2 (Spring 2002): 10. See also Anne Bigelow, "Sharing Saints, Shrines, and Stories: Practicing Pluralism in North India" (PhD diss., University of California, Santa Barbara, 2004). See also Park, *Sacred Worlds,* 261, citing S. M. Bhardwaj, "Single Religious Shrines, Multiregion Pilgrimages," *National Geographical Journal of India* 33 (1987); and A. Sievers, "The Significance of Pilgrimage Tourism in Sri Lanka (Ceylon)," *National Geographic Journal of India* 33 (1987): 430–47.

37. Elizabeth Key Fowden, "Sharing Holy Places," *Common Knowledge* 8, no. 1 (2002): 146.

38. See for example Samuel Huntington, *The Clash of Civilizations and the Remaking of World Order* (New York: Simon and Schuster, 1996); Mark Juergensmeyer, *Terror in the Mind of God: The Global Rise of Religious Violence* (Berkeley: University of California Press, 2000); John L. Esposito, *Unholy War: Terror in the Name of Islam* (New York: Oxford University Press, 2002); Bruce Lincoln, *Holy Terrors: Thinking about Religion after September 11* (Chicago: University of Chicago Press, 2003); Martin E. Marty and R. Scott Appleby, eds., *The Fundamentalism Project,* vols. 1–5 (Chicago: University of Chicago Press), 1993–2004.

39. Such is the case with Sri Pada (Adam's Peak) in Sri Lanka. It is a folk site worshiped by Buddhists, Hindus, Muslims, and Christians, but each group associates it with a different figure, be it Buddha, Adam, or the Apostle Thomas. Park, *Sacred Worlds,* 261. For Jewish-Muslim cases in which parties disagree about the identity of a saint revered at a given site, see Harvey E. Goldberg, "Gravesites and Memorials of Libyan Jews," in *Grasping Land: Space and Place in Contemporary Israeli Discourse and Experience,* ed. Eyal Ben Ari and Yoram Bilu (Albany: State University of New York Press, 1997), 48, citing P. Shinar, "La recherche relative aux rapports Judéo-Musulmans dans le Maghreb contemporain," in *Les relations entre Juifs et Musulmans en Afrique du Nord, XIXe–XXe siecles,* ed. J. L. Miege (Paris: Centre National de la Recherche Scientifique, 1980).

5. Mismanaging Conflicts over Sacred Places

1. Samuel Huntington, *The Clash of Civilizations and the Remaking of World Order* (New York: Simon and Schuster, 1996); and Samuel Huntington, "The Clash of Civilizations?" *Foreign Affairs* 72 (Summer 1993): 186–94.

2. Richard M. Eaton, "Temple Desecration in Pre-modern India," *Frontline* 17, nos. 25 and 26 (December 22, 2000, and January 5, 2000); "VHP Body Threatens Stir over Prayer Ban at Mosque," *Hindustan Times,* December 14, 2000, online at www.hindustantimes.com/nonfram/151200/detCIT12.asp; "Ominous Rumblings," *Hindu,*

November 17, 2000; and "VHP Bid for Puja in Delhi Mosque," *Statesman,* November 14, 2000.

3. Moshe Dayan, *The Story of My Life* (New York: William Morrow, 1976), 293.

4. Ibid., 390–92.

5. Uzi Narkiss, *The Liberation of Jerusalem: The Battle of 1967* (London: Valentine, Mitchell, 1983), 231.

6. *New York Times,* August 10, 16, and 17, 1975.

7. *New York Times,* October 3, 4, 5, 7, 10, 16, and 18, 1976.

8. *New York Times,* October 4, 1975; October 21, 1976.

9. *New York Times,* October 9, 1979.

10. W. Claiborne, "Five Israelis Die in Arab Raid, Worst Ever in West Bank," *Washington Post,* May 3, 1980.

11. A. Rabinovich, "Muslims and Jews Share Tomb of the Patriarchs," *Straits Times,* October 10, 1992.

12. D. Fisher, "Disputed Tomb of the Patriarchs," *Los Angeles Times,* March 29, 1986.

13. W. Ries, "Palestinian Protests Erupt after Muslim Prayers," UPI, February 19, 1988; and "Hebron Incidents," *Jerusalem Post,* December 31, 1989.

14. See, for example, "Israeli Soldier Kills Mom of 10 Who Stabbed His Partner," *Toronto Star,* September 15, 1986; B. Hepburn, "Israeli Settler Kills Axe Attacker—West Bank Incident Leaves Palestinian Dead," *Toronto Star,* November 15, 1993; and "Jewish Settler Killed on Way to West Bank Holy Site," *Los Angeles Times,* May 29, 1993.

15. "Gunman Slays 20 at Site of Mosque," *New York Times,* February 25, 1994; "Mosque Massacre Incites Arab Rioting," *New York Times,* February 26, 1994; and B. Hutman and A. Pinkas, "Wave of Riots after Hebron Massacre; Kiryat Arba Doctor Slays 39; Over 29 Palestinians Die in Aftermath," *Jerusalem Post,* February 27, 1994.

16. Richard D. Hecht, "The Construction and Management of Sacred Time and Space: *Sabta Nur* in the Church of the Holy Sepulcher," in *NowHere: Space, Time, and Modernity,* ed. Roger Friedland and Deirdre Boden (Berkeley: University of California Press, 1994), 189, citing Diane Herbert, "The Effect of the Status Quo of 1852 on the Christian Communities Inhabiting the Church of the Holy Sepulcher in Jerusalem" (M.A. thesis, University of California, Santa Barbara, 1985), 21.

17. Raymond Cohen, *Saving the Holy Sepulcher: How Rival Christians Came Together to Rescue Their Holiest Shrine* (Oxford: Oxford University Press, 2008), 8–9, 17–19, and 168; and Raymond Cohen, "No Exit from Calvary: Israel's Stewardship of the Church of the Holy Sepulcher," paper presented at the annual conference of the Association of Israel Studies, Ra'anana, Israel, June 11–13, 2007.

18. Cohen, *Saving the Holy Sepulcher,* 28–34 and throughout.

19. Shmuel Berkovits, *The Battle for the Holy Places: The Struggle over Jerusalem and the Holy Sites in Israel, Judea, Samaria, and the Gaza District* (OrYehuda, Israel: Hed Arzi, 2000), 235–36; Cohen, *Saving the Holy Sepulcher,* 214.

20. Cohen, *Saving the Holy Sepulcher,* p.212.

21. Hecht, "Construction and Management," 189.

22. Ibid., 236.

23. Cohen, *Saving the Holy Sepulcher.*

24. Ibid.

25. Berkovits, *Battle for the Holy Places,* 278–80; Cohen, *Saving the Holy Sepulcher,* 194–200. Cohen suspects that the chapel doors were locked by Israeli policemen to curry favor with the Ethiopian government.

26. Cohen, *Saving the Holy Sepulcher,* 165, citing David Holden, "The Unholy Row over the Tomb of Christ," *Saturday Evening Post,* April 9, 1966, 86.

27. K. N. Panikkar, "A Historical Overview," in *Anatomy of a Confrontation: The Rise of Communal Politics in India,* ed. Sarvepalli Gopal (London: Zed Books, 1991); Sita Ram Goel, *Hindu Temples: What Happened to Them* (New Delhi: Voice of India, 1998); Ifrah Zilberman, *Yerushalayim ve-Ayodyah: Deyokana shel Haktsanah Datit-Politit* (Jerusalem: Mekhon Yerushalayim Leheker Yisrael, 1997); and Roger Friedland and Richard Hecht, "The Bodies of Nations: A Comparative Study of Religious Violence in Jerusalem and Ayodhya," *History of Religions* 38, no. 2 (November 1998): 101–49.

28. Paola Bacchetta, "Sacred Space and Conflict in India: The Babri Masjid Affair," *Growth and Change* 31, no. 2 (Spring 2000): 255–84; Ashgar Ali Engineer, ed., *The Babri-Masjid Ramjanmabhoomi Controversy* (Delhi: Ajanta, 1990); and Peter van der Veer, " 'The Gods Must be Liberated!' A Hindu Liberation Movement in Ayodhya," *Modern Asian Studies* 21, no. 2 (1987): 283–301.

29. Narain Harsh, *The Ayodhya Temple Mosque Dispute: Focus on Muslim Sources* (Delhi: Penman, 1993).

30. Bacchetta, "Sacred Space," 265; Jitendra Bajaj, ed., *Ayodhya and the Future of India* (Madras; Center for Policy Studies, 1993).

31. Friedland and Hecht, "Bodies of Nations," 144.

32. Hans Bakker, "Ayodhya: A Hindu Jerusalem: An Investigation of 'Holy War' as a Religious Idea in the Light of Communal Unrest in India," *Numen* 38, fasc. 1 (June 1991): 99.

33. Friedland and Hecht, "Bodies of Nations," 138, citing Christophe Jaffrelot, *The Hindu Nationalist Movement in India* (New York: Columbia University Press, 1996), 398–401.

34. Friedland and Hecht, "Bodies of Nations," 102.

35. Ashis Nandy S. Trivedy, S. Mayaram, and A. Yagnik, *Creating a Nationality: The Ramjanmabhumi Movement and the Fear of the Self* (Delhi: Oxford University Press, 1995). Understandably, counts of the participants in various stages of the event differ. Friedland and Hecht, "Bodies of Nations," relying on *New York Times* reports of the Ayodhya crisis, count 300,000 *kar sevaks* in Ayodhya at the time, of which 40,000 approached the mosque but only 1,200 actually participated in the demolition.

36. Bacchetta, "Sacred Space," 257.

37. Friedland and Hecht, "Bodies of Nations," 103.

38. Debasish Mukherji and Ajay Upreti, "Making of the Mandir," *Week* (India), June 7, 1998.

39. Zilberman, *Yerushalayim ve-Ayodyah;* Friedland and Hecht, "Bodies of Nations."

40. I use "Camp David" as a shorthand for the Israeli-Palestinian negotiations that began under U.S. auspices at Camp David, Maryland, in July 2000 and ended at Taba, Egypt, in January 2001, including offers made in December 2000. I use the term "Temple Mount" to refer to the site known to Jews as "Har Habayit" and to Muslims

as "al Haram al Sharif" because this is the most common designation of the site in English.

41. Gilad Sher, *Just beyond Reach: The Israeli-Palestinian Peace Negotiations, 1999–2001* (Tel Aviv: Miskal-Yedioth Ahronoth Books and Chemed Books, 2001), 197 and 406. Alternative explanations for the failure of the negotiations are offered by, for example, Hussein Agha and Robert Malley, "Camp David: The Tragedy of Errors," *New York Review of Books* 48, no. 13 (August 9, 2001), reprinted in *Journal of Palestine Studies* 31, no. 1 (Autumn 2001): 62–75; Deborah Sontag, "Quest for Middle East Peace: How and Why It Failed," *New York Times,* July 26, 2001, reprinted in *Journal of Palestine Studies* 31, no. 1 (Autumn 2001): 75–85; and Charles Enderlin, *Shattered Dreams: The Failure of the Peace Process in the Middle East, 1995–2002,* trans. Susan Fairfield (New York: Other Press, 2003).

42. Sher, *Just beyond Reach,* 181, my translation.

43. Menahem Klein, *The Jerusalem Problem: The Struggle for Permanent Status,* trans. Haim Watzman (Gainesville: University Press of Florida, 2003), 80, quoting *Ha'aretz,* January 25, 2001.

44. Sher, *Just beyond Reach,* 172; Enderlin, *Shattered Dreams,* 206 and 208.

45. Bernard Wasserstein, *Divided Jerusalem: The Struggle for the Holy City* (New Haven: Yale University Press, 2001), 343, citing *Jerusalem Post,* August 13, 2000. The leaders of Iran, Saudi Arabia, and Syria exerted similar pressure on Arafat not to compromise over Jerusalem.

46. Enderlin, *Shattered Dreams,* 266.

47. Ibid., 253.

48. Mary Curtius, "Holy Site Paramount among Obstacles to Mideast Peace; Religion: Much of the Israeli-Palestinian Dispute Comes Down to a 36-Acre Compound in Jerusalem," *Los Angeles Times,* September 5, 2000. See also Sher, *Just beyond Reach,* 266; Klein, *Jerusalem Problem,* 76; Enderlin, *Shattered Dreams,* 205.

49. Sher, *Just beyond Reach,* 209.

50. Ibid., 233.

51. Shimon Shifer and Nahum Barnea, "It All Collapsed over Jerusalem" (in Hebrew), *Yedioth Aharonot,* July 26, 2000, 4.

52. Klein, *Jerusalem Problem,* 165.

53. Aryeh Dayan, "Barak Began Referring to the Holy of Holies," *Ha'aretz,* December 10, 2002.

54. Menahem Klein, *Shattering a Taboo: The Contacts towards a Permanent Status Agreement in Jerusalem, 1994–2001* (Jerusalem: Jerusalem Institute for Israel Studies, 2001), 20–21, my translation.

55. Sher, *Just beyond Reach,* 131, 265, and 330–31.

56. The members blocked from participating were Avraham Burg and Rabbi Michael Melchior. Menahem Klein, *A Possible Peace between Israel and Palestine: An Insider's Account of the Geneva Initiative,* trans. Haim Watzman (New York: Columbia University Press, 2007), 36 and 114.

57. Klein, *Shattering a Taboo,* 18 and 21, my translation.

58. Klein, *Jerusalem Problem,* 161–63.

59. Dayan, "Barak Began Referring to the Holy of Holies."

60. Shmuel Berkovits, *How Dreadful Is This Place! Holiness, Politics, and Justice in Jerusalem and the Holy Places in Israel* (Jerusalem: Carta, 2006), 36.

61. Klein, *Jerusalem Problem,* 78.

62. Ibid., 85, citing *Ha'aretz,* January 5, 2001. For a ruling prohibiting the division of Jerusalem, see advertisement by Rabbi Joseph Yithak HaCohen Gutnik in *Ha'aretz,* July 26, 2000, A8. For rabbinical refusal to accept Palestinian rule over the Temple Mount and proposals to construct a synagogue on the site, see Ross Dunn, "Temple Mount Synagogue 'May Provoke War,'" *Times,* London, August 8, 2000; and Etgar Lefkovits, "Rabbinate Denies Accepting Palestinian Administration on the Temple Mount," *Jerusalem Post,* July 4, 2000.

63. See Reuven Hammer, "Jewish Connection to the Temple Mount," *Jerusalem Post,* February 28, 2001.

64. *Yedioth Aharonot,* September 8, 2000.

65. Press Conference with Foreign Journalists by Acting Foreign Minister Shlomo Ben-Ami, Jerusalem, August 23, 2000 (Israel, Ministry of Foreign Affairs). Ben-Ami's disdain for the religious aspects of the negotiations also found expression during the Camp David negotiations, where Ben-Ami characterized the Jerusalem issue as consisting of two aspects: "The concrete and the mythological." Enderlin, *Shattered Dreams,* 219. Even after the collapse of the negotiations, Ben-Ami remained uninterested in the religious or even archaeological components of the dispute, as he revealed in an interview with Shmuel Berkovits in 2001. See Berkovits, *How Dreadful Is This Place!* 37–38.

66. Shibley Telhami, "Camp David II: Assumptions and Consequences," *Current History* 100, no. 642 (January 2001): 13–14.

67. Klein, *Possible Peace,* 29 and 116.

68. Lee Hockstader, "Jerusalem, City of Faith, Defies Rational Solution," *International Herald Tribune,* July 21, 2000, 1, quoting Akiva Eldar, journalist for *Ha'aretz.*

69. Flora Lewis, "Danger Mounts, but the Mideast Time Isn't Ripe," *International Herald Tribune,* August 1, 2000, 6.

70. Some of the more complex solutions considered included a "Vatican" model, a condominium model, sovereign custodianship, discussions of residual, functional, differential, and associate sovereignty, expansion of the disputed area into a "sacred basin," or the establishment of Jerusalem as a *corpus separatum.* For discussions of various proposals to resolve the Jerusalem question, see for example Moshe Hirsch and Kobi Michael, *International Involvement in the "Holy Basin" Area in Jerusalem: Analysis of Possible Options* (Jerusalem: Jerusalem Institute for Israel Studies, 2003); Ruth Lapidoth and Moshe Hirsch, eds., *The Jerusalem Question and Its Resolution: Selected Documents* (Dordrecht: Nijhoff and the Jerusalem Institute for Israel Studies, 1994); Moshe Hirsch, Deborah Housen-Couriel, and Ruth Lapidoth, *Whither Jerusalem? Proposals and Positions concerning the Future of Jerusalem* (The Hague: Nijhoff, 1995); Eliezer Glaubach-Gal, *Jerusalem, the Permanent Resolution: All Proposals, All Considerations, All Solutions* (Tel-Aviv: Yedioth Aharonot, 1996); Joel L. Kramer, *Jerusalem: Problems and Prospects* (New York: Praeger, 1980); Naomi Chazan, *Negotiating the Non-negotiable: Jerusalem in the Framework of an Israeli-Palestinian Settlement,* occasional paper no. 7 (Cambridge, MA: International Security Studies Program, 1991); Marshall J. Breger, "Religion and Politics in Jerusalem," *Journal of International Affairs* 50, no. 1 (Summer 1996): 90–118.

71. Berkovits, *How Dreadful Is This Place!* 23–26.

72. Agha and Malley, "Camp David," 71.

73. Brian Knowlton, "Mideast Talks Collapse," *International Herald Tribune,* July 26, 2000, 4; Marc Lacey and David E. Sanger, "Again, Clinton Is Left Frustrated at Mideast," *International Herald Tribune,* July 27, 2000, 7.

74. This idea was proposed in the "Clinton Plan" of December 23, 2000, which included suggestions about the division of the city of Jerusalem as well. Sher, *Just beyond Reach,* 361. The idea of dividing the Temple Mount vertically was also suggested, at different points in the conference, by Egypt and France. It may have originated with the Israeli architect Tuvia Sagiv. Berkovits, *How Dreadful Is This Place!* 102–3; and Enderlin, *Shattered Dreams,* 281.

75. See Klein, *Jerusalem Problem,* 73; Shlomo Goren, *Torat Hamedina* (Tel-Aviv: Hemed, 1996), 278–87; and rabbinical sources cited in Berkovits, *How Dreadful Is This Place!* 35–36 and 119–20.

76. Clinton's solution also collided with archaeological interests. Israeli archaeologists opposed the idea of dividing sovereignty vertically because such an arrangement would block Israeli access to the ruins under the Mount, short of cutting an opening into the Western Wall. More important, several eminent archaeologists believe that the Jewish Temple stood at an elevation higher than the current Temple Mount platform. Israeli rights under the platform would thus afford no sovereignty over the ruins of that temple. Archaeologists were yet another group of experts that had not been consulted prior to negotiations. Berkovits, *How Dreadful Is This Place!* 35–37.

77. Ibid., 25–26 and 33–34.

78. Dayan, "Barak Began Referring to the Holy of Holies"; Moshe Amirav, *The Palestinian Struggle for Jerusalem* (Jerusalem: Jerusalem Institute for Israel Studies, 2003).

79. Ruth Lapidoth has presented her argument in, among others, "Sovereignty in Transition," *Journal of International Affairs* 45, no. 2 (Winter 1992), 325–46; "Jerusalem and the Peace Process," *Israel Law Review* 28, nos. 2–3 (Spring–Summer 1994), 402–34; "Redefining Authority: The Past, Present, and Future of Sovereignty," *Harvard International Review* 17, no. 3 (Summer 1995), 8–11 and 70–71; and *Jerusalem: Some Legal Aspects* (Jerusalem: Jerusalem Institute for Israel Studies, 1997).

80. Eetta Prince-Gibson, "Sense, Sensibility, and Sovereignty," *Jerusalem Post,* June 29, 2006, 9.

81. Several of these incidents are discussed in Roger Friedland and Richard Hecht, *To Rule Jerusalem* (Berkeley: University of California Press, 2000); Bernard Wasserstein, *Divided Jerusalem: The Struggle for the Holy City* (New Haven: Yale University Press, 2001); Nadav Shragai, *Har Ha-merivah: Hama'avak al Har Ha-Bayit: Yehudim u-Muslemim, Dat u-Politikah Meaz 1967* (Jerusalem: Keter, 1995); Berkovits, *Battle for the Holy Places;* and others.

82. "Shrine to Hatred: At Joseph's Tomb, Centuries-Old Disputes Cannot Be Laid to Rest," *Washington Post,* October 28, 2000; "Settlers Pessimistic after Israeli Retreat," *Baltimore Sun,* October 17, 2000.

83. "IAF Attacks Jericho after Synagogue Burned," *Jerusalem Post,* October 13, 2000; "On Both Sides, Toll is Personal," *Washington Post,* October 14, 2000.

84. "Religious Symbols and Sensitivities at Core of Mideast Strife," *CNN International,* October 10, 2000.

85. "Mideast Clash Is Becoming an All-Out Religious War," *Los Angeles Times,* October 28, 2000; "Efrat Preparing 'Zionist Response' to Synagogue Desecration," *Jerusalem Post,* October 29, 2000.

86. "American Tourist Vandalizes Western Wall with Red Paint," *CNN International,* December 28, 2000.

87. Figure based on statistics gathered by B'Tselem, the Israeli Information Center for Human Rights in the Occupied Territories, at http://www.btselem.org/english/ Statistics/Casualties.asp (accessed December 2007).

88. The distinction between a "logic of consequences" and a "logic of appropriateness" was introduced by Max Weber and developed by James G. March and Johan P. Olsen in *Rediscovering Institutions* (New York: Free Press, 1989).

6. The Foundations and Limits of Religious Authority

1. H. L. Savage, "Pilgrimages and Pilgrim Shrines in Palestine and Syria after 1095," in *The Art and Architecture of the Crusader States,* ed. H. W. Hazard, vol. 4 of *A History of the Crusades,* ed. K. M. Setton (Madison: University of Wisconsin Press, 1977).

2. Giovanni Villani, *Villani's Chronicle,* trans. Rose E. Selfe (London: Archibald Constable, 1906), 320.

3. Dante Alighieri, *Inferno,* canto 18, in *The Divine Comedy,* trans. Lawrence Grant White (New York: Pantheon Books, 1948), 30–31.

4. The basilica of St. John Lateran was added in 1350. Santa Maria Maggiore joined the list in 1390. In 1575, Pope Gregory XIII added the churches of San Sebastiano, San Lorenzo Outside the Walls, and Santa Croce in Gerusalemme. Pope John Paul II added the Catacombs to the jubilee sites in 1983 and the Sanctuary of the Madonna of Divine Love in 2000. Anonymous, *Holy Year 2000: The Great Jubilee* (Rome: Lozzi Roma, 1999).

5. Yaroslav Trofimov, "This Chapel Is Sort of like a Checkroom for Spiritual Baggage," *Wall Street Journal,* January 13, 2000.

6. Alex Beam, "Time Has Come Once Again to Indulge Yourself," *Boston Globe,* February 2, 2000, D1.

7. Villani, *Villani's Chronicle,* 321.

8. Garry Wills, *Lincoln at Gettysburg: The Words That Remade America* (New York: Simon & Schuster, 2006).

9. Harold W. Turner, *From Temple to Meeting House* (The Hague: Mouton, 1979).

10. Roger Friedland and Richard Hecht, "The Politics of Sacred Place: Jerusalem's Temple Mount/al-Haram al-Sharif," in *Sacred Places and Profane Space,* ed. Jamie Scott and Paul Simpson-Housley (New York: Greenwood Press, 1991), 55.

11. John Searle, *The Construction of Social Reality* (New York: Free Press, 1995).

12. Anthony Giddens, *The Constitution of Society: Outline of the Theory of Structuration* (Berkeley: University of California Press, 1984). For structuration theory in international relations, see Alexander Wendt, "Anarchy Is What States Make of It," *International Organization* 46, no. 2 (Spring 1992): 391–425; and Alexander Wendt, *Social Theory of International Politics* (Cambridge: Cambridge University Press, 1999).

13. For a discussion of idea entrepreneurs and their role in initiating the spread of ideas, see, for example, Martha Finnemore, "Constructing Norms of Humanitarian

Intervention," in *The Culture of National Security,* ed. Peter Katzenstein (New York: Columbia University Press, 1996), 153–85; Martha Finnemore and Kathryn Sikkink, "International Norm Dynamics and Political Change," *International Organization* 54, no. 4 (Autumn 1998): 887–917; and Peter M. Haas, ed. *Knowledge, Power, and International Policy Coordination* (Columbia: University of South Carolina Press, 1997).

14. I thank Arnie Eisen for sharing this insight with me.

15. The Hebrew jubilee year, commanded in Leviticus 25 and 27, recurred every fifty years. In this year, Israelites were to desist from working the land, to return lands to those who had been forced to sell land owing to poverty, and to free those who were forced into servitude by poverty. In drawing on the Hebrew term, Boniface alluded not only to the theme of cyclical celebration but also to the motif of routinely releasing individuals from obligations previously incurred.

16. Entry for "Consecration" in *The Catholic Encyclopedia,* ed. Charles G. Hebermann et al. (New York, 1937). Also online at http://www.newadvent.org/cathen/04276a.htm.

17. Similarly, a cloth containing a relic is placed on the altar during the consecration of a Greek Orthodox church. Douglas Davies, "Christianity," in *Sacred Place,* ed. Jean Holm and John Bowker (London: Pinter, 1994), 42.

18. F. E. Peters, *Jerusalem: The Holy City in the Eyes of Chroniclers, Visitors, Pilgrims, and Prophets from the Days of Abraham to the Beginnings of Modern Time* (Princeton: Princeton University Press, 1985), 197.

19. Ibid., 116, citing G. Le Strange, *Palestine under the Muslims* (Beirut: Khayats, 1965).

20. For skeptical analyses of this account, see Peters, *Jerusalem,* 197; and F. E. Peters, *Jerusalem and Mecca: The Typology of the Holy City in the Near East* (New York: New York University Press, 1986), 94.

21. Ian Lustick has applied Gramsci's argument regarding hegemonic ideas to political conflicts over territory in *Unsettled States, Disputed Lands: Britain and Ireland, France and Algeria, Israel and the West Bank–Gaza* (Ithaca, NY: Cornell University Press, 1993). See Antonio Gramsci, *The Modern Prince and Other Writings,* ed. Louis Marks (New York: International Publishers, 1957); and Antonio Gramsci, "Notes on Italian History," in *Selections from the Prison Notebooks of Antonio Gramsci,* ed. Quintin Hoare and Geoffrey Nowell-Smith (New York: International Publishers, 1971). See Lustick, *Unsettled States,* 470 n. 2 for additional references.

22. Jacob Neusner, *First Century Judaism in Crisis: Yohanan ben Zakkai and the Renaissance of Torah* (New York: Ktav, 1982); Louis Finkelstein, *Akiba: Scholar, Saint, and Martyr* (New York: Atheneum, 1975); Heinrich Graetz, "The Sanhedrin at Jabne," in Graetz, *History of the Jews* (Philadelphia: Jewish Publication Society of America, 1956), 321–37.

23. Simon Dubnow, *History of the Jews,* trans. Moshe Spiegel (South Brunswick, NJ: T. Yoseloff, 1967–73), 30–33; Louis Finkelstein, *The Jews: Their History, Culture, and Religion* (New York: Harper, 1960), 1:144–53.

24. Jacob Neusner, *A Life of Rabban Yohanan ben Zakkai* (Leiden: Brill, 1962), 156, citing Tractate Rosh Hashanah 4.1, Babylonian Talmud, Rosh Hashanah 29b.

25. Peters, *Jerusalem,* 135–36, citing Eusebius of Caesarea, *Life of Constantine* 3.25–3.33, trans. and ed. F. Winkelman (Berlin, 1975).

26. Karen Armstrong, *Jerusalem: One City, Three Faiths* (New York: Ballantine Books, 1997), 229, citing Eutychius, *Annals;* Elizabeth Key Fowden, "Sharing Holy Places," *Common Knowledge* 8, no. 1 (2002): 140.

27. Muslims place the tomb of Moses (Nebi Mousa) in the Judean desert, whereas Jews believe that the location of Moses' tomb, somewhere near Mount Nebo east of the Jordan, is unknown. Muslims pray at the tomb of John the Baptist in Damascus, but Christians worship his tomb in Ephesus, Turkey. Christians revere the Church of the Holy Sepulcher as the location of the bones of Adam, while Jews place his tomb in Hebron. Along similar lines, Protestant Christians are not parties to the sectarian dispute in the Church of the Holy Sepulcher because the Protestant movement identifies a separate site, located outside the walls of Jerusalem, as the place of the crucifixion and resurrection of Jesus. The Garden Tomb, as it has come to be called, is one of the most popular Protestant sites in the Holy Land today, visited by some fifty thousand tourists a year.

28. Other charismatic leaders who succeeded in shifting the location of sacred sites, in addition to the popes mentioned at the beginning of this chapter, include the seventeenth-century Jewish mystic Shabbtai Tzvi and the Sikh guru Arjan Dev. When Tzvi, recognized by thousands of devotees as the long-awaited Messiah, was excommunicated by the rabbis of Jerusalem but received enthusiastically in Gaza, he declared the latter city to be the new sacred center of his religion, a proclamation enthusiastically embraced by his followers. See Gershom Sholem, *Sabbatai Sevi: The Mystical Messiah, 1626–1676* (Princeton: Princeton University Press, 1973), 288. Guru Arjan Dev, founder of the Sikh temple in Amritsar, named the most prominent site for ritual ablution in the temple after "the 68 Holy Places" (Ath Sath Tirath), a reference to the primary Hindu pilgrimage sites. Rather than visit these sites, the guru argued, Sikhs could fulfill their religious obligation by bathing inside the Harimandir. This minimized friction between Hindus and Sikhs at traditional Hindu sites of worship while channeling Sikh pilgrims toward Amritsar.

29. Barry Bearak, "Over World Protests, Taliban Are Destroying Ancient Buddhas," *New York Times,* March 4, 2001, 10; and "U.N. Pleads with Taliban Not to Destroy Buddha Statues," *New York Times,* March 3, 2001, A3.

30. G. S. Godkin, *Life of Victor Emmanuel II* (London: Macmillan, 1880), 193–99, citing Letter from Pius IX to Victor Emmanuel, February 14, 1860; S. Halperin, *Italy and the Vatican at War; A Study of Their Relations from the Outbreak of the Franco-Prussian War to the Death of Pius IX* (Chicago: University of Chicago Press, 1939); A. Gallenga, *The Pope and the King: The War between the Church and State in Italy* (London: S. Tinsley, 1879); O. Chadwick, *A History of the Popes: 1830–1914* (Oxford: Clarendon Press, 1998).

7. Successful Conflict Management: Jerusalem, 1967

1. Ehud Sprinzak, *The Ascendance of Israel's Radical Right* (Oxford: Oxford University Press, 1991), 288. Gershom Gorenberg has chimed in, calling the Temple Mount "the most contested piece of real estate on earth." Gershom Gorenberg, *The End of Days: Fundamentalism and the Struggle for the Temple Mount* (New York: Free Press, 2000), 11.

2. J. Goldberg, "Jerusalem Endgame: Israel's Y2K Problem," *New York Times Magazine,* October 3, 1999.

3. Susan Sered, "Rachel's Tomb: Societal Liminality and the Revitalization of a Shrine," *Religion* 19, no. 1 (January 1989:, 27–40; Susan Sered, "Rachel's Tomb and the Milk Grotto of the Virgin Mary: Two Women's Shrines in Bethlehem," *Journal of Feminist Studies in Religion* 2, no. 2 (1986): 7–22.

4. David Horovitz, "Faithful Come to Rachel's Tomb," *Jerusalem Post,* November 10, 1989; "10,000 Pray for Peace," *Jerusalem Post,* August 21, 1990.

5. For a summary of these developments, see Nadav Shragai, *The Story of Rachel's Tomb* [Hebrew: *Al Em ha-Derekh: Sipuro Shel Kever Rachel*] (Jerusalem: Gates for Jerusalem Studies, 2005).

6. "Bomb Dismantled Outside Holy Site," Associated Press, January 1, 1982.

7. See for example, "Car Gutted in Attack," *Jerusalem Post,* July 22, 1991; "Soldier Killed in Accidental Shooting Near Rachel's Tomb," *Jerusalem Post,* January 28, 1992; "Five Hurt in Bethlehem Shooting Incident," *BBC Summary of World Broadcasts,* July 4, 1985.

8. H. Keinon, "Thousands Make Pilgrimage to Rachel's Tomb," *Jerusalem Post,* October 17, 1994.

9. Nadav Shragai, "The Palestinian Authority and the Jewish Holy Sites in the West Bank: Rachel's Tomb as a Test Case," *Jerusalem Viewpoints* (Jerusalem: Jerusalem Center for Public Affairs, December 2007).

10. Evelyn Gordon, "Livnat: Document Shows Holy Sites More Important to Jews," *Jerusalem Post,* July 20, 1995, 2; Evelyn Gordon, "Five No-Confidence Motions Defeated," *Jerusalem Post,* July 25, 1995, 3; Herb Keinon, "Thousands Pray at Rachel's Tomb; Worshippers Fear Palestinian Takeover of Holy Site," *Jerusalem Post,* July 28, 1995, 2; Herb Keinon, "Rabin: New Road to Link Gilo to Rachel's Tomb," *Jerusalem Post,* July 26, 1995, 2; Jon Immanuel, "Jews Will Be Barred from Holy Sites under PA Control," *Jerusalem Post,* September 13, 1995, 1.

11. Uzi Benziman, *Yerushalayim, Ir Lelo Homa* [Jerusalem, the City without a Wall] (Jerusalem: Shoken, 1973), 20.

12. Quoted in Uzi Narkiss, *The Liberation of Jerusalem: The Battle of 1967* (London: Valentine Mitchell, 1983), 52.

13. Shabtai Teveth, *Moshe Dayan* (London: Weidenfeld and Nicolson, 1972), 335. For a discussion of government deliberations concerning the city, see Michael Brecher, *Decisions in Crisis: Israel, 1967 and 1973* (Berkeley: University of California Press, 1980), 265, 273.

14. Eli Landau, *Jerusalem the Eternal: The Paratroopers' Battle for the City of David* (Tel Aviv: Otpaz, 1968), 167; Iser Harel and Motta Gur, eds., *The Lion's Gate: The Battle over Jerusalem as Experienced by Warriors of the Paratrooper Brigade* (Tel Aviv: Ministry of Defense Publications, 1972); Abraham Rabinovich, *The Battle for Jerusalem, June 5–7, 1967* (Philadelphia: Jewish Publication Society of America, 1972); Uzi Narkiss, *Soldier of Jerusalem* (London: Valentine Mitchell, 1997); Robert Slater, *Warrior Statesman: The Life of Moshe Dayan* (New York: St. Martin's Press, 1991), 271.

15. Teveth, *Moshe Dayan,* 336. Pope Paul VI had appealed for the armies to spare the holy sites of Jerusalem and expressed hope that the city would become "a refuge for the unarmed and the wounded, a symbol for all men of hope and peace." Quoted

in Hal Kosut, ed., *Israel and the Arabs: The June 1967 War* (New York: Facts on File, 1968), 88. For an assessment of dissenting views, see Eric H. Cline, *Jerusalem Besieged: From Ancient Canaan to Modern Israel* (Ann Arbor: University of Michigan Press, 2004), 355 n. 75.

16. Benziman, *Yerushalayim,* 29.

17. Harel and Gur, *Lion's Gate,* 161.

18. Rabinovich, *Battle for Jerusalem,* 455–59.

19. Narkiss, *Liberation of Jerusalem,* 222; and Slater, *Warrior Statesman,* 271.

20. Narkiss, *Soldier of Jerusalem.*

21. Moshe Dayan, *The Story of My Life* (New York: William Morrow, 1976), 387–88; and Narkiss, *Soldier of Jerusalem,* 26.

22. Kosut, *Israel and the Arabs,* 155.

23. Dayan, *Story of My Life,* 387–88; and Narkiss, *Liberation of Jerusalem,* 26.

24. Kosut, *Israel and the Arabs,* 155; Michael Dumper, *The Politics of Jerusalem since 1967* (New York: Columbia University Press, 1997), 46.

25. Meron Benvenisti, *Mul Hachoma Hasgura* [The Torn City, in Hebrew] (Jerusalem: Weidenfeld and Nicolson, 1973), 231–32.

26. Kosut, *Israel and the Arabs,* 185.

27. Nadav Shragai, "Rabbi Goren Asked Uzi Narkiss to Blow Up the Mosques on the Temple Mount Right After the Conquest of the Western Wall," *Ha'aretz,* December 31, 1997, A1 and B3 (my translation).

28. Benvenisti, *Mul Hachoma Hasgura,* 242.

29. H. Eugene Bovis, *The Jerusalem Question: 1917–1968* (Stanford: Hoover Institution Press, 1971), 108.

30. Benvenisti, *Mul Hachoma Hasgura,* 239–41.

31. Brecher, *Decisions in Crisis,* 74; "Rabbi Goren Conducts Halachik Research to Ascertain the Boundaries of the Temple Mount," *Hatzofe,* June 23, 1967, 10; "Police to Guard the Sacred Sites in Jerusalem," *Hatzofe,* August 1, 1967, 1. All headlines from *Hatzofe* cited here are my translations of the Hebrew originals.

32. Hagai Huberman, "Rabbi Shlomo Goren and PM Mota Gur in a Combined Interview Commemorating 25 Years for the Liberation of Jerusalem," *Hatzofe,* May 25, 1992, 5–12, citing Mota Gur; Narkiss, *Liberation of Jerusalem,* 219; Nadav Shragai, *Har Ha-Merivah: Hama'avak al Har Ha-Bayit: Yehudim u-Muslemim, Dat u-Politikah Meaz 1967* [The Temple Mount Conflict, in Hebrew] (Jerusalem: Keter, 1995), 35, citing Yisrael Eldad.

33. Shragai, *Har Ha-Merivah,* 72.

34. Ibid., 61.

35. Shmuel Berkovits, *Ha-Ma'amad Ha-Mishpati shel Ha-Mekomot Ha-Kedoshim bi-Yerushalayim* [The Legal Status of the Holy Places in Jerusalem, in Hebrew] (Jerusalem: Jerusalem Institute of Israel Studies, 1997), 56.

36. Ibid., 66.

37. Dumper, *Politics of Jerusalem,* 44.

38. Berkovits, *Ha-Ma'amad Ha-Mishpati,* 49–50, quoting from High Court of Justice rulings 650/88 and 222/68 (my translation).

39. In 1971, 51.7 percent opposed the prohibition; in 1981, 53.4 percent opposed it. *Ha'aretz,* July 12, 1981, 3.

40. Ian Lustick, *For the Land and the Lord: Jewish Fundamentalism in Israel* (Washington, DC: Council on Foreign Relations, 1988); Sprinzak, *Ascendance of Israel's Radical Right,* 94–99.

41. Sprinzak, *Ascendance of Israel's Radical Right,* 98–99 and 283–84.

42. Benvenisti, *Mul Hachoma Hasgura,* 247–48.

43. Shaul Shefer, *Har Habayit, Nezer Tifartenu* (Jerusalem: Shefer), 61; Rabbi Yisrael Ariel, "Hatfila Bamikdash Ubehar Habayit," in *Hama'alot Leshlomo,* ed. Yitzhak Alfasi (Jerusalem, 1998); and Rabbi Mordechai HaCohen, *Habyit VeHa'aliya* (Jerusalem: Yad Rama, 1978).

44. Karen Armstrong, *Jerusalem: One City, Three Faiths* (New York: Ballantine Books, 1997), 299–300; F. E. Peters, *Jerusalem: The Holy City in the Eyes of Chroniclers, Visitors, Pilgrims and Prophets from the Days of Abraham to the Beginnings of Modern Time* (Princeton: Princeton University Press, 1985), 279.

45. "Oral Law Conference Concludes," *Hatzofe,* August 31, 1967, 4.

46. Armstrong, *Jerusalem,* 320; Peters, *Jerusalem,* 144, 173, 193–94. A student of Nachmanides and the famous Jewish explorer Benjamin of Tudela were among those Jews who had prayed on the Temple Mount.

47. Rabbi Shlomo Goren, *Sefer Har Habayit* [The Temple Mount Book] (Jerusalem: Hotsa'at Ha'Idra Raba, 1993), 11; Alfasi, *Hama'alot Leshlomo,* 269; Huberman, "Rabbi Shlomo Goren."

48. Shragai, *Har Ha-Merivah,* 72 (my translation).

49. Yisrael Medad, "Har Habayit Beyadam," *Nekuda,* vol. 209, November 1997, citing Chief Israeli Rabbi Eliyahu Bakshi Doron, *Hatzofe,* May 26, 1995.

50. Shragai, *Har Ha-Merivah,* 27; compare Mishnah, Tractate Kelim 6–9.

51. From the ruling, as it appeared in the Orthodox daily *Hatzofe,* October 10, 1967, 1 (my translation). "Since time immemorial": originally "MeDorey Dorot" (lit.: "For generations and generations").

52. Menahem Barsh, "It's the Destruction of a Third Temple!" [in Hebrew] *Yedioth Aharonot,* August 11, 1967, 2.

53. Dayan, *Story of My Life,* 389

54. See, for example, ad in *Ma'ariv,* August 20, 1967, 11.

55. "At the Oral Law Conference: The Entry into the Temple Mount and the Construction of the Temple," *Ha'aretz,* August 29, 1967, 2.

56. See Yitzhak Raphael, ed., *Text of the Tenth Annual Oral Law Conference at the Rabbi Kook Institute* (Jerusalem, 1967). Also in the introduction of Goren, *Sefer Har Habayit.*

57. "The Battle over the Temple Mount between the Rabbis and the Halachik Experts" [in Hebrew], *Ma'ariv,* August 31, 1967, 2; "A Rabbi Insulted," *Hatzofe,* September 2, 1967, 2.

58. Raphael, *Text of the Tenth Annual Oral Law Conference,* 5; "The Most Debated Issue at the Oral Law Conference Is Goren's Lecture That Did Not Take Place" [in Hebrew], *Ma'ariv,* August 29, 1967, 3.

59. Raphael, *Text of the Tenth Annual Oral Law Conference,* 9 (my translation).

60. Menahem Barsh, "It Is Too Early to Issue a Halachik Ruling" [in Hebrew], *Yedioth Aharonot,* August 29, 1967, 3.

61. Yehuda Elitzur, "Two Placards Raising Three Doubts," *Hatzofe,* October 13, 1967, 3.

62. For opinions for and against access to the Mount in one leading religious newspaper, see, for example, Menahem Libman, "Who Does the Temple Mount Belong To?" *Hatzofe,* August 22, 1967, 2; Moshe Ishon, "Historical Facts Confirm: Maimonides Prayed on the Temple Mount," *Hatzofe,* August 25, 1967, weekend supplement, 3; Rabbi Dr. Michael Greiber, "May Jews Enter the Temple Mount?" *Hatzofe,* September 2, 1967, 2; Rabbi Yehuda Gershoni, "On Entering the Temple Mount This Time," *Hatzofe,* September 8, 1967, 4; Rabbi Gershon Arieli, "On the Prohibition to Enter the Temple Mount," *Hatzofe,* September 12, 1967, 2; Rabbi Moshe Kamelhar, "The Temple Mount Debate," *Hatzofe,* September 22, 1967; Y. Bar-Tora, "Entering the Temple Mount," *Hatzofe,* September 24, 1967, 2. (All article title translations are my own.)

63. "The Chief Rabbis Will Discuss Goren's Prayer on the Temple Mount Tonight" [in Hebrew,] *Yedioth Aharonot,* August 16, 1967, 1 and 20; and "Unterman Refused to Meet Goren" [in Hebrew], *Yedioth Aharonot,* August 17, 1967, 4.

64. Shragai, *Har Ha-Merivah,* 33.

65. "Rabbi Goren Will Announce His Intention to Cancel Sabbath Prayers on the Temple Mount," *Ha'aretz,* August 17, 1967, 3.

66. Sprinzak, *Ascendance of Israel's Radical Right,* 284; and Dayan, *Story of My Life,* 389.

67. Shragai, *Har Ha-Merivah,* 51–82; and Sprinzak, *Ascendance of Israel's Radical Right,* 251–89.

68. One group went as far as to spend $25,000 for what it (mistakenly) believed were Lebanese cedar-wood beams from the first Temple. Shragai, *Har Ha-Merivah,* 96; and Sprinzak, *Ascendance of Israel's Radical Right,* 286.

69. Shragai, *Har Ha-Merivah,* 60.

70. Dumper, *Politics of Jerusalem,* 171; Shragai, *Har Ha-Merivah,* 340–63. Israel was condemned for its responses by a unanimous UN Security Council resolution. See J. Bodreault and Y. Salaam, "U.S. Official Statements: The Status of Jerusalem" (Washington, DC: Institute for Palestine Studies, 1992), 88.

71. Shragai, *Har Ha-Merivah,* 380.

72. Sprinzak, *Ascendance of Israel's Radical Right,* 284.

73. Andrew Album, "A Tunnel to Turmoil," *Middle East,* no. 261 (November 1996): 5–7; Joel Greenberg, "Comeback Kid: Arafat's Second Wind," *New Republic* 215, no. 17 (October 21, 1996): 10–12.

74. Shragai, *Har Ha-Merivah,* 377–78, 311.

75. Dumper, *Politics of Jerusalem,* 42, 171–72, 264.

76. Shragai, *Har Ha-Merivah,* 370–72.

77. "The Battle of the Dome: Jerusalem," *Economist* 323, no. 7760 (May 1992): 45–46.

78. Shragai, *Har Ha-Merivah,* 307–9.

79. Berkovits, *Ha-Ma'amad Ha-Mishpati,* 67.

80. Shragai, *Har Ha-Merivah,* 376.

81. A. Rabinovich, "Tense Coexistence at the Tomb of the Patriarchs," *Jerusalem Post,* October 9, 1992.

82. Norman L. Zucker, *The Coming Crisis in Israel* (Cambridge: MIT Press, 1975), 82–86.

83. Huberman, "Rabbi Shlomo Goren."

84. Nadav Shragai, "Increasing Numbers of Rabbis Are Allowing Jews to Enter Temple Mount," *Ha'aretz,* May 10, 2007; Nadav Shragai, "Dozens of Rabbis Ascend Temple Mount in Unprecedented Visit," *Ha'aretz,* May 14, 2007.

8. Successful Conflict Management: Mecca, 1979

1. This section draws on Desmond Stewart, *Mecca* (New York: Newsweek, 1980); Sayyed Hossein Nasr and Ali Kazuyoshi Nomachi, *Mecca the Blessed, Medina the Radiant* (Hong Kong: Odyssey Books, 1997); and Mohamed Amin, *Journey of a Lifetime: Pilgrimage to Makkah* (Nairobi: Camerapix, 1978).

2. Al Qur'an, trans. Ahmed Ali (Princeton: Princeton University Press, 1988). I use Ahmed Ali's translation of the Qur'an throughout this chapter, except where a cited source has provided its own translation.

3. See for example Sahih Bukhari 1.3.104 and 2.26.657 and others. These are available at the USC-MSA Compendium of Muslim Texts, http://www.usc.edu/dept/MSA/ (accessed December 15, 2007). See also Moulana Abdul Quddus Hashmi, "Ka'ba Episode: A Historical Perspective," in *Islamic Order* 1, no. 4 (1979): 7–8.

4. According to F. Wuestenfeld, the boundaries are determined by walking distance from Mecca: 1½ hours of journey on the road to Medina, 3½ hours along the road to Yemen, 5½ hours on the road to Ta'if, 3½ hours along the road to Iraq, and 5 hours along the road to Jedda. F. Wuestenfeld, *Geschichte der Stadt Mekka nach den arabischen Chroniken bearbeitet* (Leipzig, 1861), 113, cited in F. E. Peters, *Jerusalem and Mecca: The Typology of the Holy City in the Near East* (New York: New York University Press, 1986), 109.

5. The event is captured in the Qur'an, Sura 105.

6. See G. R. Hawting, "Al-Hudaybiyya and the Conquest of Mecca: A Reconsideration of the Tradition about the Muslim Takeover of the Sanctuary," in *Jerusalem Studies in Arabic and Islam,* 6 (1986): 1–25.

7. See, for example, Karen Armstrong, *Muhammad: A Biography of the Prophet* (New York: HarperCollins, 1992), 243–45.

8. Moulana Abdul Quddus Hashmi, "Ka'ba Episode." Abdul Quddus lists five additional minor incidents.

9. Joseph A. Kechichian, "The Role of the Ulama in the Politics of an Islamic State: The Case of Saudi Arabia," *International Journal of Middle East Studies* 18, no. 1 (February 1986): 60.

10. John Sabini, *Armies in the Sand: The Struggle for Mecca and Medina* (London: Thames and Hudson, 1981), 68, 94, and 209.

11. Shahram Chubin and Charles Tripp, "Iran–Saudi Arabia Relations and Regional Order," Adelphi Paper 304 (Oxford: Oxford University Press, 1996).

12. The following pages draw on Ayman al-Yassini, *Religion and State in the Kingdom of Saudi Arabia* (Boulder, CO: Westview Press, 1985); George Retz, "Wahhabism and Saudi Arabia," in *The Arabian Peninsula: Society and Politics,* ed. Derek Hopwood (Totowa, NJ: Rowman and Littlefield, 1972); Aharon Layish, "Ulema and Politics in Saudi Arabia," in *Islam and Politics in the Modern Middle East,* ed. Martin Heper and

Raphael Israeli (London: Croom Helm, 1984); Alexander Bligh, "The Saudi Religious Elite (Ulema) as Participant in the Political System of the Kingdom," *International Journal of Middle East Studies* 16, no. 4 (1985): 37–50; and Kechichian, "Role of the Ulama."

13. Kechichian, "Role of the Ulama," 55–57.

14. Al-Yassini, *Religion and State,* 55.

15. Kechichian, "Role of the Ulama," 1.

16. Al-Yassini, *Religion and State,* 55.

17. Layish, "Ulema and Politics," 47.

18. Ibid., 35.

19. John L. Esposito, *Islam and Politics* (Syracuse, NY: Syracuse University Press, 1987), 104.

20. Bligh, "Saudi Religious Elite," 40. The quote is from a British report, "Jedda Report," December 13, 1942, paragraph 5.

21. Bligh, "Saudi Religious Elite," 41.

22. Yvonne Y. Haddad, "The Arab-Israeli Wars, Nasserism, and Islamic Identity," in *Islam and Development,* ed. John L. Esposito (Syracuse, NY: Syracuse University Press, 1980), 239, and in Esposito, *Islam and Politics,* 107.

23. Yvonne Y. Haddad, "Operation Desert Storm and the War of Fatwas," in *Islamic Legal Interpretation: Muftis and Their Fatwas,* ed. Muhammad Khalid Masud, Brinkley Messick, and David S. Powers (Cambridge: Harvard University Press, 1996), 299–301.

24. Kechichian, "Role of the Ulama," 58.

25. Yaroslav Trofimov, *The Siege of Mecca: The Forgotten Uprising in Islam's Holiest Shrine and the Birth of Al Qaeda* (New York: Doubleday, 2007), 30.

26. Louis J. Cantori, "Religion and Politics in Egypt," in *Religion and Politics in the Middle East,* ed. Michael Curtis (Boulder, CO: Westview Press, 1981), 79.

27. Roger M. Savory, "Sovereignty in a Shi'i State," in Curtis, *Religion and Politics,* 134–38.

28. Al-Yassini, *Religion and State,* 79 and 135.

29. Counts of the number of pilgrims, insurgents, or counterinsurgency forces involved in the crisis differ widely, as do claims regarding the number of pilgrims initially released by the insurgents. Trofimov suggests that there were tens of thousands of pilgrims in the shrine, a reasonable number given the pilgrimage season, of which the vast majority escaped or were allowed to leave early on. Kechichian cites the French *Le Point* to the effect that there were fifteen hundred insurgents involved. See Trofimov, *Siege of Mecca,* 102; Kechichian, "Role of the Ulama," 70 n. 21, citing *Le Point,* no.385 (February 4, 1980): 53.

30. See for example Edward Cody, "Armed Men Seize Mecca's Great Mosque," *Washington Post,* November 21, 1979, A1; Edward Cody, "Saudis Press to End Siege at Mecca," *Washington Post,* November 22, 1979, A1; Edward Cody, "Saudis Capture Most of Gunmen Holding Mosque," *Washington Post,* November 23, 1979, A1.

31. Pascal Menoret, "Fighting for the Holy Mosque: The 1979 Mecca Insurgency," in *Treading on Hallowed Ground: Counterinsurgency Operations in Sacred Spaces,* ed. C. Christine Fair and Sumit Ganguly (New York: Oxford University Press, 2008), 119., citing Nasir Al-Huzaymî, *Ayâm ma' Juhaymân* [Days with Juhayman] (Riyadh: n.p., 2007), 16.

32. Trofimov, *Siege of Mecca,* 28.

33. Ibid., 42. Kechichian claims that Utaybi was among those arrested and released. Kechichian, "Role of the Ulama," 59.

34. Kechichian, "Role of the Ulama," 60.

35. Trofimov, *Siege of Mecca,* 30.

36. James Buchanan, "The Return of the Ikhwan—1979," in *The House of Saud,* ed. David Holden and Richard Johns (London: Sidgwick and Jackson, 1981), 515, citing Juhayman al-Utaybi, Pamphlet 3: "The Call of the Brethren."

37. Menoret, "Fighting for the Holy Mosque," 125.

38. Al-Yassini, *Religion and State,* 126; and Trofimov, *Siege of Mecca,* 48.

39. Menoret, "Fighting for the Holy Mosque," 125.

40. "Fighting Continues at Moslem Shrine," Associated Press, November 24, 1979.

41. Menoret, "Fighting for the Holy Mosque," 129–30.

42. Aly Mahmoud, "International News," Associated Press, November 30, 1979.

43. Trofimov, *Siege of Mecca,* 85–86.

44. Barry Shlachter, "Pakistani Troops Took Five Hours to Aid Embattled Embassy," Associated Press, November 22, 1979; Stuart Auerbach, "Pakistanis Attack, Burn U.S. Embassy," *Washington Post,* November 22, 1979, A1; Trofimov, *Siege of Mecca,* 104–16.

45. Trofimov, *Siege of Mecca,* 112, 137–38, and 143.

46. Ibid., 86–87.

47. Muhammad Khalid Masud, Brinkley Messick, and David S. Powers, "Muftis, Fatwas, and Islamic Legal Interpretation," in *Islamic Legal Interpretation: Muftis and Their Fatwas,* ed. Masud, Messick, and Powers (Cambridge: Harvard University Press, 1996), 19.

48. William Powell, *Saudi Arabia and Its Royal Family* (Secaucus, NJ: Lyle Stuart, 1982), 320. This account is confirmed in part by Holden and Johns, *House of Saud.* Trofimov rejects this version of events outright but does recount a failed assault on the mosque by the Sixth Paratroop Battalion of the Saudi army, attacking on foot, that annihilated much of the battalion. Trofimov, *Siege of Mecca,* 125–34.

49. Bligh, "Saudi Religious Elite," 48. Menoret claims that the fatwa was published on the twenty-fifth; Trofimov argues that it was published on the twenty-third. Menoret, "Fighting for the Holy Mosque," 138 n. 41; Trofimov, *Siege of Mecca,* 150–51.

50. Trofimov, *Siege of Mecca,* 128.

51. "Text Pronouncement Issued by the Ulema of the Kingdom of Saudi Arabia," *BBC Summary of World Broadcasts,* November 26, 1979; "International News," Associated Press, November 25, 1979.

52. Trofimov, *Siege of Mecca,* 99. These included the amassing of an army of seventy thousand Jews in Isfahan, to be destroyed by the Mahdi with the aid of Jesus Christ, as well as the existence of walls surrounding Damascus, behind which the Mahdi was to await Jesus.

53. Kechichian, "Role of the Ulama," 61. For the theological underpinnings of the fatwa, see Kechichian, ibid., throughout.

54. Foreign Broadcast Information Service—Middle East and Africa, November 26, 1979, C4.

55. Trofimov, *Siege of Mecca,* 151.

56. Edward Cody, "Saudi Religious Leadership Advocates Strict Punishment for Mosque Siege," *Washington Post,* November 26, 1979, A14; and "Saudi Troops Corner Last Extremists at Mosque," Associated Press, November 26, 1979.

57. Trofimov, *Siege of Mecca,* 221.

58. Menoret, "Fighting for the Holy Mosque," 130, citing http://www.gign.org/groupe-intervention-gign/missions-zoom.php?id=8 and Fahd Al-Qahtanî, *Zilzâl Juhaymân fî Makka* [Juhayman's Earthquake in Mecca] (London: Organisation of the Islamic Revolution in the Arabian Peninsula, 1987), 230; Trofimov, *Siege of Mecca,* 222.

59. Ghassan Salame, "Political Power and the Saudi State," in *The Modern Middle East: A Reader,* ed. Albert Hourani, Phillip S. Khoury, and Mary C. Wilson (Berkeley: University of California Press, 1993), 586.

60. "Saudi Arabian Embassy Denies Reports That French Anti-terrorist Commandos Assisted Saudi Forces," *Washington Post,* January 29, 1980; *Le Point,* no. 384 (January 28, 1980): 64–65; corroborated by Jean-Michel Gourevitch, "La Mecque: Le Point confirme," *Le Point,* no. 385 (February 4, 1980): 53.

61. Trofimov, *Siege of Mecca,* 172–73.

62. Al-Yassini, *Religion and State,* 128.

63. Trofimov, *Siege of Mecca,* 239.

64. Al-Yassini, *Religion and State,* 129.

65. Menoret, "Fighting for the Holy Mosque," 135 citing Alexei Vassiliev, *The History of Saudi Arabia* (London: Saqi, 2000), 397, and Al-Huzaymî, *Ayâm ma' Juhaymân,* 5; and Trofimov, *Siege of Mecca,* 241.

66. Trofimov, *Siege of Mecca,* 7.

67. Ibid., 21, 124, and 153.

68. Ibid., 247, citing Peter Bergen, *The Osama bin Laden I Know: An Oral History of al Qaeda's Leader* (New York: Free Press, 2006), 23; and Jason Burke, *Al Qaeda: The True Story of Radical Islam* (London: I. B. Tauris, 2004), 58.

69. Menoret, "Fighting for the Holy Mosque," 133, citing Francois Burgat and Mohammed Sbitli, "Les Salafis au Yemen ou la modernisation malgré tout," *Chroniques Yéménites* 12 (2002).

9. Lessons from Conflicts over Sacred Places

1. Madeleine Albright, *The Mighty and the Almighty: Reflections on America, God, and World Affairs* (New York: HarperCollins, 2006), 75. Robert Seiple was ambassador-at-large for international religious freedom, a position established in 1998 and held by John Hanford as of 2009. The Office of International Religious Freedom in the State Department promotes religious freedom worldwide and publishes reports about religious discrimination. It is not, however, designed to provide expertise on global or regional religious issues. Seiple was the author, with Dennis R. Hoover, of *Religion and Security: The New Nexus in International Relations* (New York: Rowman and Littlefield, 2004).

2. Mark Tully and Satish Jacob, *Amritsar: Mrs. Gandhi's Last Battle* (London: Jonathan Cape, 1985); Lt. Gen. K.S. Brar, *Operation Bluestar: The True Story* (New Delhi: UBSPD, 1993); C. Christine Fair, "The Golden Temple: A Tale of Two Sieges," in *Treading on Hallowed Ground: Counterinsurgency Operations in Sacred Spaces,* ed., C. Christine Fair and Sumit Ganguly (Oxford: Oxford University Press, 2008), 37–65.

3. Menahem Klein, *The Jerusalem Problem: The Struggle for Permanent Status,* trans. Haim Watzman (Gainesville: University Press of Florida, 2003), 162–63.

4. Ibid., 134.

5. On explaining versus understanding, see Martin Hollis and Steve Smith, *Explaining and Understanding International Relations* (Oxford: Oxford University Press, 1991). On interpretivism versus naturalism, see Mark Bevir and Asaf Kedar, "Concept Formation in Political Science: An Anti-naturalist Critique of Qualitative Methodology," *Perspectives on Politics* 6, no. 3 (September 2008): 503–18.

6. See, for example, Muhammad Qasim Zaman, *The Ulama in Contemporary Islam* (Princeton: Princeton University Press, 2002); Joseph A. Kechichian, "The Role of the Ulama in the Politics of an Islamic State: The Case of Saudi Arabia," *International Journal of Middle East Studies* 18, no. 1 (February 1986): 53–71; and Julie Taylor, "Prophet Sharing: Strategic Interaction between Muslim Clerics and Middle East Regimes," *Journal of Islamic Law and Culture* 10, no. 1 (April 2008): 41–62.

7. Robert Bradnock and Roma Bradnock, *South Asian Handbook* (Bath, UK: Trade & Travel, 1993), 467.

8. Ibid., 465.

9. T. N. Bhan, "At the Foot of Vishnu," *Kashmir,* Government of India, Ministry of Information and Broadcasting, Publications Division, May 1953, vol. 3, no. 5, p. 95.

10. Victoria Schofield, *Kashmir in the Crossfire* (London: I. B. Tauris, 1996), 272.

11. Rajesh Kadian, *The Kashmir Tangle: Issues and Options* (Boulder, CO: Westview Press, 1993), 123.

12. Robert Bradnock and Roma Bradnock, *India Handbook 2001* (Bath, UK: Bradnock Handbooks, 2000), 533; and Holger Kersten, *Jesus Lived in India: His Unknown Life before and after the Crucifixion* (New Delhi: Penguin Books, 1981).

13. Mohammad Yasin and Madhavi Yasin, *Mysteries and Glimpses of Kashmir* (Delhi: Raj, 1996), 17–18.

14. Schofield, *Kashmir in the Crossfire,* 197; Alastair Lamb, *The Kashmir Problem: A Historical Survey* (New York: Frederick A. Praeger, 1968), 74; Sumit Ganguly, *The Crisis in Kashmir: Portents of War, Hopes of Peace* (Princeton, NJ: Woodrow Wilson Center Press, 1997), 53; Gowher Rizvi, "India, Pakistan, and the Kashmir Problem, 1947–1972," in *Perspectives on Kashmir: The Roots of Conflict in South Asia,* ed. Raju G. C. Thomas (Boulder, CO: Westview Press, 1992), 69; and Pervaiz Iqbal Cheema, "Pakistan, India, and Kashmir: A Historical Review," in Thomas, *Perspectives on Kashmir,* 104.

15. Alexander Evans, "Reducing Tension Is Not Enough," *Washington Quarterly* 24, no. 2 (2001): 181–93; Ganguly, *Crisis in Kashmir,* 94–95.

16. Vernon Hewitt, *Towards the Future? Jammu and Kashmir in the Twenty-first Century* (Cambridge, UK: Portland Books, 2001), 168; Schofield, *Kashmir in the Crossfire,* 258–59; and Ganguly, *Crisis in Kashmir,* 119–20.

17. Schofield, *Kashmir in the Crossfire,* 272; and Ganguly, *Crisis in Kashmir,* 124–27.

18. Ganguly, *Crisis in Kashmir,* 151–52.

19. "Gunmen Disguised as Holy Men Kill 24 in Kashmir," Reuters, *New York Times,* July 13, 2002.

20. David Rohde, "Nine Hindus Die in Attack on Pilgrims in Kashmir," *New York Times,* August 7, 2002, A8.

21. "Commandos Storm Indian Hindu Temple after 29 Killed," Reuters, *New York Times,* September 24, 2002.

22. See, for example, John A. Vasquez, *The War Puzzle* (Cambridge: Cambridge University Press, 1993); John A. Vasquez and Marie T. Henehan, "Territorial Disputes and the Probability of War, 1816–1992," *Journal of Peace Research* 38, no. 2 (March 2001): 123–38; Michael Brecher, Jonathan Wilkenfield, and Sheila Moser, *Crises in the Twentieth Century,* vol. 1 (New York: Pergamon Press, 1988); Paul Hensel, "Charting a Course to Conflict: Territorial Issues and Interstate Conflict, 1816–1992," in *A Road Map to War: Territorial Dimensions of International Conflict,* ed. Paul F. Diehl (Nashville: Vanderbilt University Press, 1999), 115–46; and Barbara F. Walter, "Explaining the Intractability of Territorial Conflict," *International Studies Review* 5, no. 4 (December 2003): 137–53.

23. For an expanded version of this argument and empirical evidence, see Ron E. Hassner, "The Path to Intractability: Time and the Entrenchment of Territorial Disputes," *International Security* 31, no. 3 (Winter 2006–7): 107–38.

24. Hagai Segal, *Yamit, sof: ha-ma 'avak la-'atsirat ha-nesigah be-Sinai* [Yamit, the End, in Hebrew] (Gush Katif, Israel: Midreshet ha-darom, 1999).

25. For religious interpretations of these borders, see Naftali Kraus, "Parasha Upshara," *Ma'ariv,* February 2, 1998; Rabbi Ya'akov Ariel, "Maavak Yamit Berei Hahalacha," *Tchumin,* vol. 3 (Alon Shvut, Israel: Tzomet, 1982); Yossi Ninve, "Concerning the Borders of the Land of Israel according to the Bible," in *The State of Israel and the Land of Israel,* ed. Adam Doron (Tel-Aviv: Beit Berl, 1988); Rabbi Paul Laderman, "The Land of Israel and the State of Israel in Jewish Religious Movements—Past and Present," in ibid.; Moshe Brawer, *Israel's Boundaries Past, Present, and Future* (Tel Aviv: Yavneh, 1988). The following support the view that Begin never considered Camp David to compromise his commitment to the borders of biblical Israel: Robert C. Rowland, *The Rhetoric of Menachem Begin: The Myth of Redemption through Return* (New York: University Press of America, 1985), 202; Shlomo Avineri, "History versus Security," *Jerusalem Post International Edition,* June 1–7, 1980, 13.; Mordechai Karniel, *The Heritage of Menachem Begin* (Jerusalem: Psagot, 1999), 28–31; Mordechai Karniel, *Menachem Begin: Portrait of a Leader* (Jerusalem: Reuven, 1998), 13–17, 27; and Theodore Draper, "A Revealing Memoir of Camp David," *New York Times,* May 17, 1981.

26. Segal, *Yamit,* 10–11, 47. The views were most radically expressed in Yoel Ben-Nun, "Lo Taguru," *Nekuda* 42 (April 7, 1982): 4–7. Begin responded by breaking with the movement and accusing its members of suffering from a "Messiah syndrome." Arye Naor, *Begin in Power: A Personal Testimony* (Tel Aviv: Yediot Aharonot, 1993), 163.

27. Ehud Sprinzak, *The Ascendance of Israel's Radical Right* (Oxford: Oxford University Press, 1991), 104

28. Gideon Aran, *Eretz Yisrael Beyn Dat Upolitika: Hatnua Leatzirat Hanesiga Besinai Ulekacheha* [The Land of Israel between Religion and Politics: The Movement to Stop the Withdrawal from Sinai and Its Lessons, in Hebrew] (Jerusalem: Jerusalem Institute for Israel Studies, 1985), 59–60.

29. Etta Bick, "Policy, Protest, and the Pulpit: Rabbis and the Territorial Politics of the Holyland," paper presented at the annual conference of the Association for Israel Studies, Tucson, Arizona, May 2005.

30. Bradley Burston, "Countdown: Will Settler Synagogues Face the Bulldozer's Blade?" *Ha'aretz,* April 26, 2005, citing Gaza rabbi Yosef Elnikaveh. The Israeli High Court of Justice resolved the issue of destroying synagogues by ordering these synagogues to be relocated in whole or in symbolic part (walls, decorative designs, stained glass, etc.) to Israel proper. Yuval Hoaz, "High Court Orders 2 Synagogues Moved from Gaza to Israel," *Ha'aretz,* August 23, 2005.

31. Yitzhak Reiter, "'All of Palestine Is Holy Muslim *Waqf* Land': A Myth and Its Roots," in *Law, Custom, and Statute in the Muslim World: Studies in Honor of Aharon Layish,* ed. Ron Shaham, (Leiden, The Netherlands: Brill, 2006).

32. Isak Svensson, "Fighting with Faith: Religion and Conflict Resolution in Civil Wars," *Journal of Conflict Resolution* 51, no. 6 (December 2007): 934, citing Elizabeth Harris, "The Cost of Peace: Buddhists and Conflict Transformation in Sri Lanka," in *Can Faiths Make Peace? Holy Wars and the Resolution of Religious Conflicts,* ed. P. Broadhead and D. Keown (London: I. B. Tauris, 2007).

33. Usama bin Muhammad bin Laden, "Ladanese Epistle: Declaration of War; Expel the Infidels from the Arab Peninsula," August 1996. This was followed in February 1998 by "Jihad against the Jews and Crusaders: World Islamic Front Statement."

34. The concept of civil religion, initially proposed by Jean-Jacques Rousseau, received its modern application in the writings of Robert N. Bellah. See Bellah, "Civil Religion in America," *Dedalus* 96, no. 1 (Winter 1967): 1–21; and Bellah, *Beyond Belief: Essays on Religion in a Post-traditionalist World* (Berkeley: University of California Press, 1991). The monuments on the National Mall in Washington, DC, offer the most obvious example of American civil-religious sacred space, as does the former site of the World Trade Center in New York City.

35. For the role of memorials, cemeteries, and the cult of the fallen soldier in modern nationalism, see Rudy Koshar, *From Monuments to Traces: Artifacts of German Memory, 1870–1990* (Berkeley: University of California Press, 2000); George L. Mosse, *Fallen Soldiers: Reshaping the Memory of the World Wars* (New York: Oxford University Press, 1990); Reinhart Koselleck and Michael Jeisman, eds., *Der politische Totenkult: Kriegerdenkmäler in der Moderne* [The Political Cult of the Dead: War Memorials in the Modern Era, in German] (Munich: Fink, 1994); and George W. White, *Nationalism and Territory* (Lanham, MD: Rowman and Littlefield, 2000).

36. David Scott Palmer, "Overcoming the Weight of History: Getting to Yes in the Peru-Ecuador Dispute," paper presented at the International History Institute, Boston University, February 28, 2000, 21; David Scott Palmer, "Peru-Ecuador Border Conflict: Missed Opportunities, Misplaced Nationalism and Multilateral Peacekeeping," *Journal of InterAmerican Studies and World Affairs* 39, no. 3 (Autumn 1997): 109, citing George McBride, "Ecuador-Peru Boundary Settlement," typescript, unpublished report to the U.S. Secretary of State, Washington DC, 1949, 1.

37. Gabriel Marcella and Richard Downes, Introduction, in *Security Cooperation in the Western Hemisphere: Resolving the Ecuador-Peru Conflict,* ed. Marcella and Downes (Miami, FL: North-South Center Press, 1999), 15 n. 15, citing Paco Moncayo, "Entrevista de Marcelo Gullo al Gral," *Sí,* February 7, 1997.

38. Manpreet Sethi, "Novel Ways of Settling Border Disputes: The Peru-Ecuador Case," *Strategic Analysis,* IDSA, 23, no. 10 (January 2000), www.ciaonet.org/olj/sa.

39. David R. Mares, "Political-Military Coordination in the Conflict Resolution Process: The Challenge for Ecuador," in Marcella and Downes, *Security Cooperation,* 177–78, 186–89.

40. Luigi R. Einaudi, "The Ecuador-Peru Peace Process," in *Herding Cats: Multiparty Mediation in a Complex World,* ed. Chester A. Crocker (Washington, DC: United States Institute for Peace, 1999), 424.

41. Contrast Steven J. Brams and Alan D. Taylor, *From Cake Cutting to Dispute Resolution* (Cambridge: Cambridge University Press, 2002).

42. Carlos Espinosa, "Exorcising the Demons of War: Memory, Identity, and Honor in the Ecuador-Peru Peace Negotiations," working paper 98/99–2 (Cambridge: David Rockefeller Center for Latin American Studies, Harvard University), 23; and Marcella and Downes, Introduction, 234.

43. Espinosa, "Exorcising the Demons of War," 28–29.

44. Ibid., 3 and 25–26.

45. Ibid., 28–29.

46. Ibid., 33.

47. Beth A. Simmons, "Territorial Disputes and Their Resolution: The Case of Ecuador and Peru," *Peaceworks* 27 (Washington, DC: United States Institute of Peace, April 1999), 12.

48. Espinosa, "Exorcising the Demons of War," 34–35.

49. Simmons, "Territorial Disputes," 18; Fernando Bustamante, "Ecuador: Putting an End to Ghosts of the Past?" *Journal of InterAmerican World Affairs* 34, no. 4 (Winter 1992–93): 195–224.

50. Monica Herz and Joao Pontes Nogueira, *Ecuador vs. Peru: Peacemaking amid Rivalry* (New York: Lynne Rienner, 2002), 78; Bryce Wood, *Aggression and History: The Case of Ecuador and Peru* (New York: Columbia University, Institute of Latin American Studies, 1978), 233.

51. Palmer, "Overcoming the Weight of History," 13–15.

52. Espinosa, "Exorcising the Demons of War," 31.

53. Ibid., 35; and Herz and Nogueira, *Ecuador vs. Peru,* 78–79.

54. Espinosa, "Exorcising the Demons of War," 3 and 36.

55. Amos Harel and Jonathan Lis, "High Alert amid Warnings of Temple Mount Attack," *Ha'aretz,* April 7, 2005.

56. Nadav Shragai, "A Mounting Sense of Urgency," *Ha'aretz,* December 30, 2004; Amos Harel, "Pulling for the Pullout," *Ha'aretz,* June 10, 2005.

57. "Israel Begins Running Web Camera at Contested Excavation Site," *New York Times,* February 16, 2007, 11; Isabel Kershner, "Some Work Delayed near Jerusalem Holy Site," *New York Times,* February 13, 2007, 3.

58. "Priests Scuffle inside Bethlehem Church," Associated Press, December 27, 2007.

59. Raymond Cohen, *Saving the Holy Sepulcher: How Rival Christians Came Together to Rescue Their Holiest Shrine* (Oxford: Oxford University Press, 2008), 161.

60. "The Other Illegal Outpost," *Jerusalem Post,* July 2, 2003; Matthew Gutman, "Interior Ministry Razes Controversial Nazareth Mosque," *Jerusalem Post,* July 2, 2003.

61. "Israel Halts Mosque Construction Near Major Christian Shrine," *Ha'aretz,* January 9, 2002; Karin Laub, "Blood from a Stone: Muslims Defiant at Nazareth Mosque Dedication," *ABC News On Line,* February 15, 2000.

62. "Pyramid Presents Religious Quandary for Suburban Mexicans," Associated Press, *CNN World News,* http://www.wwrn.org/article.php?idd=21081&sec=73&cont=6.

63. Keith Bradsher, "Under the Giant Buddha, a Tussle over Tourists," *New York Times,* October 25, 2002.

64. Ralph Blumenthal, "Humble Church Is at Center of Debate on Eminent Domain," *New York Times,* January 25, 2006, A11.

65. Brandon Bailey, "Calpine Geothermal Plans Are Drawing Some Heat: Power Project Threatens Sacred Sites, Tribe Says," *San Jose Mercury News,* February 12, 2006; Michelle Berditschevsky and Peggy Risch, "Claiming the Highlands: Geothermal Mining Confronts an Ancient Native Tradition," *Terrain Magazine,* Summer 2000; Eric Bailey, "A Power Struggle: Electric vs. Spiritual," *Los Angeles Times,* July 17, 2002; Shadi Rahimi, "Battle Heats Up over Geothermal Energy Facility," *Indian Country Today,* April 20, 2007.

66. Matt McKinney and Rafael Frankel, "Cambodian-Thai Enmity at Root of Riots; Reports of Slur Open Old Wounds," *Boston Globe,* February 2, 2003.

67. "Thailand Suspends Cambodian Ties," *CNN World News,* January 30, 2003.

68. Nirmal Ghosh, "Cambodia to Pay Thailand $10m for Riots Damage," *Straits Times,* March 18, 2003; and David Barboza, "Cambodian Pique at Thais Lingers," *New York Times,* April 19, 2003.

69. "Balkans Flare Up," *New York Times,* March 31, 2004, 22.

70. Nicholas Wood and David Binder, "Treasured Churches in a Cycle of Revenge," *New York Times,* April 3, 2004, 9.

71. Samuel P. Huntington, *The Clash of Civilizations and the Remaking of World Order* (New York: Simon and Schuster, 1996).

72. Huntington declares religion to be "the most important…of all the objective elements which define civilizations" (ibid., 42) and "the foundations on which the great civilizations rest" (47, citing Christopher Dawson, as well as 59). The clash of civilization is replacing conflicts between states because religion is replacing ideology and is increasingly intruding on international affairs (54). Religion has become "a central, perhaps *the* central, force that motivates and mobilizes people" and "the most profound difference that can exist between people" (66 and 254).

73. Ibid, 67–8, 129–130, 245 and 292.

74. In order of publication, these volumes, all edited by Martin E. Marty and R. Scott Appleby and published by the University of Chicago Press, are *Fundamentalisms and Society: Reclaiming the Sciences, the Family, and Education* (1993); *Fundamentalisms Observed (1994); Fundamentalisms Comprehended* (1995); *Fundamentalisms and the State: Remaking Polities, Militance, and Economies* (1996); and *Accounting for Fundamentalisms: The Dynamic Character of Movements* (2004).

75. The authors amend this, to some extent, in a separate text that functions as a summary of the Fundamentalism Project: Gabriel A. Almond, R. Scott Appleby, and Emmanuel Sivan, *Strong Religion: The Rise of Fundamentalisms around the World* (Chicago: University of Chicago Press, 2003).

76. Clifford Geertz, "Thick Description: Toward an Interpretive Theory of Culture," in *The Interpretation of Cultures* (New York: Basic Books, 1973).

Index

Page numbers in italics refer to photographs.

Saud, Faysal al, king of Saudi Arabia,
141, 142
Saud, House of, 139–142
Saud, Khalid al, king of Saudi Arabia, 147
Saud, Muhammad al, 139–140
Saud, Sultan al, crown prince of Saudi Arabia,
146
Saudi Arabia, 64, 65, 198n45
political legitimacy, 142
Wahhabi revival, 150
Saudi National Guard, 146, 148
Saudi ulema
House of Saud and, 139–142
influence of, 142–144
Mecca crisis and, 147–151, 159
Schneerson, Rabbi Meir, 130
Second Gulf War (2003), 60–62
Selimiye Mosque (Nicosia), 52
Shahak, Amnon, 81
sharing sacred spaces, 53, 65–67
See also sacred spaces, conflict over, misman-
agement
Sharon, Ariel, 87
al-Shaykh, Shaykh Abd Allah, 140
Shehab al-Din, tomb of, 172
Shiprock. See *Tsé Bit' A'i*
shrines, 2, 24–32, 48, 65–66, 136, 167
See also mosques; sacred spaces; temples
Sinai settlements, evacuation of, 165
al-Sistani, Grand Ayatollah Ali, 61
Six Day War (1967), 117–118
social constructivist approach to the study of
sacred space, 6–7, 94–98, 154–155
Solomon's judgment, 37, 38, 42
Sophornius, patriarch of Jerusalem, 105
Sri Amarnath cave (Srinagar), 161–163
Sri Lanka, 1, 166, 195n39
Sri Pada (Sri Lanka), 195n39
St. Catherine's monastery (Sinai peninsula), 25
St. John Lateran, Basilica of (Rome), 201n4
St. Peter, Basilica of (Rome), 31, 63
Stupa of a Thousand Images (Gyantse), 45
Supreme Court of Israel, 122, 131, 214n30
synagogues, 17, 24, 27–29, 33, 49, 57, 63, 66, 87,
103–104, 132, 165, 214n30

Tabernacle, 48
Taliban, 108
Talmud, 103
Tamimi, Sheikh Tatzir, Palestinian Muslim
cleric, 90
Temple Lot (Independence), 55
Temple of Apollo (Delphi), 18–20, 23
Temple of Buddha's Tooth (Kandy), 1

Temple Mount, x, xii–xvi, 22, 23, 113
access to, *112,* 131
boundaries of, 47
centrality of, 29
disputes, 12, 172
forced syncretism and, 56–57, 58
indivisibility of, 113–114
Jordan and, 131
partition strategy, 72
rabbinical ruling (1967), 13, 121–129, 158–159
religious counterruling (1986), 129
sectarian competition over access to, 86–87
security challenges, 115
symbolism of, 131–132
uniqueness of, 49
violence and, xiii–xvi, 129–130
See also Camp David negotiations
Temple Mount Faithful movement, 129–130
temples, 1, 2, 17, 24–33, 60, 63
Buddhist, 47
Greek and Roman, 18, 23, 56–57
Hindu, 4, 30, 45, 57, 63, 71, 78, 161–163,
185n3, 191n20, 192n28
Mormon, 49, 55
Shinto, 30, 47–49, 63
See also Angkor Wat (Cambodia); Ayodhya
crisis; Borobudur Temple Java); Golden
Temple (Amritsar); Hanumangarhi
(Temple of Hanuman); Jewish Temple;
Kashi Vishwanath Temple (Varanasi);
Kukulcan, Temple of (Chichen Itza);
sacred spaces, institutionalization of;
shrines; Temple Lot (Independence);
Temple Mount (Jerusalem); Temple of
Apollo (Delphi); Temple of Buddha's
Tooth (Kandy); Temple Square
(Salt Lake City)
Temple Square (Salt Lake City), 31, 32
territorial disputes, 13–14, 154, 159–171
civil-religious sacred spaces and, 166–169
entrenchment, 163–166
resolution of, 168–171
sacred spaces, interaction with, 161–163
Theodosius, Roman emperor, 20
thick religion methodology, 14, 154, 177–179
tirtha (Sanskrit pilgrimage site), 46
Tomb of Adam, 203n27
Tomb of Moses, 203n27
Tomb of Rabbi Shimon bar Yohai (Meron), 55
Tomb of Rachel (Bethlehem), 115–116
Tomb of Samuel (Jerusalem), 65
Tomb of the Patriarchs (Hebron), 73–74, 116
torii (Shinto gateway), 47
Tsé Bit' A'i (New Mexico), 59